Unrivaled

A VOLUME IN THE SERIES

Cornell Studies in Security Affairs

Edited by Robert J. Art, Robert Jervis, and Stephen M. Walt

A list of titles in this series is available at cornellpress.cornell.edu.

Unrivaled

*Why America Will Remain
the World's Sole Superpower*

MICHAEL BECKLEY

Cornell University Press

Ithaca and London

Cornell University Press gratefully acknowledges receipt of a grant from the Faculty Research Awards Committee at Tufts University, which aided in the publication of this book.

First published 2018 by Cornell University Press

Printed in the United States of America

Library of Congress Cataloging-in-Publication Data

Names: Beckley, Michael, author.
Title: Unrivaled : why America will remain the world's sole
    superpower / Michael Beckley.
Description: Ithaca : Cornell University Press, 2018. | Series: Cornell
    studies in security affairs | Includes bibliographical references
    and index.
Identifiers: LCCN 2018004047 | ISBN 9781501724787 (cloth ; alk. paper)
Subjects: LCSH: United States—Foreign relations—21st century. |
    United States—Foreign relations—China. | China—Foreign
    relations—United States. | Unipolarity (International relations) |
    Hegemony. | Great powers.
Classification: LCC E895 .B43 2018 | DDC 327.73009/05—dc23
LC record available at https://lccn.loc.gov/2018004047

To Mom and Dad
For everything

Contents

Acknowledgments

I am deeply grateful to many people for making this book possible. Chief among them are six outstanding mentors that guided my path from student to professor. Ryan Mills, Melissa Wade, and Carrie Rosefsky Wickham taught me how to teach and inspired me to become an educator. Richard Betts, Andrew Nathan, and Robert Jervis supervised my Ph.D. dissertation and shaped how I think about international relations.

I would not have been able to write a book like this if I did not work at two wonderful institutions, Tufts University and Harvard's Kennedy School of Government, where scholars are encouraged to study big questions and not to worry too much about traditional academic boundaries. I would particularly like to thank Kelly Greenhill, Richard Eichenberg, Natalie Masuoka, Nimah Mazaheri, Steven Miller, Malik Mufti, Dennis Rasmussen, Elizabeth Remick, Tony Smith, Jeffrey Taliaferro, and Stephen Walt for their support.

I owe tremendous thanks to the faculty at Dartmouth's Dickey Center for International Understanding, my academic home away from home, where I received help at every stage of writing this book, from developing the ideas to tracking down the data to writing the proposal. I am especially grateful to Stephen Brooks, Jeffrey Friedman, Jennifer Lind, Daryl Press, Benjamin Valentino, and William Wohlforth for expert feedback.

Over the years, many friends have had a hand in this project. Stefano Recchia not only studied with me, but also had the (dis)pleasure of living with me for most of graduate school. He has been like an older brother, showing me the ropes in academia and how to live a balanced life. Mike Horowitz has helped me in countless ways, from research to writing to negotiating the academic job market. I will never be able to return the favor, but I hope to pass it on. Jonathan Markowitz has spent hours brainstorming with me, reading my work, and imposing much-needed rigor on my research. His influence is everywhere in this book, but most prominent in chapter 2. Nuno Monteiro and Paul MacDonald offered trenchant comments on the second version of the manuscript. Their shrewd criticism prodded me to write a completely revamped, third version of the book—a grueling task that was well worth the effort.

The Smith Richardson Foundation provided generous financial support for my research and helped put me through graduate school. For that, I am eternally grateful. I thank my editor at Cornell University Press, Roger Haydon, along with the series editors and anonymous referee for giving the book a voice. The beautiful map in chapter 4 was produced by Noah Rose, Thomas Lucic, and Shaan Shaikh. A portion of that chapter was previously published as "The Emerging Military Balance in East Asia: How China's Neighbors Can Check Chinese Naval Expansion," *International Security* 42, no. 2 (fall 2017). I am indebted to the editors of *International Security* for allowing me to use that material here.

My grandparents did not live to see this book, but as members of the Greatest Generation they helped inspire it. Laverne and John Beckley answered the call of duty in World War II and were beloved members of their community throughout their lives. Lillian and Tom Iwata were imprisoned in Japanese-American internment camps while their brothers served in the 442nd Regimental Combat Team, the most decorated military unit of its size and length of service in American history. One of those brothers, Robert Mizukami, received a Purple Heart. Another, William Mizukami, made the ultimate sacrifice. As I wrote this book, I thought often about their service to a great nation at a dark time in its history.

Diane Beckley and Jennifer Brouwer are two of my role models. They climbed the corporate ladder at a time when women were almost totally shut out of the boardroom. Now they serve as pillars of their community, shaping local government, donating to charity, and spreading love and joy to neighbors. As a frequent recipient of that love, joy, and charity—and as the father of a daughter—I send them my deepest thanks.

Throughout the years of research and writing, my wife, Silvana, has been my best friend and sharpest critic, providing incisive feedback, unwavering support, good humor, and timely kicks in the rear. She scrutinized every word of this book, except for this paragraph, and her wise judgment vastly improved the final product. More important, her love and laughter lifted my spirits and made me whole. This book would not exist without her, and my life would not be nearly as fulfilling.

My greatest thanks go to my parents, Barbara and Dennis, who have devoted more love and encouragement to me than I can possibly express, let alone repay. Their support for my education alone was monumental. They sacrificed their material comfort to send me to college, and they took it upon themselves to educate me throughout my childhood. My Mom raised me to appreciate good writing by reading to me almost every night. My Dad taught me how to do proper research by walking me through my first study, a third-grade science project that proved that baking soda and vinegar can turn a wine bottle into a cannon. Together my parents have filled my life with many happy memories and valuable lessons that I draw on every day. The older I get, the more grateful I become, and the more I realize that Mom and Dad were right about just about everything. I dedicate this book to them.

Unrivaled

Why America?

By most measures, the United States is a mediocre country. It ranks seventh in literacy, eleventh in infrastructure, twenty-eighth in government efficiency, and fifty-seventh in primary education.[1] It spends more on healthcare than any other country, but ranks forty-third in life expectancy, fifty-sixth in infant mortality, and first in opioid abuse.[2] More than a hundred countries have lower levels of income inequality than the United States, and twelve countries enjoy higher levels of gross national happiness.[3]

Yet in terms of wealth and military capabilities—the pillars of global power—the United States is in a league of its own. With only 5 percent of the world's population, the United States accounts for 25 percent of global wealth, 35 percent of world innovation, and 40 percent of global military spending.[4] It is home to nearly 600 of the world's 2,000 most profitable companies and 50 of the top 100 universities.[5] And it is the only country that can fight major wars beyond its home region and strike targets anywhere on earth within an hour, with 587 bases scattered across 42 countries and a navy and air force stronger than that of the next ten nations combined.[6] According to Yale historian Paul Kennedy, "Nothing has ever existed like this disparity of power; nothing." The United States is, quite simply, "the greatest superpower ever."[7]

Why is the United States so dominant? And how long will this imbalance of power last? In the following pages, I argue that the United States will remain the world's sole superpower for many decades, and probably throughout this century. We are not living in a transitional post–Cold War era. Instead, we are in the midst of what could be called the unipolar era—a period as profound as any epoch in modern history.

This conclusion challenges the conventional wisdom among pundits, policymakers, and the public.[8] Since the end of the Cold War, scholars have dismissed unipolarity as a fleeting "moment" that would soon be swept away by the rise of new powers.[9] Bookstores feature bestsellers such as *The Post-American World* and *Easternization: Asia's Rise and America's Decline*;[10] the U.S. National Intelligence Council has issued multiple reports advising the president to prepare the country for multipolarity by 2030;[11] and the "rise of China" has been the most read-about news story of the twenty-first century.[12] These writings, in turn, have shaped public opinion: polls show that most people in most countries think that China is overtaking the United States as the world's leading power.[13]

How can all of these people be wrong? I argue that the current literature suffers from two shortcomings that distort peoples' perceptions of the balance of power.

First, the literature mismeasures power. Most studies size up countries using gross indicators of economic and military resources, such as gross domestic product (GDP) and military spending.[14] These indicators tally countries' resources without deducting the costs countries pay to police, protect, and provide services for their people. As a result, standard indicators exaggerate the wealth and military power of poor, populous countries like China and India—these countries produce vast output and field large armies, but they also bear massive welfare and security burdens that drain their resources.

To account for these costs, I measure power in *net* rather than gross terms. In essence, I create a balance sheet for each country: assets go on one side of the ledger, liabilities go on the other, and net resources are calculated by subtracting the latter from the former. When this is done, it becomes clear that America's economic and military lead over other countries is much larger than typically assumed—and the trends are mostly in its favor.

Second, many projections of U.S. power are based on flawed notions about why great powers rise and fall. Much of the literature assumes that great powers have predictable life spans and that the more powerful a country becomes the more it suffers from crippling ailments that doom it to decline.[15] The Habsburg, French, and British empires all collapsed. It is therefore natural to assume that the American empire is also destined for the dustbin of history.

I argue, however, that the laws of history do not apply today. The United States is not like other great powers. Rather, it enjoys a unique set of geographic, demographic, and institutional advantages that translate into a commanding geopolitical position. The United States does not rank first in all sources of national strength, but it scores highly across the board, whereas all of its potential rivals suffer from critical weaknesses. The United States thus has the best prospects of any nation to amass wealth and military power in the decades ahead.

For the foreseeable future, therefore, no country is likely to acquire the means to challenge the United States for global primacy. This is an extraordinary development, because the world has been plagued by great power rivalry for millennia. In the past five hundred years alone, there have been sixteen hegemonic rivalries between a ruling power and a rising power, and twelve of them ended in catastrophic wars.[16] In the first half of the twentieth century, for example, when the world was multipolar, Germany twice challenged Britain for European primacy. The result was two world wars. In the second half of the twentieth century, under bipolarity, the Soviet Union challenged the United States for global primacy. The result was the Cold War, a conflict in which the superpowers spent between 6 and 25 percent of their GDPs on defense every year, waged proxy wars that killed millions of people, and brought the world to the brink of nuclear Armageddon.

Today, by contrast, unipolarity makes a comparable level of great power competition impossible and thus makes a comparable level of conflict highly unlikely.[17]

Not the Argument

Before elaborating on the points above, let me be clear about what I am *not* arguing. First, I am not arguing that U.S. dominance is guaranteed or will last forever. The United States could easily squander its geopolitical potential. It could, for example, gut its demographic advantage by restricting high-skill immigration. It could allow demagogues and special interests to capture its political institutions and run the country into the ground. Or it could fritter away its resources on reckless adventures abroad. In addition, there are any number of events (e.g., a nuclear accident, natural disaster, or disease outbreak) that could disproportionately devastate the United States. The purpose of this book is not to argue that unipolarity is set in stone, but rather to make an educated guess about how long it will last based on present trends and current knowledge about why great powers rise and fall.

Second, I am not arguing that the United States is invincible or all-powerful. There are more than 190 countries, 7 billion people, and 197 million square miles of territory on earth. The United States cannot be present, let alone dominant, in every corner of the globe. Weaker nations can "route around" American power, doing business and calling the shots in their home regions while ignoring the United States.[18] They also can "tame" American power by, among other things, denying the United States access to their domestic markets, suing the United States in international courts, bribing American politicians, bankrolling anti-American terrorist groups, hacking U.S. computer networks, meddling in U.S. elections, or brandishing weapons of mass destruction.[19] Unipolarity is not omnipotence; it simply means that the United States has more than twice the wealth and military capabilities of any other nation. To translate those resources into influence, the United States will often have to collaborate with regional players.

Third, I am not arguing that unipolarity constitutes a Pax Americana, in which U.S. primacy guarantees global peace and prosperity. Unipolarity implies the absence of one major source of conflict—hegemonic rivalry—but it allows for, and may even encourage, various forms of asymmetric conflict and domestic decay.[20] The United States still faces serious threats at home and abroad. The purpose of this book is to clarify the scope of these threats, not to deny their existence.

Finally, I am not arguing that Americans are inherently superior to other nations or that the United States is the most wonderful place on earth. I assume that people are basically the same all around the world, and I know for a fact that citizens of some rich nations enjoy a higher quality of life than the average American. My argument, therefore, is not that Americans are exceptional or that the United States is the greatest country in the world. Instead, I argue that the United States has been blessed by exceptional circumstances that all but guarantee that it will be the most *powerful* nation. One implication of this conclusion, as I explain later, is that the United States can afford to devote a bit more of its immense resources to improving the lives of its citizens.

Plan of the Book

The plan of the book is straightforward. First, I develop a framework for measuring power and use it to assess current trends in the balance of power. Then, I build a framework for predicting power trends and use it to assess the future prospects of today's great powers. Finally, I discuss the implications of my findings for world politics and U.S. policy.

THE PILLARS OF POWER

Chapter 2 defines power and explains how to measure it. I start by showing that standard indicators exaggerate the power of populous countries because they ignore three types of costs that drain countries' economic and military resources: production, welfare, and security costs.

Production costs are the price of doing business; they include the raw materials consumed, and the negative externalities (e.g., pollution) created, during the production of wealth and military capabilities. Welfare costs are subsistence costs; they are the expenses a nation pays to keep its people from dying in the streets and include outlays on basic items like food, healthcare, education, and social security. Finally, security costs are the price a government pays to police and protect its citizens.

Needless to say, these costs add up. In fact, for most of human history, they consumed virtually all of the resources in every nation. Even today, they tie down large chunks of the world's economic and military assets.[21] Thus analysts must deduct these costs to accurately assess the balance of power.

To illustrate these points, I show that the rise and fall of the great powers and the outcomes of hundreds of international wars and disputes during the past two hundred years correlate closely with variations in countries' net stocks of economic and military resources—not with gross flows of resources. China and Russia, for example, had the largest GDPs and military budgets in the world during much of the nineteenth and early twentieth centuries, but both countries suffered from severe production, welfare, and security costs that condemned them to defeat at the hands of smaller but more efficient nations.

After reviewing this history, I develop a framework for assessing the current balance of power. I also explain why China is the most potent challenger to U.S. primacy and thus why I focus on the U.S.-China power balance in the following two chapters.

ECONOMIC TRENDS

Chapter 3 analyzes economic trends for the United States and China. The main conclusion is that the United States is several times wealthier than China, and the absolute gap is growing by trillions of dollars each year. China's economy is big but inefficient. It produces high output at high costs. Chinese businesses suffer from chronically high production costs, and China's 1.4 billion people generate massive welfare and security burdens. The United States, by contrast, is big and efficient, producing high output at relatively low costs. American workers and businesses are seven times more productive than China's on average, and with four times fewer people than China, the United States has much lower welfare and security costs. Gross domestic product and other popular indicators create the false impression that China is overtaking the United States economically. In reality, China's economy is barely keeping pace as the burden of propping up loss-making companies and feeding, policing, protecting, and cleaning up after one-fifth of humanity erodes China's stocks of wealth.

MILITARY TRENDS

Chapter 4 analyzes the U.S.-China military balance, both overall and within East Asia. The results are stark: the United States has five to ten times the military capabilities of China, depending on the type of military forces in question, and maintains a formidable containment barrier against Chinese expansion in East Asia. In a war, China could potentially deny the U.S. military sea and air control within a few hundred miles of China's territory, but China cannot sustain major combat operations beyond that zone, and the United States retains low-cost means of denying China sea and air control throughout the East and South China seas as well as preventing China from accomplishing more specific objectives, such as conquering Taiwan.

The widespread perception that China is poised to dominate East Asia and close the military gap with the United States stems from a neglect of production, welfare, and security costs. My analysis takes these factors into account. I show, for example, that Chinese weapons systems are roughly half as capable as the United States' on average; Chinese troops, pilots, and sailors receive less than half the training of their American counterparts and have limited operational experience and no combat experience; China's personnel costs are at least 25 percent higher than the United States'; and homeland security operations consume at least 35 percent of China's military budget and bog down half of China's active-duty force, whereas the U.S. military outsources such operations and their costs to civilian agencies.

Of course, U.S. military assets are dispersed around the world whereas China's are concentrated in East Asia. The United States, however, is involved in most regions by choice and can redeploy forces from one area to another without seriously jeopardizing its security. China, by contrast, has to keep most of its military on guard at home, because it suffers from twice the level of domestic unrest as the United States and shares sea or land borders with nineteen countries, five of which fought wars against China within the last century and ten of which still claim parts of Chinese territory as their own. Crucially, many of these countries have developed the means to deny China sea and air control throughout most of its near seas—even without U.S. assistance.

In sum, despite much talk of the rise of China, the United States maintains a huge economic and military lead, and the trends are generally in its favor. For China or any other nation to catch up to the United States, they will need to grow their power base much faster than they currently are. How likely is that?

FUTURE PROSPECTS

Chapter 5 analyzes the future prospects of the great powers and shows that the United States has the best foundation for growth.

I begin by critiquing two theories that currently dominate discussions about why great powers rise and fall—balance-of-power theory and convergence theory. Both of these theories suggest that unipolarity will be short lived.[22] Balance-of-power theory holds that weak states usually gang up on strong states and force a redistribution of international power.[23] Convergence theory holds that poor countries grow faster than rich countries, thus rising challengers inevitably overtake reigning hegemons.[24]

I argue that these theories do not apply today. Balance-of-power dynamics are muted, because the United States is too powerful and far away for other major powers to balance against.[25] Currently, no country can afford a sustained military challenge to U.S. primacy, and all of America's potential rivals are packed together in Eurasia and therefore are more likely to fight each other than band together against the distant United States.[26] To back up this argument, I show that balancing against the United States has been sporadic since 1991 while bandwagoning with the United States has been widespread.

Convergence theory, on the other hand, is underspecified.[27] Sometimes poor countries grow faster than rich countries and sometimes they fall further behind. In the late nineteenth century, for example, Germany, Japan, and the United States rose relative to Britain whereas Austria-Hungary, France, Russia, China, India, and the Ottoman Empire declined. These and other historical examples show that convergence is conditional; it depends on additional factors that, so far, have not been incorporated into theories of international change.

To address this shortcoming, I develop a new framework for projecting the rise and fall of nations. Drawing on studies from the field of economics, I show that sustained economic growth depends on three broad factors: geography, institutions, and demography.

The ideal geography for growth is one with abundant natural resources, transport infrastructure, and buffers from enemies.[28] The ideal government is one that is capable yet accountable, meaning that it is strong enough to provide services and maintain order, but sufficiently divided to prevent corruption and the violation of private property rights.[29] Finally, the ideal population is large, young, and educated.[30]

After presenting the evidence linking these factors to economic growth, I use indicators of each to assess the future prospects of the eight most powerful countries: the United States, China, Russia, Japan, Germany, the United Kingdom, France, and India.

I find that the United States has, by far, the best growth fundamentals. Geographically, the United States is a natural economic hub and military fortress. It has enormous stocks of natural resources, more natural transport infrastructure than the rest of the world combined, and is surrounded by "friends and fish" (Canada, Mexico, and two huge oceans) whereas all the other major powers border powerful rivals. Institutionally, the United States is so-so. The small and divided U.S. government does a poor job redistributing wealth, but it fosters entrepreneurship and innovation; spurs reform after policy blunders; and helps the United States suck up investment, technology, and human capital from other nations. Demographically, the United States has the most productive population, and its working-age population is set to grow during this century, unlike the populations of its competitors.

Potential challengers each have several weaknesses. China, the only country that is anywhere close to challenging U.S. primacy, has especially dismal growth prospects. In the coming decades, China will lose a third of its workforce and age faster than any society in history, with the ratio of workers to retirees shrinking from 8-to-1 today to 2-to-1 by 2050; its institutions fuel corruption, stifle entrepreneurship, and stymie reform after policy mistakes; its natural resources have dwindled due to overuse

7

and pollution; and it is encircled by more than a dozen hostile countries. Russia has vast stocks of natural resources, but its institutions are more corrupt and less effective than China's, and it has a declining and extremely unhealthy population and a vulnerable geographic location. Japan, Germany, and the United Kingdom have slightly more effective and less corrupt institutions than the United States (France lags slightly behind), but they have small and shrinking populations and few natural resources. India will soon have the largest and youngest population among the great powers, but it trails the other great powers in virtually every other category.

In sum, the United States has the most potential for future growth, in addition to an enormous economic and military lead. Unipolarity is not guaranteed to endure, but present trends strongly suggest that it will last for many decades.

IMPLICATIONS

Chapter 6 concludes by discussing the implications of unipolarity for world politics and U.S. policy. The most important implication is the absence of hegemonic rivalry. During the past five hundred years, there has been a hegemonic competition between a rising power and a ruling power every thirty years on average.[31] Seventy-five percent of these feuds ended in war, and even many of the "peaceful" cases were vicious cold wars. Today, by contrast, the United States does not face a peer competitor. As a result, there is less warfare in the world than in any period in modern history.[32]

Unipolarity, however, is not totally conducive to peace and prosperity. In the remainder of chapter 6, I highlight several dangers.

First, unipolarity may undermine crisis stability between the United States and weaker nations.[33] American military superiority could embolden the United States to stand firm in a crisis while simultaneously encouraging weaker nations to shoot first, before the U.S. military can wipe out their offensive forces. This "use it or lose it" dynamic can turn minor incidents into major wars. I discuss how the United States can avoid such scenarios with China, Russia, and North Korea.

Second, unipolarity will tempt the United States to fight stupid wars of choice in areas of little strategic value.[34] I explain where and when such imperial temptations will be most severe and propose ways to contain them.

Third, without a superpower rival, American national unity may dissolve, and special interests may capture the country's institutions and stifle reform and innovation.[35] The analyses of U.S. institutions in chapter 5 suggest that polarization, gridlock, and corruption are already infecting the American system of government. I highlight these trends and assess various proposals to reverse them.

Finally, unipolarity could undermine the liberal world order.[36] As the world's sole superpower, the United States is more capable than other nations of providing global governance, but it may have less incentive to do so given its secure location and vast stocks of wealth. In the coming decades the United States could become a "global power without global interests," turning inward while leaving others to maintain international security, prop up the global economy, and defend human rights.[37] Arms buildups, insecure sea-lanes, and closed markets are only the most obvious risks of a return to U.S. isolationism.[38] Less obvious are problems, such as climate change, water scarcity, refugee crises, and disease, which may fester without a leader to rally collective action. I discuss these threats to global security and explain why the United States can and should help address them.

The Pillars of Power

The balance of power is the motor of world politics, playing a role as central as the role of energy in physics and money in economics.[1] Power, however, is like love; it is "easier to experience than to define or measure."[2] Just as a person might have trouble saying "I love you 3.6 times more than her," scholars have trouble quantifying power, because there are many ways to conceptualize it.[3] In this chapter, I define power, develop a framework for measuring it, and show that this framework does a better job than existing approaches at tracking the rise and fall of great powers and predicting the outcomes of international disputes and wars.

Conceptual Issues

RESOURCES VERSUS OUTCOMES

Power can be measured in two main ways.[4] The most common approach, and the one I adopt in this book, measures power by tallying the wealth and military assets of each country. The logic of this "power as resources" approach is simple. Wealth enables a country to buy many forms of influence through aid, loans, investment, and bribes and to cultivate soft power by, among other things, funding global propaganda campaigns, building awesome skyscrapers, and hosting international expos.[5] Military resources (e.g., troops and weapons), on the other hand, enable a country to destroy enemies, attract allies, and run extortion rackets, extracting concessions and favors from weaker countries through threats of violence and offers of protection.[6]

Some scholars, however, define power in terms of outcomes.[7] Power, they argue, is first and foremost about winning. It is the ability of a country to prevail in a dispute, attract followers, and set the agenda of international negotiations.[8] Measuring power, these scholars argue, therefore requires a "power as outcomes" approach that involves observing international events—such as wars or diplomatic negotiations—and then determining the extent to which the participants shaped the outcomes in line with their respective interests.

Both definitions of power have virtues. The power as outcomes approach usefully tells us who got what, when, and how on a specific issue. It also helps explain cases in which the side with fewer resources prevailed. Such David versus Goliath cases are not uncommon; in fact, they account for roughly 25 percent of all international disputes and wars.[9] Materially weak countries can defeat better-endowed opponents through smart strategy, or dumb luck, or by running more risks or bearing greater costs.[10] By defining power in terms of outcomes, analysts can account for these nonmaterial factors and measure power with a greater degree of granularity than the power as resources approach.

Yet the power as outcomes approach has several weaknesses that limit its usefulness for what I hope to accomplish in this book. First, I want to assess the overall balance of power—that is, the balance of power across a broad range of issues—but the power as outcomes approach is inherently issue specific. The reason is that evaluating outcomes requires knowing the preferences of the actors involved; in other words, figuring out which country won a dispute (the outcome) requires first establishing what each country wanted to happen in the first place (preferences). Preferences, however, are not fixed—different countries, at different times, want different things—so while we might know a country's preferred outcome regarding a particular event, it is difficult, if not impossible, to know the preferences of many countries across hundreds of events over long periods of time. Thus the great strength of the power as outcomes approach—its specificity—becomes a weakness when the goal is to assess the overall balance of power.

A second limitation of the power as outcomes approach is that it is only useful for analyzing past events. After all, analysts must wait for an outcome to occur before they can study it. In this book, however, I want to make an educated guess about the balance of power in the decades ahead. To do that, I need a measure of power that can be projected into the future.

Third, the power as outcomes approach sometimes leads to nonsensical conclusions. For example, North Vietnam defeated the United States in the Vietnam War (1965–73), but it would be strange to argue that North Vietnam, a fledgling country where most of the population was living on less than a dollar per day, was more powerful than the United States, a globally engaged superpower with a $3 trillion economy, dozens of allies, and thousands of nuclear weapons. A better interpretation of the war's outcome would be that power has limits, and that North Vietnam defeated the United States, not because it was more powerful, but because it was more resolved (i.e., more willing to suffer and bear costs in pursuit of its objectives). In short, power alone does not determine outcomes; grit, luck, and wisdom matter too. The power as resources approach usefully untangles power from these other elements whereas the power as outcomes approach lumps them together.

For these reasons, I ultimately adopt the power as resources approach. I do so, however, using a hybrid model: I measure power in terms of resources, but I use data on outcomes to evaluate the relative validity of different resource indicators. Specifically, I determine which indicators of resources most accurately track the rise and fall of the great powers and predict the winners of international disputes and wars. This dual approach captures the best of both worlds; it yields a measure of power that is both historically valid and generalizable, one that faithfully reflects the past but also can be applied to the present and projected into the future.

GROSS VERSUS NET

Power resources can be measured in gross or net terms. Most standard indicators, such as gross domestic product (GDP) and military spending, are gross indicators, meaning that they do not deduct costs. Such indicators overstate the power of populous countries, because they count the benefits of having a big population—namely, the ability to mobilize a large workforce and raise a big army—but not the costs of having many people to feed, police, protect, and serve.

A big population is obviously an important power asset.[11] Luxembourg, for example, will never be a great power, because its workforce is a blip in world markets and its army is smaller than Cleveland's police department. A big population, however, is no guarantee of great power status, because people both produce and consume resources. One billion peasants will produce immense output, but they also will consume most of that output on the spot, leaving few resources left over to buy global influence or build a powerful military.

To rank among the most powerful nations in the world, a state needs to amass a large stock of resources, and to do that a state must be populous *and* prosperous. It must produce high output at low costs. It must not only mobilize vast inputs, but also produce significant output *per unit of input*. In short, a nation's power stems, not from its gross resources, but from its net resources—the stock of resources left over after subtracting costs.[12]

What costs? There are three main types that erode countries' power resources: production, welfare, and security costs. Production costs are the price a nation pays to generate wealth and military capabilities. They include the raw materials consumed, and the negative externalities (e.g., pollution) spewed out, during the production process. Welfare costs are subsistence costs; they are the expenses a nation pays to keep its people alive and include outlays on basic items like food, healthcare, education, and social security. Finally, security costs are the price a government pays to police and protect its citizens.

These costs tie down large chunks of every country's assets. To accurately assess the balance of power, therefore, analysts must deduct them by using net indicators.

STOCKS VERSUS FLOWS

Resources can be measured as stocks or flows. Stocks refer to accumulated resources; they are a nation's stash, or stockpile, of wealth and military assets. Flows, on the other hand, measure annual increases and decreases (i.e., inflows and outflows) of resources. Stocks and flows each tell us something important about a country. Stocks tell us about a country's total resources at a given moment in time. Flows, by contrast, tell us about a country's trajectory; that is, whether its resources are increasing or decreasing, and by how much.

In the long run, say over many decades, stocks and flows will point in the same direction; a country that enjoys sustained net inflows of resources will eventually accumulate large stocks. Over shorter periods of time, however, stocks and flows can point in opposite directions. For example, a country could experience a net outflow of resources for several years, but still retain huge stocks of wealth and military assets, just as a family of aristocrats with a large estate can blow through millions of dollars and still be fabulously wealthy. Conversely, a country experiencing a short-term influx of resources may, nevertheless, have meager stocks, just as a young sports star from a poor family can earn a high salary but still have little wealth in the bank.

In sum, flows provide a glimpse of a country's recent performance, but not a sense of a country's total wealth and military assets. For that reason, I measure the balance of power in terms of net stocks of resources and use flow measures only to gauge trends in the balance of power.

Indicators

Enough said about conceptual issues. More needs to be said about how, exactly, to measure power, which means discussing specific indicators. In the next three subsections, I show that the most commonly used indicators of wealth, military capabilities, and overall power ignore costs and stocks. After highlighting this problem, I explain how analysts can fix it by using net stock indicators.

WEALTH INDICATORS

The most commonly used measure of aggregate wealth is GDP, which records the value of all goods and services produced within a country over a fixed period of time. GDP has been described as "the leading indicator" and "the Zeus of the statistical pantheon" because governments, organizations, and analysts around the world use it to gauge states' relative economic standing.[13] As Zachary Karabel explains:

> No single number has become more central to society in the past fifty years. Throughout the world, GDP has become a proxy for success and for failure,

for sentiment about the future and sense of well-being in the present. It has the power to win or lose elections, overthrow governments, start popular movements. . . . Public debates about the economy in every country in the world today are framed by whether GDP is growing or contracting and by how much. It is a convenient reference point for news and for politicians. After all, it's one number, rarely more than three digits, and almost anyone can grasp that if that number goes up, it's good, and if it goes down, it's bad. As goes GDP, so goes the nation, whether that nation is the United States or China.[14]

Despite the widespread use of GDP, however, few people know what it actually measures. In particular, it is rarely recognized that GDP measures gross flows of resources and therefore does not deduct costs or measure long-term wealth accumulation.

For example, GDP counts production costs (inputs and externalities) as output. Spending money always increases GDP, even if the funds are wasted on boondoggles. In fact, the most common method of calculating GDP is called the "expenditure method" and involves simply adding up all of the spending done by the government, consumers, and businesses in a country in a given time period.[15] Thus hiring workers always increases GDP, even if they spend all day getting drunk in the break room. Boosting production always increases GDP, even if the goods rot on the shelf and tons of toxic waste are produced in the process. In fact, a country can increase its GDP by dumping toxic waste in the streets and then hiring millions of workers and spending billions of dollars to clean it up.

GDP also does not deduct welfare costs. Money spent feeding people is counted the same as money earned selling supercomputers on world markets. Consequently, populous countries generate considerable economic activity simply by existing. Even a nation caught in a Malthusian hell, in which all output is immediately devoured and living standards and technological progress are stagnant, will post a large GDP if it has a big population.

In addition, GDP counts many security costs as economic output. GDP does not distinguish between guns and butter; a $100 million gulag shows up the same as a $100 million innovation center. Hence, GDP fails to account fully for the economic costs of conflict. In fact, GDP usually rises when a country mobilizes for war. To be sure, defense spending can sometimes yield economic dividends—for example, the Internet and GPS began as U.S. military research projects—but in general, resources devoted to policing and protection drain wealth rather than create it.[16]

How can analysts address these shortcomings of GDP? The ideal solution would be to deduct costs and measure net stocks of resources directly. For example, if a country cuts down a forest to build a new office park, then the value of the forest would show up as a loss on the country's balance sheet. If a country spends $50 billion fighting a war—or growing food to feed its people or cleaning up toxic waste or hosting the Olympics—then $50 billion would be deducted from its stock of assets. In short, there would be no free lunch.

The obvious drawback to such an approach, however, is that compiling balance sheets for every country is a painstaking process that requires substantial data and time. Fortunately, the World Bank and the United Nations (UN)—working with dozens of economists from leading universities and research organizations—have taken up the task and published databases that measures countries' wealth stocks from the 1990s to the present in three areas: produced capital (man-made items such as machinery, buildings, infrastructure, software); human capital (the population's education, skills, and working life span); and natural capital (water, energy resources, arable land).[17]

These databases are still being refined, but they provide a rough first look at national stocks of wealth.[18] In chapter 3, therefore, I begin my analysis of economic trends by presenting data from each database on countries' stocks of produced, human, and natural capital. I then provide a more detailed analysis by presenting data on the subcomponents of each type of capital. For example, I supplement the produced capital indicators with measures of productivity, innovation, and debt; I supplement the human capital indicators with information on the education, health, and organization of each country's population; and I supplement the natural capital indicators with data on each country's reserves of natural resources and rates of depletion. This layered analysis grafts "qualitative flesh onto quantitative bones," combining the rigor and mathematical precision of a quantitative index with the granularity of detailed case research.[19]

MILITARY INDICATORS

Most analysts measure military power with gross "bean counts" of military spending, troops, and weapons. Journalists, for example, usually focus on military spending.[20] Academics typically use the Composite Indicator of National Capability (CINC), which is an index that combines military spending with data on troops, population, and industrial output.[21] Similarly, governments usually size up foreign rivals in terms of military expenditures and head-to-head force comparisons.[22] In the U.S. Department of Defense, for example, analysts use force densities, attrition coefficients, and firepower scores—all of which are basically measures of gross manpower or firepower.

Like GDP, these standard military metrics do not deduct production, welfare, or security costs. In military affairs, production costs refer to the number of assets needed to produce a given level of force and are mainly a function of skill, technology, and distance; a military with skillful personnel and superior technology operating from nearby bases will use fewer resources to accomplish a mission than a military with low skill and outdated technology fighting far from home. Crude counts of military assets gloss over these factors and sometimes yield wildly inaccurate estimates of the military balance as a result.

For example, in 1990, U.S. defense planners, using numerical force comparisons, predicted that the United States would suffer between 2,500 and 48,000 casualties if it invaded Iraq, which had the fourth largest military in the world at the time.[23] In 1991, however, a U.S.-led coalition, operating from secure bases near the combat theater, decimated Iraq's army and killed 35,000 Iraqi troops while losing only 240 attackers. Subsequent research showed that this lopsided outcome stemmed from the United States' superior skill and technology, factors that standard metrics largely missed.[24]

Standard military indicators also ignore welfare costs. A country's military budget is tallied the same regardless of how much is spent on food, housing, uniforms, medical care, pay, and pensions for the troops. These personnel costs, however, are not trivial; in many countries, they account for one-third of the military budget and can balloon to 50 percent or more for large armies, especially after wars.[25] Countries that can limit these costs, and concentrate funds on weapons, literally get more bang for the buck.

Finally, standard military indicators do not deduct security costs, which refer to military assets used for internal security and border defense missions. Military units that are bogged down quelling rebellions or defending borders against foreign invasions cannot project power abroad. Deducting security costs thus accounts for the fact that two nations with identical militaries may, nevertheless, wield vastly different levels of military power if one country is surrounded by enemies and wracked by domestic instability whereas the other is stable and surrounded by allies.

How can analysts incorporate these costs into military assessments? Unfortunately, there are no databases of net military stocks currently available. In chapter 4, therefore, I manually account for production, welfare, and security costs by comparing the relative skill and technology of each nation's military units; deducting the resources each nation devotes to welfare and homeland security; and conducting operational analyses of the most likely scenarios for war involving the United States and China, the main challenger to U.S. primacy.

OVERALL POWER INDICATORS

As the discussion above makes clear, measuring net stocks of resources is a tedious process that requires substantial data and time. Policymakers and scholars, however, sometimes want a single "headline" indicator that provides a parsimonious estimate of the overall balance of power and for which data are available for many countries stretching back many years. Several such indicators are widely used by scholars, policy analysts, and journalists. Unfortunately, all of them measure gross flows of resources rather than net stocks.

The most popular headline indicator is GDP. Proponents of GDP argue that it serves as a solid proxy for overall power because it represents a country's raw productive potential.[26] Although GDP is technically an economic indicator, proponents argue that it captures both economic and military capacity, because states can easily convert economic resources into military might. In short, GDP is fungible; it can be turned into "any mix of military, economic, and political" resources, just as a person can use cash to buy many forms of influence.[27]

After GDP, the most popular headline indicators of power are indexes of "war potential." Some of these indexes simply tally each nation's military spending, number of troops, or both. Others combine military spending and troops with gross economic output and population size.[28] For example, the U.S. National Intelligence Council, a body that advises the president on long-term security threats, measures power with an indicator that combines military spending, R&D spending, GDP, and population. The logic of combining these factors is that power ultimately depends on the ability to win major wars, and doing that requires a big army backed by substantial industrial might.

Among scholars, the most commonly used indicator of war potential is the CINC index mentioned earlier, which combines military spending, troops, population, urban population, iron and steel production, and energy consumption.[29] Data from CINC are available for most countries from 1816 to 2010 and have been used in more than a thousand peer-reviewed studies, including seminal studies on the causes of war, alliance politics, international cooperation, trade, nuclear proliferation, and democratization.[30]

Despite its widespread use, however, CINC suffers from the same problem as GDP: it is a gross measure that does not deduct costs. CINC, for example, counts military units the same regardless of their level of skill or technology, the costs of supporting those units, or the number of wars they have to fight. CINC also treats military spending and energy consumption (inputs) as if they were outputs. Thus a country can increase its CINC score by making enemies and then raising a huge, oil-guzzling army to attack them. Ultimately, CINC, like GDP, is a one-dimensional indicator; it only measures the gross size of a country's resources, not how efficiently a country uses its resources.

In sum, what is needed is a single indicator that can account for both size and efficiency and for which there are data covering many countries over many years. Does such an indicator exist?

In an oft-cited statistical reference, the historian Paul Bairoch suggested that the "strength of a nation could be found in a formula combining per capita and total GDP."[31] Bairoch did not elaborate on this point, but subsequent research suggests that he was on to something: as noted, scholars already believe that GDP represents the gross size of a state's economic and military resources, and there is a large body of literature showing that GDP per capita serves as a reliable proxy for economic and military efficiency.

Economists, for example, use GDP per capita to measure economic development, because rich countries are, almost by definition, more efficient and innovative than poor countries (the main exceptions to this rule are petrostates, like Saudi Arabia, that can grow rich simply by pulling oil out of the ground). Military studies also show that the higher a country's GDP per capita, the more efficiently its military fights in battle.[32] The reason is that a vibrant civilian economy helps a country produce advanced weapons, train skillful military personnel, and manage complex military systems.

GDP per capita therefore provides a rough but reliable measure of economic and military efficiency. This finding is not surprising, because population size is the main driver of production, welfare, and security costs—the bigger a country's population, the more people the government has to protect and provide for—so dividing GDP by population effectively controls for many of the costs that make the difference between a state's gross and net resources. Combining GDP with GDP per capita therefore yields an indicator that accounts for size and efficiency, the two main dimensions of net resources.

To create a rough proxy for net resources, therefore, I follow Bairoch's advice by simply multiplying GDP by GDP per capita, creating an index that gives equal weight to a nation's gross output and its output per person. This two-variable index obviously does not measure net stocks of resources directly, nor does it resolve all of the shortcomings of GDP and CINC. But by penalizing population, it provides a better sense of a nation's net resources than GDP, CINC, or other gross indicators.

Future studies can experiment with ways to improve this measure by adjusting the weights or, even better, by expanding the databases produced by the World Bank and UN or developing new measures of net stocks of resources. For now, however, multiplying GDP by GDP per capita yields a primitive proxy that can be used to demonstrate the importance of net resources in international politics. The next section does just that.

The Historical Record

RESEARCH DESIGN

A brief look at the history of world politics over the past two centuries supports my claim that power is a function of net stocks of resources. To illustrate this point, I conduct case studies of extended great power rivalries in which one nation had a preponderance of gross resources whereas the other had a preponderance of net resources. I focus on "extended" rivalries, meaning geopolitical competitions that lasted for several decades or longer, because they provide more information about each nation's relative power than does a single war or crisis. I focus on great powers, because minor power competitions are often shaped by great power politics and thus may not reveal much information about the relative power of the minor powers themselves. And I focus on cases in which one side had a preponderance of gross resources while the other side had a preponderance of net resources, because these cases constitute head-to-head tests of the importance of gross versus net resources in geopolitical competition.

According to widely used datasets, there have been fourteen great power rivalries since 1816 that lasted at least twenty-five years.[33] From this list, I select the rivalries with the largest gaps between the balance of gross and net resources. I measure gross resources as the average of one nation's share of the sum of the two sides' GDPs and CINC scores; and I measure net resources by calculating that same nation's share of the sum of the two sides' GDP x GDP per capita. In doing so, I am effectively using GDP and CINC as representatives for the standard, gross approach to measuring power; and using GDP x GDP per capita as the representative for my alternative, net approach. I calculate the gap between the balance of gross and net resources for each year of the rivalry by subtracting the latter from the former and taking the absolute value of the difference. I then calculate the average gap for each rivalry. These averages are displayed in descending order in table 2.1.

To keep this chapter at a reasonable length, I do not analyze every rivalry but instead focus on the rivalries with the largest gaps, which I arbitrarily define as those with at least a 20 percentage-point difference between the average balance of gross resources and the average balance of net resources. Six cases meet this criterion, however I ultimately exclude two of them—France vs. China (1860–1929) and Britain vs. the Soviet Union (1946–1992)—because these rivalries were sideshows in larger geopolitical competitions and thus do not constitute independent cases: in the nineteenth century, France challenged China only after Britain had already brought China to its knees in the Opium Wars; and during the Cold War, Britain's rivalry with the Soviet Union was shaped by the larger U.S.-Soviet rivalry. Excluding these two cases leaves me with four cases for further study, which are highlighted in bold in table 2.1.

Before analyzing these cases, it is worth noting that the nine cases with the largest gaps between the balance of gross and net resources, including the four cases I study below, involve China or Russia. This is not surprising because China and Russia are the only countries in the past two hundred years to have led the world in gross resources while lagging behind other great powers in net resources. Their experience in competitions with less populous but more developed countries thus provides the most straightforward test of my contention that power stems from net rather than gross resources.

Table 2.1 Extended great power rivalries, 1816–1992

Rivalry	Years	Percentage-point gap between balance of gross resources and balance of net resources
Britain vs. China	**1839–1911**	33
France vs. China	1860–1929	32
Britain vs. Soviet Union	1946–92	29
United States vs. Soviet Union	**1946–92**	26
Germany vs. Russia	**1891–1917**	22
Japan vs. China	**1874–1945**	21
Russia/Soviet Union vs. China	1857–1992	19
Britain vs. Russia	1833–1907	18
Japan vs. Russia	1853–1992	13
Britain vs. Germany	1853–1992	10
Britain vs. Italy	1911–47	10
France vs. Germany	1830–1945	5
United States vs. Britain	1816–1903	4
Germany vs. Italy	1914–45	4
Austria-Hungary vs. Italy	1843–1930	insufficient data

Sources: Maddison 2003; Singer, Bremer and Stuckey 1972; Bennett 2017; Klein, Goertz, and Diehl 2006.

BRITAIN VERSUS CHINA, 1839–1911

By standard gross indicators, China looked like a superpower in the nineteenth and early twentieth centuries. It had the largest GDP and military in the world until the 1890s, and the second largest GDP and military until the 1930s.[34] During this time, however, China suffered a "century of humiliation" in which it lost huge chunks of territory and most of its sovereign rights, fighting at least a dozen wars on its home soil and losing every single one of them.

Among these conflicts were two "opium wars" with Britain.[35] For centuries, European merchants had traveled to China to swap silver for tea and silk. In the nineteenth century, however, British traders discovered that they could make more money by growing opium in India and selling it on the black market in China.[36] Despite China's long-standing ban on opium, British dealers smuggled into China nearly twelve tons of opium per year, enough to keep 3 million addicts high year round.[37] To pay for this influx of narcotics, Chinese citizens spent 400 tons of silver annually, a ruinous sum that eroded 20 percent of China's wealth from 1828 to 1836.[38]

To stem the opium epidemic, the Chinese government declared a war on drugs in 1839. Chinese officials began seizing opium from British merchants and dumping it into the sea. Britain responded by sailing sixteen warships into Chinese waters and sinking China's navy. From 1839 to 1842, in what is now called the First Opium War, British forces occupied most of China's major coastal cities and brought Beijing to the brink of famine by blockading the Grand Canal, the critical lifeline linking the Chinese capital to China's main rice fields in the south.

Overmatched, the Chinese government capitulated in 1842 and signed the Treaty of Nanjing, which gave Britain $21 million in reparations, a perpetual lease on Hong Kong, access to five port cities, unprecedentedly low Chinese tariffs, and immunity from Chinese law for British citizens living in China.

Fifteen years later, Britain upped the ante by demanding full economic access to all of China and the right to sell opium legally throughout the country. When the Chinese government resisted, Britain again used military force, sparking what is now known as the Second Opium War. In January 1858, British forces occupied Guangzhou, the largest port in China, and in April 1858 British forces, joined by French troops and Russian and American diplomats, occupied Tianjin, the commercial hub of northern China only 100 miles from Beijing.

China mustered little resistance to the invasion, in part because China's military was busy suppressing the Taiping Rebellion, the bloodiest internal uprising in human history (estimated 20 to 30 million dead). In June 1858, therefore, the Chinese government signed the Treaty of Tianjin, granting Britain and its allies access to ten new treaty ports, freedom of travel throughout China, freedom of navigation on the Yangtze River, reparation of 6 million silver taels, and the legal right to sell opium in China.

When the Chinese government dragged its feet honoring these terms, British and French forces marched on Beijing, burned down the emperor's Summer Palace, and forced the Chinese government to sign a new treaty—the Treaty of Beijing—that quadrupled China's reparations bill, added Tianjin to the list of open treaty ports, and incorporated the Kowloon Peninsula and Stonecutter's Island into Britain's colony at Hong Kong. Over the next fifty years, China would be forced to sign a dozen more "unequal treaties" with Britain, France, Russia, the United States, Germany, and Japan.

Clearly Britain was more powerful than China during the nineteenth century. This fact, however, is not captured by standard gross metrics: China's GDP and defense budget were more than twice the size of Britain's, and China's army of 800,000 troops dwarfed the 7,000-troop force that Britain sent to China to fight the Opium Wars.[39]

China's weakness is only apparent when costs are taken into account. Figure 2.1 provides a first-cut assessment and hints at what more detailed research makes clear: China suffered from greater production, welfare, and security costs than Britain and thus had fewer resources to draw on in their

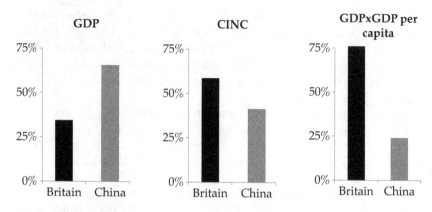

Figure 2.1. British and Chinese relative shares of power resources in 1870.

Source: Maddison 2003; Singer, Bremer, and Stuckey 1972.

many disputes. Whereas Britain comes out far ahead of China when power is measured by my proxy for net resources (GDP x GDP per capita), Britain never overtook China in terms of GDP, and CINC suggests, nonsensically, that China and Britain were equally matched in the mid-nineteenth century and that China surpassed Britain in power in 1907, five years before the Chinese government collapsed.

What were these costs? First, China was far less productive than Britain. The average unskilled worker in London generated three to six times the output of the average laborer in Beijing, and each British industrial worker generated sixteen to thirty-three times the output of each Chinese industrial worker.[40] British workers were not only healthier and better educated than Chinese workers on average, they also had superior technology. British looms, for example, could produce twenty times the output of a Chinese hand worker, and British power-driven "mules" (spinning machines) had two hundred times the capacity of Chinese spinning wheels.[41]

Second, China's massive population, which was thirteen times larger than Britain's, generated substantial welfare costs. China's "welfare ratio" (its economic output divided by the costs of providing its population with food, clothing, and shelter) was stuck at "bare bones subsistence" levels throughout the nineteenth century, except during the Taiping Rebellion in the 1850s when the ratio dipped below subsistence and millions of people starved to death.[42] In Britain, by contrast, economic production was four times subsistence levels in 1820 and more than ten times subsistence by 1900.[43]

Third, China's sprawling territory generated severe security costs. The Chinese government faced twenty-five major uprisings each year on average, so the central government had to keep taxes low to appease local rulers while simultaneously keeping military spending high to maintain large internal security forces.[44] These competing demands plunged China into fiscal crisis. China's tax revenues in the nineteenth century were 50 percent lower than they were in the *seventeenth century* and were five times smaller than Britain's in aggregate and a hundred times smaller on a per capita basis.[45] Meanwhile, China's military spending consumed 50 to 70 percent of government revenues in peacetime and 100 percent or more during wars.[46] The fact that China lost all of its wars in the nineteenth century compounded these fiscal problems, because China had to pay the victors massive indemnities that typically exceeded the annual revenues of the Chinese government.[47]

Production, welfare, and security costs also drained China's military resources. China's military was unskilled and underequipped compared to Britain's. As one study concludes: "In all areas of equipment—weaponry, forts, and most critically ships—Chinese equipment lagged behind that of the British . . . the British had long moved into the era of firepower, while parts of the Chinese army hung on to bows, swords, spears, and rattan shields."[48]

The best Chinese firearm was the matchlock, a muzzle-loading musket developed in the fifteenth century that required soldiers to light a match each time it was fired; British regiments, by contrast, were equipped with flintlocks or breech-loading percussion locks. Chinese warships carried ten cannons each whereas British ships had 120 or more, and Chinese cannons lacked sights and swivels and thus could not target moving objects, like British ships and soldiers. Hopelessly outgunned, some Chinese defenders tied firecrackers to monkeys and planned to hurl the weaponized animals onto British ships.[49] British firepower, however, was so lethal that Chinese troops never got close enough to make the throw.

Without a viable offensive option, Chinese defenders mostly huddled in their forts, allowing the British to pick when and where to fight. Repeatedly during the Opium Wars, therefore, Chinese armies of thousands were routed in minutes by a few hundred, or even a few dozen, British troops.

Security costs also degraded China's military power. China's forces were "scattered through the empire, far too busy with domestic peace-keeping duties (killing bandits or rebels; carrying out disaster relief; guarding prisons; policing smugglers) to be spared for the quarrel with the British."[50] At any given time, 50,000 Chinese soldiers were in transit around the country suppressing revolts. Consequently, Chinese garrisons typically had only a quarter of their troops on hand to counter British assaults. When the British attacked Tianjin in 1840, for example, only 600 of the registered 2,400 Chinese soldiers arrived in time for the battle.[51]

Britain, of course, had to fight far from home, but it had a series of secure bases in Asia that allowed it to project power around China's periphery, thus nullifying China's home-field advantage.[52] The lethal combination of naval supremacy and secure forward-operating sites enabled Britain to seize the initiative in numerous battles. For example, during the First Opium War, it took the British fleet thirty-five days to mass near China and capture Zhoushan, an island strategically located between Shanghai and Ningbo. Overstretched Chinese ground forces, by contrast, took five months to rally a counteroffensive, which ultimately failed.[53]

JAPAN VERSUS CHINA, 1874–1945

China's misery did not end with the Opium Wars. In the latter half of the nineteenth century, Japan became determined not to suffer the same fate as China, so it revamped its government, economy, and military and began seizing territory and resources in East Asia. When China tried to stand in the way of Japan's imperialist plans, Japan went on a rampage, quickly defeating China militarily in 1894 and forcing it to sign the Treaty of Shimonoseki, which ceded the Liaodong Peninsula, Formosa (present-day Taiwan), and the Pescadores to Japan. China also was forced to recognize Korea's independence—which effectively meant that Korea would become a vassal of Japan, no longer of China—and to give Japan commercial rights in China and pay a massive indemnity.[54]

After pocketing these gains, Japan annexed Korea in 1910, and when World War I broke out in 1914, Japan entered the war on the Allies' side and seized the German-controlled city of Qingdao on China's Shandong Peninsula. Japan then presented China with the infamous "Twenty-One Demands" that basically called for China to become a Japanese ward. The United States forced Japan to abandon its most punishing demands, but Japan still extracted substantial territorial and economic concessions from China.

A little over a decade later, Japan expanded its presence in northeast China, establishing a colony there called Manchukuo in 1932, and bringing the Chinese provinces of Jehol and Hebei under Japanese control in 1933. In 1934, the Japanese government declared that East Asia was Japan's sphere of influence and warned other great powers not to defend China. Then in 1937, Japan staged a full-scale invasion. By the time World War II began in Europe in 1939, Japan controlled most of eastern China plus Taiwan and its outlying islands. Japanese expansion stopped only when it ran afoul of the United States, which decisively defeated Japan in 1945.

Obviously Japan was more powerful than China during their rivalry. Yet by standard metrics, China appeared to have far greater power resources (figure 2.2). China's population, GDP, and military were several times larger than Japan's, but Japan had greater net resources because it was much more efficient than China, with lower production, welfare, and security costs.

For starters, Japanese industry was more productive than China's. In 1913, Japan's labor productivity was three times greater than China's overall, and by 1930, Japan was producing 150 times as much iron and steel as China and controlled 80 percent of the global silk market, China's top export industry.[55]

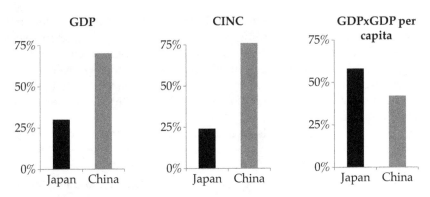

Figure 2.2. Chinese and Japanese relative shares of power resources in 1930.

Source: Maddison 2003; Singer, Bremer, and Stuckey 1972.

Welfare costs also worked in Japan's favor. While Chinese economic output hovered around subsistence levels in the early twentieth century, Japan's economy grew five times faster than its population, "making it possible to feed the increasing number of Japanese born every year with enough left over to finance both the government's modernization efforts and investment in the modern sectors of the economy."[56] Whereas agriculture tied down 80 percent of China's workforce and accounted for 65 percent of China's GDP in the 1930s, it occupied only 47 percent of Japan's workforce and made up 15 percent of its economy.[57]

Security costs took a smaller toll on Japan's economy than China's. Military spending consumed half of China's government revenues in the first three decades of the twentieth century, and if indemnities are included, then China's security spending totaled 85 to 100 percent of government revenues.[58] In Japan, by contrast, the government allocated only 7 to 11 percent of its funds to the military, and this spending was more than offset by the wealth Japan seized from China.[59] For example, the indemnity Japan received after the Sino-Japanese war in 1895 equaled one-third of Japan's GDP that year and paid for the expansion of Japan's army, navy, railways, telephone lines, and iron industry.[60]

In military affairs, it was a similar story.[61] As one study concludes: "Chinese forces lost every major confrontation on the battlefield . . . and were inferior in organization, equipment, training, and leadership to the Japanese Army."[62] China had one rifle for every three soldiers and one artillery piece for every six thousand soldiers, and 80 percent of Chinese hand grenades failed to explode.[63] Japanese soldiers, by contrast, not only had modern firearms, but also tanks, armored vehicles, combat aircraft, and chemical weapons, which they used indiscriminately on Chinese troops and civilians.

Only 27 percent of Chinese officers received any formal training,[64] and few Chinese units had field doctors, so even minor wounds often resulted in death.[65] The Chinese military also lacked modern communication and transport equipment—according to one government report, there were only six thousand motorized vehicles in the entire country, and half were inoperable—so messages were sent via runners, and soldiers moved around the country on foot.[66] As a result, Chinese forces had a limited combat radius, a situation that made counterattacks and timely reinforcement nearly impossible.

Chinese military power also was undermined by welfare costs. As one study concludes:

> The typical Chinese military unit spent the bulk of its time and energy simply trying to preserve its existence. It expected to have to take care of its own needs, including food, clothing, conscripts, weapons, and transportation. Fighting consumed too much energy, so fighting was done only when absolutely necessary. When sufficiently desperate, soldiers would not hesitate to pillage the very same people they were supposed to protect. This in turn provoked numerous incidents of friction between the army and the civilian population. Probably the worst case occurred in Honan during the early phase of Operation Ichigo. When the Chinese troops retreated in defeat, more soldiers were killed by the indignant local population than by the Japanese.[67]

Finally, Chinese forces suffered substantial security costs because China was internally divided prior to the Japanese invasion; indeed, the period from 1916 to 1928 is called the "Warlord Era" because China was chopped up among rival military cliques. The Nationalist Party, led by Chiang Kai-Shek, took control of China in 1928, but its rule was contested by warlords, Muslims, and communists. During the war with the Japanese, therefore, the Chinese government had to station troops throughout the country to prevent domestic rivals from seizing power or seceding.[68] With its forces dispersed, the Chinese military often found itself outnumbered in battles with the Japanese despite its four-to-one advantage in troops overall.[69]

GERMANY VERSUS RUSSIA, 1891–1917

For most of the nineteenth century, Russia had the largest GDP and military in Europe. During this time, however, Russia suffered "a steady slackening of power and prestige" and a series of crushing military defeats that culminated in the collapse of the Russian Empire in 1917.[70]

Russia had two main goals in the nineteenth and early twentieth centuries: to expand its empire in the Middle East and Asia while maintaining a balance of power in Europe. This strategy was wrecked in 1871 by the formation of Germany.[71] Although Russia initially allied with Germany and Austria-Hungary to contain France, Russia's traditional rival, the rapid growth of German power and disputes with Austria-Hungary in the Balkans compelled Russia to switch sides and ally with France in 1894. Germany, finding itself squeezed between two hostile powers, responded by building up its military and launching a preventive war to eliminate the Russian and French threat once and for all.[72]

The result—World War I—was catastrophic for Russia: Germany annihilated Russia's army; exacted a large indemnity; and forced Russia to give up territory comprising parts of modern-day Estonia, Latvia, Lithuania, Poland, Belarus, and Ukraine. Only Germany's defeat by a coalition led by Britain, France, and the United States saved Russia from bearing the full brunt of these losses. Nevertheless, Russia was devastated by the war, and by 1920 it was engulfed in a bloody civil war and accounted for a mere 2 percent of European industry. Russia would not return to the ranks of the great powers until the 1930s as the Soviet Union.

What explains Russia's poor performance? The main issue was that Russia carried greater production, welfare, and security costs than Germany and thus had far fewer net resources available for geopolitical competition (figure 2.3).

For starters, in the early twentieth century, Russia was "the least developed European power," lagging behind its neighbors in terms of per capita income, output per worker, and other measures of economic development such as literacy and health.[73] In 1910, Russia was only 40 percent as productive as Germany overall and 20 percent as productive in heavy industries.[74]

In addition, most of Russia's economic output was consumed by welfare costs. Russia's GDP grew steadily during the nineteenth century, but nearly all of this growth stemmed from population growth.[75] The demands of feeding this growing population forced 90 percent of Russia's labor force

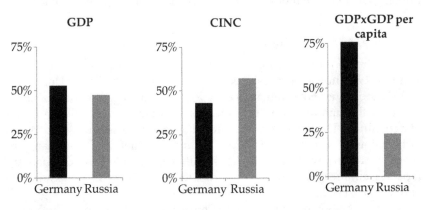

Figure 2.3. German and Russian relative shares of power resources in 1905.

Source: Maddison 2003; Singer, Bremer, and Stuckey 1972.

into agriculture, which accounted for half or more of Russia's entire eco-nomic output even as late as 1913.[76] With so many mouths to feed, Russia failed to accumulate wealth at the rate of other great powers: while the real per capita wealth of Germany grew 3 percent annually from 1890 to 1917, Russia's increased by only 1 percent.[77]

Security costs also took a large toll on Russia's economy. With a territory that stretched across one-sixth of the Earth's landmass, Russia had to main-tain large military forces just to police its own borders and prevent remote regions from breaking away.[78] From 1870 to 1913, peacetime defense spend-ing consumed 5 percent of Russia's GDP and 80 percent of the Russian gov-ernment's revenues annually. In Germany, by contrast, peacetime defense spending accounted for 3 percent of GDP.[79]

Russia's army was twice the size of Germany's and was backed by a big-ger budget, but Germany's advantages in technology and skill enabled it to outfight Russia on a soldier-for-soldier basis. Whereas German troops were well-trained and armed, a majority of Russian troops were untrained con-scripts sent into battle without rifles, where they were expected to scavenge weapons from the dead.[80] Russia also lacked railroads in its western regions, so it had extreme difficulty moving its armies around the Russo-German border.[81] Germany, on the other hand, had a well-developed rail-road system, so it could move its forces quickly to that same border.

Security costs also sapped Russian military power. As Yale Historian Paul Kennedy notes, "The great part of the Russian army was always pinned down by internal garrison duties, by police actions in Poland and the Ukraine, and by other activities, such as border patrol."[82] As a result, "in every war waged by Russia throughout the reign [of the Russian Empire], its generals were chronically embarrassed by a shortage of troops."[83] This shortage became acute in the five years prior to World War I, when mass uprisings increased tenfold and the Russian Revolution gathered pace.[84]

UNITED STATES VERSUS SOVIET UNION, 1946–92

Russia temporarily fell from the ranks of the great powers after World War I. In 1922, however, Russia reconstituted itself as the Soviet Union, and in 1928 the Soviet government, led by Josef Stalin, began modernizing the economy through forced industrialization and the ruthless collectivization of agriculture. The Soviet Union suffered enormous losses in World War II, but it gained power in relative terms because its chief rivals, Germany and Japan, were utterly destroyed. As the allies dismantled the German and Japanese empires, the Soviet Union gobbled up territory in Eastern Europe and northeast Asia.

By 1945, the Soviet Union was the most powerful nation in Europe; by the 1950s it was widely regarded as a superpower; and by the 1970s, the Soviet Union led the world by most measures of gross resources, including

CINC, army size, nuclear weapons, military spending, gross industrial output, R&D intensity, and employment of scientists and engineers.[85] In 1977, Ray Cline, the U.S. Central Intelligence Agency's chief Soviet analyst, famously combined many of these gross indicators into a single power index and concluded that the Soviet Union was twice as powerful as the United States and getting stronger.[86]

Yet between 1970 and 1991, the Soviet Union lost two million square miles of territory—a chunk of land nearly twice the size of India—and all of its client states in Eastern Europe, withdrew in defeat from Central Asia, accepted onerous arms-control agreements, and opened up sectors of its economy to Western corporations.[87] Rather than orchestrate a soft landing for its rival, the United States engaged in "intense predation" by backing independence movements within the Soviet Union and absorbing a reunited Germany into NATO.[88] In 1989, the Soviet Union called off the Cold War, and in 1991 the Soviet Union itself broke apart into fifteen states, leaving the United States standing as the world's sole superpower.[89]

How could this happen? With the benefit of hindsight, it is clear that the Soviet Union, for all of its vast size, was an inefficient state lumbering under large production, welfare, and security costs (figure 2.4).

The Soviet Union literally had the "worst performing economy in the world" in the 1970s and 1980s: its productivity was negative, its output-capital ratios declined steadily, and it became the first industrialized nation in history to record peacetime declines in life expectancy and infant mortality.[90] The Soviets grew their economy during this time, but did so mainly through "perspiration rather than inspiration"—by working harder, not smarter.[91] By the 1980s, Soviet industries were using twice as many raw material and energy inputs as American industries but producing half the output.[92]

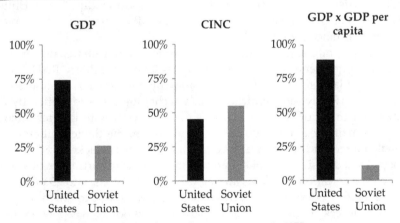

Figure 2.4. U.S. and Soviet relative shares of power resources in 1975.

Source: Maddison 2003; Singer, Bremer, and Stuckey 1972.

The U.S. productivity advantage was particularly pronounced in high-technology sectors.[93] The Soviet Union employed nearly twice as many scientists and engineers as the United States and spent nearly twice as much on R&D as a share of GDP.[94] But the Soviet Union's massive science projects (so-called Projects of the Century) failed to produce breakthroughs and succeeded only in swallowing up ever-greater shares of Soviet resources.[95] Although R&D spending and scientific employment steadily increased from the 1960s to the 1980s, the number of Soviet inventions, prototypes, patents, profitable products, and international scientific prizes declined sharply relative to those of the United States.[96] In 1985, U.S. technology companies sold 7 million computers while the Soviet Union produced only 9,000.[97]

Welfare costs also eroded Soviet wealth. Soviet social assistance programs depleted half of government revenues annually.[98] Food subsidies alone consumed 30 percent of the Soviet budget in the 1980s.[99] In the United States, by contrast, all food, housing, and other social assistance programs combined accounted for less than 10 percent of the budget.[100] By the 1980s, the only industry generating profits in the Soviet Union was the oil industry, and according to Soviet estimates, nearly 75 percent of annual oil revenues were spent on entitlements for food, housing, and social programs.[101]

Security costs also took their toll on Soviet wealth. Defense spending consumed roughly 40 percent of the Soviet budget and 15 to 20 percent of GDP—a share at least four times the U.S. level.[102] Both superpowers had globe-spanning military commitments, but as Dartmouth scholars Stephen Brooks and William Wohlforth have shown, the "relative costs of the United States' empire by invitation were not nearly as large as the imperial costs faced by the Soviets, who arguably confronted modern history's worst case of imperial overstretch."[103] The Soviet Union spent 2 to 4 percent of its GDP annually propping up the economies and militaries of its allies with aid, arms transfers, implicit trade subsidies, and export credits.[104] The United States, by contrast, spent 0.3 percent of its GDP annually on all forms of foreign assistance combined.[105]

The Soviet military, too, suffered from production, welfare, and security costs. Despite spending 2 to 3 percent of its GDP on military R&D, Soviet technology lagged behind U.S. technology by a generation or more in fifteen of the twenty most critical military technologies, as identified by the U.S. Department of Defense, and was merely on par with U.S. technology in the remaining five categories.[106] Furthermore, the Soviet military was hobbled by a rigid command structure, and its officers lacked initiative; its troops lacked basic skills, like map reading; language barriers created serious communication problems among different divisions; and 25 percent of Soviet forces were made up of fresh conscripts with little to no training.[107]

Soviet forces trained so little in part because Soviet weapons systems were so fragile; for example, Soviet fighters required overhauls at triple the rate of many Western aircraft, and Soviet tank engines wore out after

500 hours or less of use.[108] Plagued by equipment failures, the government kept most weapons systems "packed away like a family's best china," using them only for special exercises once or twice a year.[109] The resulting skill deficiencies, plus the technology issues mentioned above, probably made a Soviet conquest of Central Europe impossible.[110]

Finally, and perhaps most important, the Soviet military confronted an extremely hostile security environment.[111] By the 1980s, the United States had six times as many allies as the Soviet Union. Facing a robust Western containment barrier abroad and disaffected citizens at home, the Soviet Union had to expend significant resources just to defend its borders and prevent restive regions and satellite countries from breaking away. The United States, by contrast, enjoyed a secure home base in the Western Hemisphere and dozens of rich allies around the world. It therefore had more leeway to choose where and when to project military power and was able to offload part of the burden of defending the free world to others.

ADDITIONAL EVIDENCE

The historical cases discussed above strongly suggest that power is a function of net stocks of resources, not gross flows. But does this pattern hold for other cases? In a separate and more technical study, I demonstrate that the relationship between power and net stocks of resources does, in fact, apply broadly to all states, not just to the great powers.[112]

Specifically, I show that victory and defeat in hundreds of international disputes and wars over the past two hundred years has depended mainly on which side had larger net stocks of resources. Gross flow indicators, by contrast, perform little better than a coin toss at predicting the winners and losers of these conflicts. Israel, for example, had a smaller economy, military, and population than its Arab neighbors but nevertheless won most of its disputes and wars with them, because it was more economically and militarily efficient and, thus, had a larger net stock of resources to draw on.

I also show that net indicators perform better than gross indicators as a control variable when plugged into statistical models of international relations. Many quantitative studies control for power to isolate correlations among other variables (e.g., between the level of trade between two countries and their likelihood of going to war, between a country's regime type and the likelihood that it signs international treaties, etc.). I replicate a random sample of two dozen studies and substitute measures of gross and net resources to see how each power indicator affects the models' in-sample goodness of fit, which measures how well the model accounts for the variance in the data. Substituting measures of net resources for gross resources improves the model fit roughly 75 percent of the time.

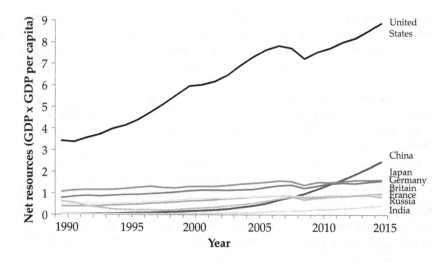

Figure 2.5. Net resources (GDP × GDP per capita) of the great powers, purchasing power parity, constant 2011 international dollars.

Source: World Bank 2016.

From Past to Present

The rise and fall of the great powers and the outcomes of international disputes and wars over the past two hundred years show that net stocks of wealth and military assets are the key pillars of power. By contrast, gross indicators systematically overstate the power of populous countries.

With this point in mind, I now turn to the current balance of power. Chapter 3 analyzes trends in the international distribution of wealth, and chapter 4 analyzes military trends. In both chapters, I focus on China, because it is the only country that could match the United States in net resources anytime soon. This point is clearly shown in figure 2.5.

Japan, France, the United Kingdom, and Germany are almost as efficient as the United States, but they lack the size necessary to contend for superpower status. Russia has neither the size nor the efficiency to contend. India will soon have the world's largest population, but it is nowhere close to rivaling China in net resources, let alone the United States. If the United States faces a peer competitor in the twenty-first century, therefore, it will surely be China.

Economic Trends

The United States is several times wealthier than China, and the absolute gap is growing by trillions of dollars each year. Obviously this conclusion cuts against the conventional wisdom that China is an economic juggernaut. It also flies in the face of data showing that China has a bigger GDP (measured by purchasing power parity) and a faster economic growth rate than the United States. Nevertheless, the large and persistent wealth gap between the United States and China is real and can be documented with considerable evidence.

Figure 3.1 provides a first look at this evidence by showing three estimates of U.S. and Chinese stocks of wealth. The first two charts display estimates of each country's total wealth and come from the United Nations' Inclusive Wealth Index and the World Bank's Comprehensive Wealth database described in chapter 2. The third is an estimate of private wealth produced by Credit Suisse. Despite using different data and methods, these indicators show a similar result: the United States is several times wealthier than China, and the absolute gap is growing by trillions of dollars. This result is similar to the picture presented by the crude indicator of net resources (GDP × GDP per capita) introduced in the previous chapter (figure 2.5).

How can China be poorer than the United States when it has a larger GDP? And how can China be trailing the United States economically when its growth rate is several times higher?

The main reason, as I explain below, is that China is big but inefficient. It produces vast output but at high costs. Chinese businesses suffer from chronically high production costs, and China's 1.4 billion people impose substantial welfare and security burdens. The United States, by contrast, is big and efficient. American businesses are among the most productive in the world, and with four times fewer people than China, the United States has lower welfare and security costs. Gross domestic product ignores the cost side of the equation and creates the false impression that China is overtaking the United States economically. In reality, China is lagging behind, because its inefficient growth model and the costs of caring for 20 percent of humanity exhaust most of its economic output.

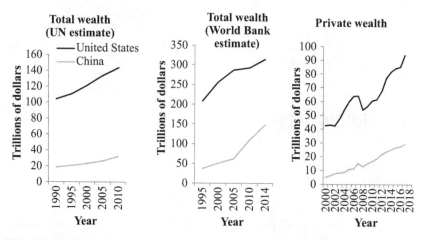

Figure 3.1. Stocks of wealth.

Note: UN estimate in constant 2005 dollars. World Bank estimate in constant 2014 dollars. Private wealth data in current dollars.

Source: UNU-IHDP 2014; Lange and Carey 2018; Credit Suisse 2017.

To develop this argument, I follow the approach of the UN and the World Bank in dividing stocks of wealth into three broad categories: human, produced, and natural capital. For each category, I present the aggregate estimates provided by the UN's Inclusive Wealth Report and the World Bank's Comprehensive Wealth database.[1] Then I dig deeper by evaluating subindicators of each type of wealth.

One cautionary note before proceeding: many of the statistics below are based on Chinese government data that probably exaggerate China's economic output. Dozens of studies have shown that Chinese officials systematically inflate China's numbers, and top Chinese leaders, including the premier and the head of China's National Statistics Bureau, have admitted as much.[2] Many economists believe that China's true economic growth rate is roughly half the government-listed rate, and some analysts argue that China's economy has not grown since the 2008 financial crisis.[3] If these claims are true, then the statistics I present below drastically understate the U.S.-China wealth gap. For the sake of conservatism, however, I take Chinese government data at face value.

Human Capital

According to the World Bank and the UN, human capital—the knowledge, skills, and labor embodied in a nation's population—constitutes more than half of the wealth of most countries and as much as 80 percent of the wealth

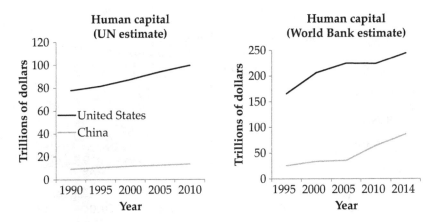

Figure 3.2. Stocks of human capital.

Note: UN estimate in constant 2005 dollars. World Bank estimate in constant 2014 dollars.

Source: UNU-IHDP 2014; Lange and Carey 2018.

of highly developed nations.[4] Figure 3.2 shows that the U.S. stock of human capital is several times greater than China's.[5] This result is surprising given that China has 1 billion more people than the United States, a higher labor force participation rate (70 percent versus 60 percent), and U.S.-China trade since 1999 may have put 2 million American manufacturing workers out of a job.[6] The reason the United States retains a larger stock of human capital despite these factors is that it has lower production, welfare, and security costs. I explain each below.

PRODUCTION COSTS

Americans workers are the most productive in the world and generate roughly seven times the output of Chinese workers on average (figure 3.3). China's labor productivity has improved since the 1970s, but remains half that of Turkey, lower than Mexico's, and roughly on par with Brazil's. There are three main reasons that American workers are more productive than Chinese workers: education, health, and organization.

Education. Americans receive twice as many years of schooling as Chinese workers on average.[7] Whereas public school is free through high school in the United States, China's government only covers the costs of elementary and middle school. At many Chinese high schools, families have to pay tuition and other expenses, and these outlays are among the highest in the world.[8] Many students drop out to avoid these fees. Consequently, 76 percent of China's working-age population has not completed

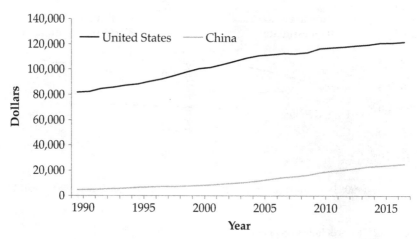

Figure 3.3. Labor productivity (GDP per worker, converted to 2016 U.S. dollars with updated 2011 PPPs).

Source: The Conference Board Total Economy Database™, May 2017. © 2017 The Conference Board, Inc. Content reproduced with permission.

high school; and roughly one-third of the children currently entering the workforce have an IQ below 90 and are barely literate or numerate.[9]

China is trying to narrow the gap in educational attainment by expanding access to higher education. Since 2000, China has doubled its number of universities and increased its tertiary enrollment rate (the share of high school graduates that enroll in college) from 8 to 30 percent.[10] Nevertheless, only 10 percent of China's workforce has a college degree, compared to 44 percent of the U.S. workforce, and the quality of Chinese universities has not kept pace with the surge in quantity.[11] Many Chinese college students describe their schools as "diploma factories," where student-teacher ratios are double the average in U.S. universities, cheating is rampant, students spend a quarter of their time studying "Mao Zedong thought," and students and professors are denied access to basic sources of information, such as Google Scholar and certain academic journal repositories.[12]

For these reasons, China still has only two of the world's top one hundred universities and only seven of the top two hundred, despite spending hundreds of billions of dollars trying to create a Chinese "Ivy League."[13] The United States, by contrast, accounts for fifty of the top one hundred universities and seventy-seven of the top two hundred.[14]

Detailed studies find that many graduates of Chinese universities lack basic reading and writing skills and less than 10 percent of Chinese engineering graduates are fit to work for a foreign multinational company.[15] According to some surveys of CEOs, the United States has a "skills gap" of roughly 4 million workers, supposedly because too many American students major in subjects like art history and philosophy instead of busi-ness, engineering, or computer science.[16] However, there are good reasons to doubt these findings: 4 million job vacancies is hardly unusual in an economy the size of America's; college enrollments in science, engineering, and business programs are actually at all-time highs; the liberal arts are quite useful for jobs in an information economy that runs on creativity and critical thinking; and careful studies suggest that CEOs may be hyping the idea of a skills gap to get the government to pay for job training programs that companies otherwise would have to pay for themselves.[17] Regardless, if CEO surveys are valid measures of human capital, then China is in trou-ble, because such surveys find that China has a skills gap of 24 million workers and is projected to have a skills gap of 40 million workers by 2030.[18]

Compounding China's talent problem is that it loses 400,000 workers every year to foreign countries in net terms, including tens of thousands of scientists and engineers and roughly 6,000 "inventors," meaning people that have registered at least one patent.[19] The total scope of China's "brain drain" problem is unknown, but U.S. government data show that the United States alone absorbs 3,500 Chinese scientists and engineers each year and nets 1 mil-lion workers annually from all foreign countries, including roughly 20,000 "inventors" and 10,000 scientists and engineers (figure 3.4).

The Chinese government is trying to reverse this brain drain by spending billions of dollars on its "1,000 Talents" scheme, which lures scholars and scientists from abroad with five-year positions at Chinese institutions and $160,000 in cash. According to the most comprehensive study of the

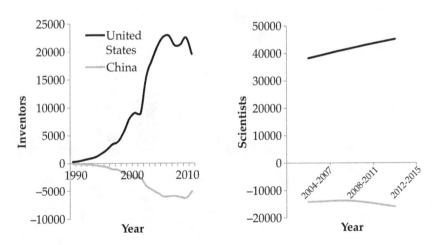

Figure 3.4. Net migration of inventors and scientists.

Note: Data on Chinese scientists only cover scientists immigrating to the United States, not to other nations.

Source: Miguelez and Fink 2013; NSF 2018.

program, however, 1,000 Talents has failed to bolster China's human capital, for several reasons:[20] more than 90 percent of the awardees have been over forty-five years old, a major problem, because scholars and scientists are generally most productive before the age of forty-five;[21] nearly 90 percent of the participants were already living in China when they received their award (Chinese universities receive $2 million for every scholar they recruit, so when schools failed to attract scholars from abroad, they simply gave awards to local scholars and collected the $2 million); 75 percent of the scholars recruited from foreign countries kept their tenured positions abroad and worked only part-time in China during the fellowship period, contributing little to China's knowledge base; and 70 percent of the recruited scholars said they intended to leave China after the fellowship.[22]

Health. The U.S. workforce is not only better educated but also healthier than China's. Figure 3.3 shows the number of years of healthy life the United States and China lose per thousand people to common diseases and injuries, a metric known as a disability-adjusted life year (DALY). China loses roughly 40 percent more years of productive life per capita on average from these major ailments (figure 3.5). According to Yanzhong Huang, a scholar at the Council on Foreign Relations, the rising costs of China's disease burden is "cancelling out the gains from economic growth"; from 2003 to 2010 China's GDP increased by 193 percent, but the costs of disease increased by 197 percent.[23]

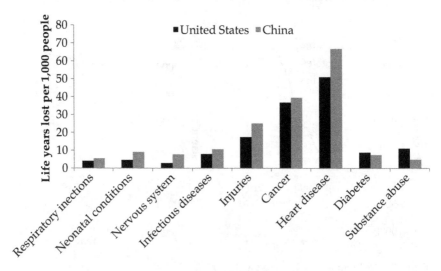

Figure 3.5. Years of life lost per 1,000 people from major diseases.

Note: Data for cancer losses are for people aged thirty to fifty-nine.

Source: WHO Mortality Database 2017.

There are three main reasons Americans are healthier than China's citizens: better healthcare, a less toxic environment, and healthier habits.

Access to healthcare in China is abysmal for all but the wealthy elite. In 2009, the government established a universal healthcare scheme, but premiums under this program are only twenty-four dollars, a sum far from sufficient to cover a basic checkup, let alone a major procedure.[24] Half of Chinese healthcare spending comes out of pocket, and many Chinese citizens avoid medical care altogether.[25] One-third of people who are told to go to a hospital decide not to because of the cost, and 80 percent of rural residents diagnosed with serious illnesses die at home because they cannot afford medical care.[26] The United States has one of the most expensive and inefficient healthcare systems in the world, as I discuss later, but it provides far greater access and care than China's system.

In addition to receiving better healthcare, American live in a less toxic environment. Air pollution is seven times worse in China than in the United States (figure 3.6) and kills 1.6 million Chinese citizens each year versus 200,000 Americans.[27] Breathing Beijing's air is the equivalent of smoking forty cigarettes a day.[28] Whereas nearly all Americans enjoy clean water out of the tap, 90 percent of China's groundwater is polluted to some degree.[29] Every year, 190 million Chinese fall ill and 60,000 die because of water pollution.[30] Combined, air and water pollution cost China an estimated 7.5 percent of GDP annually—roughly a trillion dollars—in lost productivity and medical expenses.[31]

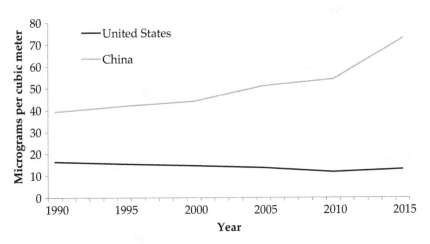

Figure 3.6. PM2.5. air pollution, mean annual exposure (micrograms per cubic meter).

Note: Population-weighted exposure to ambient PM2.5 pollution is defined as the average level of exposure of a nation's population to concentrations of suspended particles measuring less than 2.5 microns in aerodynamic diameter.

Source: World Bank 2016.

Finally, Americans generally have healthier habits than Chinese citizens. China's smoking rate, for example, is 50 percent higher than America's and projected to be 70 percent higher by 2025. China's rates of diabetes and prediabetes also recently surpassed America's, mainly because of poor nutrition.[32]The one ailment that afflicts Americans much more than Chinese citizens is substance abuse: U.S. rates of alcohol consumption are 50 percent higher than China's, and Americans are ten times more likely than Chinese citizens to die of a drug overdose.[33] As awful as America's substance abuse problem is, however, its toll does not compare to the collective toll taken by China's multiple health crises, as evidenced by the DALY data in figure 3.5. For example, the United States loses six more years of productive life per thousand people from substance abuse, but China loses sixteen more years from heart disease and another eight from cancer.

The Chinese government is working hard to solve these health problems, but the health gap between China and the United States will expand in the years ahead for a simple reason: China is aging more rapidly than any society in history. The number of Chinese aged sixty-five and older will more than triple by midcentury, from 130 million in 2015 to 410 million by 2055 (figure 3.7). At that point, senior citizens will account for nearly one-third of China's population versus only 20 percent of the U.S. population. Given that most health problems get worse with age, the graying of China's society essentially guarantees a decline in the productivity of China's workforce and an erosion of China's stock of human capital.

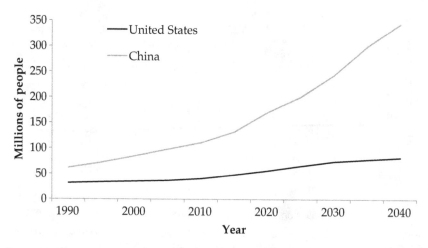

Figure 3.7. Population aged sixty-five years and older.

Source: UN Population Database 2017.

Organization. A third element of human capital is organization. A worker in Switzerland may produce more than one in Somalia, not because she is smarter or healthier, but because she works in a more organized society where resources are allocated efficiently, innovation and entrepreneurship are rewarded, and the trains run on time.

One attempt at measuring economic organization is the World Bank's "Doing Business Report," which scores countries according to the ease with which businesses can operate. In the latest report, the United States ranks seventh—after Singapore, New Zealand, Denmark, South Korea, Hong Kong, and the United Kingdom—and ahead of Sweden, Norway, and Finland. China ranks eighty-fourth, just behind Guatemala and Bosnia Herzegovina and just ahead of El Salvador and Uzbekistan. Whereas the United States is at or near the world frontier in virtually every aspect of doing business, China generally ranks in the middle of the global pack (figure 3.8). A smaller database, the World Economic Forum's Competitiveness Index, shows a similar U.S.-China gap in economic organization: the United States ranks third, behind only Switzerland and Singapore; China ranks twenty-eighth, behind Saudi Arabia and just ahead of Estonia and Thailand.

Qualitative research confirms these quantitative assessments. Numerous studies show that private companies in China face severe challenges in obtaining loans and permits, registering their business, and seeking recourse for damages and expropriation—unless they have political connections to

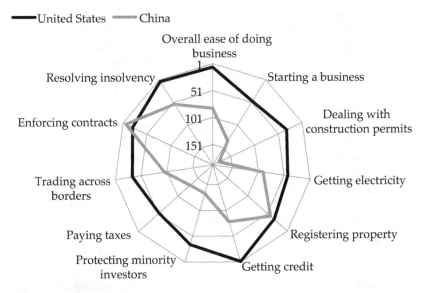

Figure 3.8. Ease of doing business. International rankings among 189 countries.

Source: World Bank 2016.

the Communist Party.[34] Entrepreneurs in China have reported spending roughly 70 percent of their time schmoozing with party members, because political connections are crucial to gain access to capital and to reduce exposure to taxes and regulations.[35] Obviously political connections help tremendously in American business as well.[36] But crony capitalism—whether measured by corruption indexes, social network analyses, or investigative reports—is several times greater in China than in the United States.[37]

WELFARE AND SECURITY COSTS

Welfare costs drain more of China's human capital than America's for one simple reason: agriculture. Whereas the United States can feed itself with only 1 percent of its workforce in agriculture, China devotes 30 percent of its workforce to farming—and still depends on food imports to feed its population.[38] China suffers a massive opportunity cost from having so many workers in the fields—the productivity level of Chinese agriculture is one-fourth that of the rest of the economy, and most of China's agricultural output is immediately consumed and therefore does not add to China's stock of wealth.[39] Economic development is, at its core, a process of structural change from agriculture to industry; the fewer farmers a nation uses to feed itself, the more workers it can mobilize to produce wealth in modern industries.[40] The United States has 99 percent of its workforce potentially available for wealth creation whereas China only has 70 percent.

The share of farmers in China's economy will decline as China's economy develops, but this process will take time given China's growing demand for food and chronically low agricultural productivity. Currently, many of China's 240 million farmers struggle to feed even themselves, because their supplies of water and land are dwindling due to pollution and overuse; in 2016, the average Chinese farmer had less than a football field of land to work with, compared to 400 football fields for the average American farmer.[41]

The United States and China devote similar shares (10 to 15 percent) of their human capital to other public welfare tasks.[42] China has a large socialist administration for a developing country, with more bureaucrats and social service workers per capita than any country in Asia except Malaysia, whereas the United States devotes a slightly smaller share of its workforce to public welfare and administration than the average developed country.[43]

Security costs, however, take a larger toll on America's human capital than China's. Although the two countries have roughly the same share of their labor forces employed in law enforcement, homeland security, and the military, the U.S. incarceration rate is five times greater than China's. With 2.2 million prisoners and another 5 million people on probation or parole, the United States leads the world in incarceration and has more people under criminal justice control than the Soviet Union imprisoned under Stalin.[44] The United States incarcerates people for acts that other countries do not consider crimes (drug possession, prostitution, accidentally violating obtuse regulations) and imposes long sentences for minor offences; under "three strikes" rules, petty thieves have been jailed for life.[45]

This prison industrial complex is not only morally abhorrent, it removes 3 percent of working-age Americans from the labor force and devastates minority communities—eight percent of black men aged twenty-five to fifty-four are institutionalized, and one in nine black children has a parent behind bars.[46] Given that children of incarcerated parents are more likely to drop out of school and develop learning disabilities and health problems, the economic and social impact of America's addiction to incarceration goes far beyond the loss of able-bodied adults.[47]

Produced Capital

The U.S. stock of produced capital—manmade goods and infrastructure— is two to three times larger than China's (figure 3.9), and this estimate understates the true gap, because one-third of China's GDP and 90 percent of its high-technology goods are produced by foreign firms that have merely set up factories in China to snap together components produced elsewhere.[48] This practice, known as "export processing," accounts for 90 percent of China's high-technology exports and 100 percent of China's trade surplus.[49] On average, of every dollar an American consumer spends on an item labeled "Made in China," 55 cents go for components and services produced in the United States.[50] In other words, more than half of the content of "Made in China" is American.[51]

Even without deducting the foreign-produced share of China's economic output, the United States still has at least two times the stock of produced capital as China. This finding may surprise people, given that China has a larger GDP in purchasing power parity terms, invests $600 billion more than the United States every year in physical capital, and has over $3 trillion in foreign exchange reserves. How can China outproduce and outinvest the United States—and own nearly $1.2 trillion in U.S. debt—yet still have a substantially smaller stock of produced capital?

The main reason, as I explain below, is that China has much higher production costs than the United States. China's rapid growth in output over the past twenty-five years has stemmed not from innovation and productivity but from capital and labor inputs; from perspiration rather than inspiration. China has been spending money to make money, and like the Soviet Union before it, China has been spending more and more to earn less and less.

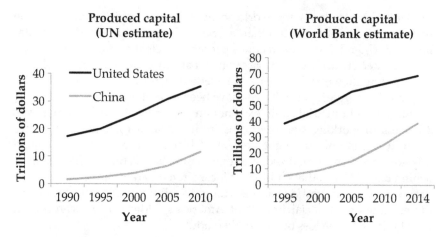

Figure 3.9. Stocks of produced capital.

Source: UNU-IHDP 2014; Lange and Carey 2018.

PRODUCTION COSTS

Gross domestic product growth is not necessarily a sign of expanding wealth. If a country spends billions of dollars building bridges to nowhere, its GDP will rise but its stock of wealth will remain unchanged or even decline. To accumulate wealth, a country needs to increase its productivity, which implies a sustained rise in output produced per unit of input, a metric that economists call total factor productivity (TFP). Mere increases in input, without an increase in the efficiency with which those inputs are used, will suffer diminishing returns and wrack up debt.

How productive is China's economy? Remarkably, 90 to 97 percent of China's economic growth since 1990 has stemmed from growth in inputs: the expansion of employment and relentless investment in physical capital.[52] China's TFP growth has not only been unspectacular, it has been virtually nonexistent, accounting for only 3 to 10 percent of China's growth during that time. By contrast, productivity improvements have accounted for 20 to 25 percent of U.S. economic growth for the past century.[53]

Many people assume that China is becoming more productive over time, but China's TFP growth rate has actually turned negative in recent years, meaning that China is producing less output per unit of input each year.[54] Meanwhile Chinese investment spending has climbed to nearly 50 percent of China's GDP—a level "unprecedented in world economic history"—and accounted for nearly all of China's economic growth.[55]

Over the same time period, American TFP has grown at roughly 1 percent a year—hardly impressive, but at least moving in the right direction—and America's output-to-capital ratio (the wealth produced for every dollar invested) has surpassed China's (figure 3.10), a remarkable development because output-to-capital ratios are usually higher in developing countries, where greenfield investment opportunities (i.e., lucrative investments in untapped areas) are more plentiful than in developed countries.

The inescapable conclusion from these numbers is that much of China's investment spending is wasted. How much, exactly, is difficult to say, but the Chinese government estimates that it blew more than $6 trillion on "ineffective investment" between 2009 and 2014.[56] This waste stems from two main sources: extravagant infrastructure projects and industrial overcapacity.

China's mega-infrastructure projects look impressive, but roughly 60 percent of them cost more to build than they will ever generate in economic returns.[57] For example, China has built more than fifty "ghost cities"—entire metropolises composed of empty office buildings, apartment complexes, shopping malls, and, in some cases, airports.[58] Americans often complain about the "crumbling" infrastructure in the United States,[59] but the World Economic Forum ranks U.S. infrastructure far ahead of China's (11th versus 42nd), partly because the United States is blessed with an abundance of natural infrastructure (e.g. internal waterways, natural harbors, etc.), a point I expand upon in chapter 5, and partly because so much of China's manmade infrastructure is useless.[60]

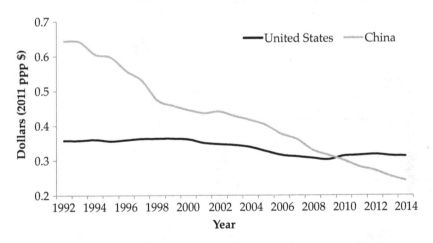

Figure 3.10. Dollars of economic output per dollar of investment (current PPP dollars).

Source: Penn World Table 2017.

Overcapacity is also common in Chinese industries, with roughly one-third of China's industrial production going to waste.[61] In industry after industry, from refining to shipbuilding to aluminum to cement, the picture is the same—supply far outpaces demand—and still expansion continues.[62] For example, China's *unused* capacity in steelmaking is greater than the *total* steel capacity of the United States, Japan, and Germany combined.[63]

Chinese officials hope that their Belt and Road initiative, which aims to reconstitute the Silk Road by investing $1 trillion in infrastructure projects in sixty-nine countries between China and Europe, can mop up excess capacity and spread Chinese influence across Eurasia.[64] The scheme may indeed boost Chinese soft power, as I discuss in chapter 5, but it also will probably exacerbate China's economic woes, because it funds hundreds of financially dubious projects in unstable countries, more than half of which have credit ratings below investment-grade.[65] The Chinese government estimates that it will lose 80 percent of the value of its investments in South Asia, 50 percent in Southeast Asia, and 30 percent in Central Asia;[66] and Chinese bankers and executives complain privately that the central government is pressuring them to undertake unprofitable projects,[67] such as building railways across Central Asia that will ship goods at more than twice the cost of shipping by sea.[68]

The unsurprising result of China's wasted investment has been a dramatic rise in debt, from 100 percent of GDP in the 1990s to more than 255 percent in 2017 (figure 3.11).[69] At $30 trillion and counting, China's debt is not only the largest ever recorded by a developing country, it has risen faster than any country's, quadrupling in absolute size between 2007 and 2017.

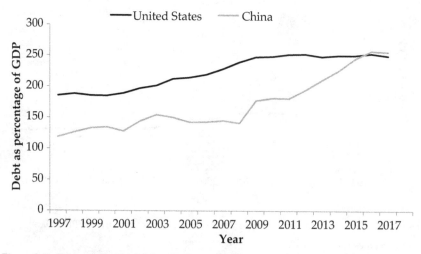

Figure 3.11. Total nonfinancial debt as a share of GDP.

Source: Bank for International Settlements 2017.

[handwritten annotation: US can sustain higher china can debt levels than]

American debt is massive too, but it has stabilized at a lower level than China's and is less burdensome. As anyone that has taken out a loan knows, the wealthier you are, the more debt you can carry. With a per capita income six times greater than China's, the United States not only has more surplus wealth to pay down its debts, but also enjoys lower interest rates.[70] The fact that the dollar is the world's reserve currency further reduces U.S. borrowing costs—an "exorbitant privilege" that saves U.S. debtors an estimated $100 billion in interest payments every year.[71]

Without these privileges, China's household and corporate borrowers have been hit with rising interest rates that now consume 20 percent of China's GDP.[72] Roughly a quarter of China's thousand biggest firms owe more money in interest than they earn in gross profits; and 45 percent of all new loans in China are being used to pay interest on old loans, a phenomenon that analysts call "Ponzi finance."[73]

Many bankers—93 percent, according to one survey—believe that China's debt is worse than the above data indicate and actually exceeds 300 percent of GDP.[74] One reason is that Chinese banks have severely underreported nonperforming loans (i.e., loans that will not be paid back). According to an analysis by Goldman Sachs, 7 percent of Chinese bank loans are nonperforming.[75] To put that number in perspective, consider that the U.S. nonperforming loan ratio peaked at 5.6 percent at the height of the 2008 financial crisis.[76]

Another reason China's debt may be understated is that many Chinese companies take loans from shadow banks, whose transactions are not included in official Chinese statistics. Such "back-alley banking" has become rampant in recent years.[77] From 2010 to 2012 alone, Chinese shadow lenders doubled their outstanding loans to $5.8 trillion—a sum equivalent to 69 percent of China's GDP and more than seven times the size of the stimulus package the United States rolled out to recover from the 2008 financial crisis—and from 2012 to 2016, Chinese shadow loans increased by an additional 30 percent each year.[78]

China may avoid a full-blown financial crisis—the state owns both the banks and their biggest corporate borrowers, and Chinese citizens have little choice but to keep their savings in state-owned banks—but writing off these bad loans will cost China somewhere between $1.5 trillion and $10 trillion, the latter figure nearly equal to China's entire GDP.[79] By comparison, during the global financial crisis, the direct cost of rescuing U.S. banks was about 8 percent of GDP.[80]

China has $3 trillion of foreign exchange reserves, but they are not a treasure-trove that the Chinese government can use to pay off its debts.[81] The Chinese government purchased these reserves with money taken from state-owned banks, most of which was deposited there by Chinese citizens. If the government were to spend that money, it would be stealing $3 trillion from the Chinese people—a move that would probably collapse the banking system, as people would not likely put more money in banks that just expropriated their life-savings.

Ultimately, the only way for China to solve its debt problem without gutting social spending is to increase its productivity, which in turn will require innovation. The Chinese government understands this point well. Since 2006, it has tripled its spending on research and development (R&D), employed more scientists and engineers than any other country, and mounted the most extensive corporate espionage campaign in history.[82]

So far, however, these measures have failed to turn China into an innovation powerhouse. As shown in figure 3.12, China lags far behind the United States by all standard measures of innovation, including profits, patents, and royalties in high-technology industries and highly cited scientific articles.

China has developed pockets of economic excellence. For example, China leads the world in some manufacturing industries—especially in the production of household appliances, textiles, steel, solar panels, and simple drones—because its huge population of poor workers and generous government subsidies enable

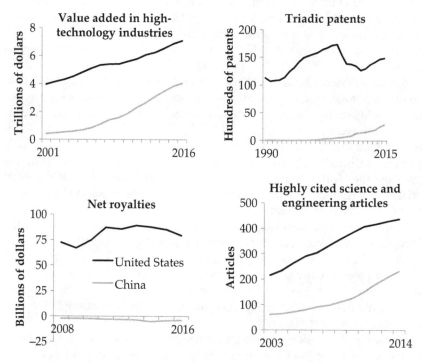

Figure 3.12. Innovation outputs.

Note: Net royalties (balance of royalty payments and receipts), value added in high-technology industries, triadic patents, and top 1 percent most-cited articles in science and engineering fields.

Source: National Science Board 2018.

it to function as the "workshop of the world," churning out commodified goods at low prices.[83] China also has the world's largest e-commerce market and mobile payments system and commands respectable shares of global markets for Internet software and communications equipment—mainly because the Chinese government restricts foreign Internet and telecommunications firms from operating in China, thereby giving Chinese firms, such as Alibaba, Baidu, and Tencent, a captive market of a billion people.[84]

However, in high-technology industries, meaning those that involve the commercial application of scientific research (e.g., pharmaceuticals, biotechnology, and semiconductors) or the engineering and integration of complex parts (e.g. aviation, medical devices, and system software), China generally accounts for small shares of global markets compared to the United States.[85] China is a major producer of many high-technology products, particularly computer and electronics technologies, but most Chinese firms in these industries are confined to low-tech, low-productivity activities, such as manufacturing and component supply whereas American firms tend to focus on product design, development, and branding—the activities in which profits and proprietary knowledge are greatest.[86]

As manufacturing has become increasingly automated with the development of 3D-printing and artificial intelligence, and as China's labor costs have risen, American firms have started "reshoring" manufacturing plants in the United States to take advantage of low energy prices, high-skilled labor, and proximity to consumers. For those reasons, Deloitte and Boston Consulting Group both project that the United States will overtake China as the world's most cost-competitive manufacturing nation by 2020.[87]

Technological leaders sometimes rest on their laurels and abandon innovative efforts in favor of "finding new markets for old products."[88] The United States may be falling into this trap. The Trump administration has proposed reducing federal nondefense R&D spending by 20 percent, a move that would continue a long-term trend of declining government support for scientific research. Over the past thirty years, the American private sector has compensated for the decline in U.S. government support and driven overall U.S. R&D spending to all-time highs.[89] However, business R&D tends to focus on incremental innovations and the application and marketing of existing technologies, not on the invention of new "disruptive" technologies. By cutting government R&D spending, the United States risks stifling basic scientific research across a range of subjects and missing out on major breakthroughs as a result.[90]

Other worrying trends include the fact that the U.S. startup rate (the share of new firms in the total number) has declined by 50 percent since 1978, and business deaths now outnumber business births for the first time in generations.[91] American corporate profits are at all-time highs, but two-thirds of U.S. economic sectors have become more concentrated among a handful of mega firms, a fact that suggests that rent seeking and price gouging, rather than innovation, caused the rise in profits.[92] For example, the four airlines that now control 80 percent of the U.S. commercial airline market (compared to 48 percent a decade ago) have profited immensely in recent years by cramming more passengers onto planes without reducing ticket prices.[93]

The overall picture of the U.S. economy, then, is one of declining dynamism. Some economists dismiss these negative trends as a temporary hangover from the Great Recession or a statistical fluke (standard industrial-era indicators may not capture the economic benefits of new technologies like digital search engines, G.P.S.-generated directions, video chat, etc.).[94] A more worrying possibility, however, is that U.S. innovation is simply not what it used to be. The Internet and smartphones are great inventions, but they may not be as revolutionary as the innovations that propelled previous eras of U.S. productivity, such as the internal-combustion engine, electrification, indoor plumbing, and commercial jetliners.[95]

Despite these worrying trends, however, the United States still outpaces China in most of the "industries of the future," which include information industries that harness big data; machine industries that design advanced tools and robots; medical industries that create new drugs and healthcare technologies; and energy industries that produce alternatives to fossil-fuels.[96] Figure 3.13 shows U.S. and Chinese relative shares of value added

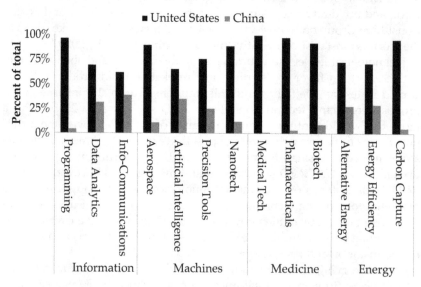

Figure 3.13. U.S. and Chinese relative shares of value added or patents in industries of the future.

Source: Graphs for programming, data analytics, aerospace, and precision tools use value-added data from National Science Board 2018. All other industries use patent data from OECD 2017 and *The Economist* 2017b.

(or patents when value-added data were unavailable) in these industries. With few exceptions, the United States has a commanding lead.

China performs well in alternative energy industries, largely because of government subsidies, as mentioned above. The same goes for supercomputers and quantum communications—two areas where China outspends the United States in R&D.[97] China also is becoming a world leader in some information and artificial intelligence (AI) industries, including digital payments and speech- and face-recognition. The main reason is that China has an abundance of data, the vital input to these industries.[98] In the past, software products were created by programmers typing code. With the advent of deep-learning algorithms, however, such products are increasingly based on reams of data. The more data available, the smarter the products will be. With nearly 730 million Internet users, China is the "Saudi Arabia of data;" just by going about their lives, China's citizens generate more data than most other countries combined.[99] In most AI sectors, America still leads China in profits, patents, and number of companies.[100] But China could rapidly close the gap unless American firms develop algorithms capable of getting smart with less data (for example, by using simulated data, including data generated from video games).[101]

For now, the United States remains at the forefront of global innovation, accounting for almost a third of global high-technology revenues, nearly double China's share.[102] China's government has ordered Chinese scientists to catch up to the United States by 2050.[103] Rather than spurring innovation, however, this mandate has fostered "a Wild West climate where top researchers, under intense pressure to produce, are tempted to fake results or copy the works of others."[104] According to a former Chinese biochemist turned whistle-blower, "misconduct is so widespread among Chinese academics that they have almost become used to it."[105] China now leads the world in retractions of scientific studies due to fraud; one-third of Chinese scientists have admitted to plagiarizing or falsifying results (versus 2 percent of U.S. scientists); and two-thirds of China's R&D spending has been lost to corruption.[106]

Chinese businesses, too, have generally failed to answer Beijing's call for innovation. From 1991 to 2015, annual sales of new products accounted for less than 14 percent of Chinese firms' annual profits.[107] For American firms, by contrast, new products accounted for 35 to 40 percent of sales revenue.[108] Over the same time period, Chinese firms' total spending on R&D as a percentage of sales revenue stalled at levels four times below the average for American firms.[109] When Chinese firms imported foreign technology, they spent less than 25 percent of the total cost on absorbing the technology, a share far lower than the 200 to 300 percent spent by Korean and Japanese firms when they were trying to catch up to the West in the 1970s.[110] As a result, many Chinese firms remain dependent on foreign technologies and manual labor and have a rudimentary level of automation and digitization:

on average Chinese enterprises have just nineteen robots per ten thousand employees; U.S. firms, by contrast, use an average of 176 robots per ten thousand employees.[111]

For all these reasons, major studies on Chinese innovation generally paint a dismal picture. A joint study by the World Bank and the Chinese government finds that "China has seen a sharp rise in scientific patents and published papers, but few have commercial relevance and even fewer have translated into new products or exports."[112] Another study by the Mercator Institute for China Studies predicts that China's national innovation policy "will probably fail in its endeavor to catalyze a comprehensive, broad-scale technological upgrading across the Chinese economy. The strategy's effectiveness is limited by the mismatch between political priorities and industry needs, the fixation on quantitative targets, inefficient allocation of funding and campaign-style overspending by local governments."[113]

WELFARE AND SECURITY COSTS

In contrast to production costs, which afflict China's stocks of produced capital much more than America's, U.S. and Chinese welfare and security costs basically cancel each other out: China spends more on food and has more unfunded pensions; the United States spends more on healthcare and security; and the two nations spend roughly equal amounts on education.

Food. China spends around $1 trillion per year on food, which is 30 percent more than the United States (figure 3.14). China's high cost of food stems from three main factors: high consumption, scarce land, and low agricultural productivity. China consumes double the meat and nine times as many cereals and grains as the United States, but has roughly half as much arable land and produces less than 70 percent as much food per hectare.[114] This imbalance will almost surely get worse, because China will have hundreds of millions more meat consumers in the coming decades barring a dramatic cultural shift toward vegetarianism.[115] Meanwhile China is projected to lose another 20 percent of its arable land to pollution and drought.[116]

Social Security. China has at least $10 trillion in unfunded pension liabilities out to 2040, a shortfall that is $2.5 trillion greater than the United States'.[117] I say "at least" $10 trillion, because other studies calculate that China's shortfall is more severe—a Bank of China/Deutsche Bank study, for example, calculates that China's shortfall will reach $10.9 trillion in 2033, while the Chinese Academy of Social Sciences estimates that by 2050 there will be a $128 trillion gap.[118] Theoretically, China could reduce its pension gap by reducing payouts to retirees. In practice, however, such cost cutting is impossible, because Chinese retirees already receive

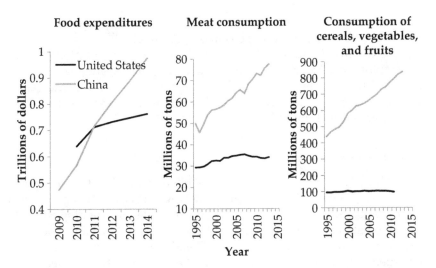

Figure 3.14. Voracious appetites.

Note: Cost and weight of annual consumption of meat, cereals, vegetables, and fruits.

Source: Food expenditure data from U.S. Department of Agriculture Economic Research Service. Food consumption data from Food and Agriculture Organization of the United Nations Statistics Division.

meager pensions—in some rural Chinese counties the basic pension is less than nine dollars per month.[119] Remarkably, these puny payouts have already exhausted China's stock of pension assets. As a result, China is paying current-year benefits with current-year contributions, a pay-as-you-go scheme that will become unsustainable as China's ratio of workers to retirees drops from 8-to-1 today to just over 2-to-1 by 2040.[120] The U.S. ratio, on the other hand, will hover at 3-to-1 and then start to rise after 2040.

Education Spending. The U.S. and Chinese governments both spend around $800 billion per year on education.[121] As noted, however, the United States provides free public school through high school whereas China's government only covers the costs of elementary and middle school.[122] To address this problem, the Chinese government has proposed a massive increase in education spending.[123] If present trends continue, China will overtake the United States in education spending in the 2020s.

Healthcare. The United States spends $3 trillion on healthcare annually, compared to China's $1 trillion.[124] The United States reaps some benefits from this largesse—as shown earlier, U.S. rates of disease are much lower than China's, and Americans have more access to advanced medical technologies and drugs than Chinese citizens—but the fiscal costs are enormous. Americans spend more than $10,000 per capita each year on healthcare and a whopping 18 percent of GDP in total.[125]

In the coming decades, China's healthcare spending will probably rise more rapidly that America's, because China's population is aging at a faster rate and China has higher rates of disease. The overall U.S.-China gap in healthcare spending, however, will probably remain greater than $1 trillion for the foreseeable future.[126]

SECURITY COSTS

The United States spends roughly $800 billion more than China per year on security (figure 3.15). This estimate, however, is based on a maximalist interpretation of U.S. security spending that includes any funding remotely related to national defense, veterans affairs, foreign policy, homeland security, or domestic law enforcement.[127] China's totals, by contrast, include only spending on "national defense" and "public security" as listed in the *China Statistical Yearbook*, a Chinese government publication. Many analysts

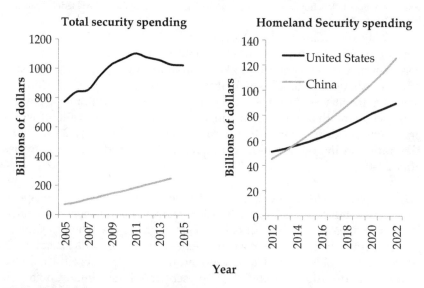

Figure 3.15. Security costs.

Note: Total security spending and homeland security spending. Homeland security spending includes border defense, internal security, and public safety spending.

Source: Data for total security spending from White House, Historical Tables, table 3.2, Outlays by Function and Subfunction, and table 4.1, Outlays by Agency; U.S. Census, compiled by usgovernmentspending.com; China data from *China Statistical Yearbook*. Homeland security spending data from Homeland Security Research Corp 2015. Reproduced courtesy of Homeland Security Research Corp., www.hsrc.biz.

believe these totals drastically understate China's true level of internal security spending, most of which is done off-budget.[128]

Regardless, the picture changes dramatically if we exclude military spending, which is arguably a source of power rather than a pure cost, and count only spending on homeland security. As shown in figure 3.15, China's homeland security costs are already greater than the United States' and are projected to rise rapidly in the coming decades. The two main reasons are that China suffers from a much higher rate of domestic unrest than does the United States and faces more serious threats to its territorial integrity.

All major political risk indices show that China suffers roughly twice as much unrest and crime per capita as the United States and typically ranks in the bottom fourth of the world in domestic stability.[129] For example, the World Bank's political stability and absence of violence index, which aggregates political risk data from more than thirty sources, ranks China 157th out of 212 countries, just ahead of Azerbaijan and Honduras, whereas the United States ranks 56th. Chinese government data paint a similar picture: so-called mass incidents (public protests or riots involving a hundred or more people) increased from 9,000 in 1993 to 280,000 in 2010;[130] and so-called social order violations, which refer to fights or cases in which large groups of citizens obstructed police from their duties, have risen from 3.2 million in 1995 to 13.9 million in 2012.[131] The Chinese government stopped releasing these figures to the public after 2012.

Unrest in China emanates from multiple sources. In Tibet and Xinjiang, which account for almost one-third of China's landmass, non-Han ethnic groups wage low-level insurgencies against the central government. In Hong Kong, residents maintain a separate political system and periodically stage large protests against Beijing's attempts to dilute their political autonomy. And throughout China, citizens harboring a variety of grievances—for example, pollution, corruption, and government land seizures—stage demonstrations that sometimes turn violent.

In addition to containing domestic unrest, China must secure its land borders, which stretch fourteen thousand miles and include boundaries with fifteen countries.[132] Most of these borders have been conflict zones at some point in China's history. Some of them remain so today.

Most notable, China shares a bitterly contested fourteen-hundred-mile border with India.[133] In the northern section, China occupies an area of Indian-claimed territory the size of Switzerland. In the eastern part, India occupies Chinese-claimed territory the size of Austria. Both sides maintain a massive military presence near the border: China has built air bases, roads, and railways capable of surging 450,000 troops to the border; India keeps four divisions on the border armed with long-range cruise missiles and backed up by two fighter squadrons. In the summer of 2017, Chinese and Indian forces had their most tense border standoff since the 1962 Sino-Indian border war.

China's eight-hundred-mile border with Vietnam also remains tense.[134] When anti-Chinese protests erupted in Vietnam in 2014 (after China placed an oil rig inside Vietnam's exclusive economic zone), China deployed thousands of troops, tanks, missile launchers, and other heavy artillery to Pingxiang city, where the 1979 Sino-Vietnamese war started. In 2014 and 2015, Chinese and Vietnamese forces exchanged fire on at least two occasions, and both countries withdrew from border peace talks in 2017.

China's other land borders are less militarized, but they still require attention and resources from Chinese security forces. China and Russia formally resolved their border dispute in 2008—the two countries fought a war there in 1969—but both countries have modernized their forces near the border and conduct military exercises simulating a Sino-Russian war.[135]

North Korea is a formal ally of China, but China stations three Group Armies (roughly 150,000 troops) and a border defense brigade near their 880-mile shared border.[136] China maintains twenty-four-hour video and aerial drone surveillance of the border, has built bunkers there to protect Chinese forces against nuclear and chemical blasts, and has surged additional units to the border on several recent occasions, including in 2010 when North Korea shelled South Korea's Yeonpyeong Island; in 2013 after the purge of Jang Song Thaek, a high-ranking North Korean official and uncle of North Korea's leader Kim Jong Un; in August 2015 after an outbreak of hostilities between North and South Korea in the Korean demilitarized zone; and in 2017 when North Korea and the United States threatened each other with nuclear annihilation.[137]

Finally, the People's Liberation Army (PLA) is engaged in a war on terror on its borders with Central Asian states, where Uighur separatists have established safe havens. China also has flooded the streets of Xinjiang with tens of thousands of paramilitary troops to enforce "grid-style social management" (aka martial law) on the population.[138]

All told, China probably spends several hundred billion dollars each year to secure its homeland. The United States, by contrast, enjoys low levels of internal unrest and is bordered by two weak neighbors, both of whom are U.S. allies. As a result, U.S. homeland security costs are less onerous than China's.

Natural Capital

The key elements of natural capital are water, energy resources, and arable land, all of which are necessary to sustain life and power agriculture and industry. According to the UN, the United States has roughly 30 percent more natural capital than China, and both countries have been depleting their stocks over time. The World Bank, however, calculates that China has nearly three times the natural capital of the United States and suggests that both nations have been growing their stocks over time (figure 3.16).[139]

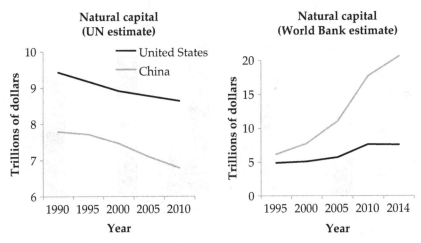

Figure 3.16. Stocks of natural capital.

Note: UN estimate in constant 2005 dollars. World Bank estimate in constant 2014 dollars.

Source: UNU-IHDP 2014; Lange and Carey 2018.

Which estimate is more accurate? Additional data suggests that the UN's estimate is closer to the mark. According to the U.S. Central Intelligence Agency, the United States has 10 percent more renewable freshwater than China (figure 3.17); and analyses by the Council on Foreign Relations, *The Economist,* and independent researchers suggest that the actual gap is much larger, because half of China's river water and 90 percent of its groundwater is unfit to drink, and 25 percent of China's river water and 60 percent of its groundwater is so polluted that the Chinese government has deemed it "unfit for human contact" and unusable even for agriculture or industry.[140] China technically has 50,000 large rivers, but more than half of them have been destroyed through pollution, overuse, climate change, or all of the above.[141]

In terms of energy resources, the United States has three times as much oil and natural gas as China and twice as much coal (figure 3.17). China has subsidized its renewable energy and nuclear power industries, but both combined still account for less than 5 percent of China's energy use compared to 12 percent of the United States'.[142] China has large reserves of oil and natural gas encased in shale basins, but China has not been able to tap them and, according to some analyses, may never do so.[143] One reason is that China's shale deposits were left behind by prehistoric lakes and, consequently, have rock layers that are more ductile and less amenable to hydraulic fracturing than the brittle marine shales in North America.[144] Another reason is that China lacks the water necessary for fracking. Each shale-gas well requires fifteen thousand tons of water a year to run, and China would need to drill thousands of wells a year to launch a successful industry. China has nowhere

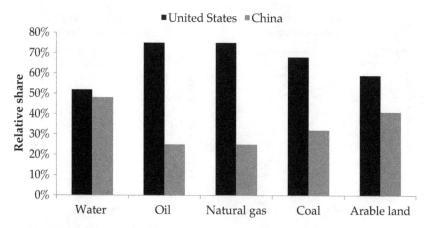

Figure 3.17. Natural endowments compared.

Note: Relative shares (percentage) of water, energy resources, and arable land.

Source: Data for water from CIA World Factbook. Data for energy resources from BP 2016. Data for land from World Bank 2016.

near that amount of water located close to its major shale basins, which are concentrated in Jilin and Liaoning, two of China's driest provinces.[145]

Finally, the United States has 45 percent more arable land than China, and again the true size of the gap is probably much larger because large chunks of China's farmland are too polluted, desiccated, or both to support agriculture. According to a recent Chinese government study, water pollution has destroyed nearly 20 percent of China's arable land, an area the size of Belgium.[146] An additional 1 million square miles of China's farmland has become desert, forcing the resettlement of 24,000 villages and pushing the edge of the Gobi Desert to within 150 miles of Beijing.[147] A recent study by Renmin University estimates that restoring China's farmland would cost $1 trillion.[148]

In sum, the United States has more water, energy resources, and arable land than China. The U.S. stock of natural capital, however, is larger than China's not only because of the size of U.S. resource endowments, but also because the United States uses its resources more efficiently and has fewer people to support with them. In other words, the United States has lower production and welfare costs.

PRODUCTION COSTS

The United States generates more than three times as much wealth from each gallon of water as China (figure 3.18). China's water use is extremely inefficient. In agriculture, only 45 percent of the water China withdraws actually makes it to crops, and in industry only 40 percent of water is

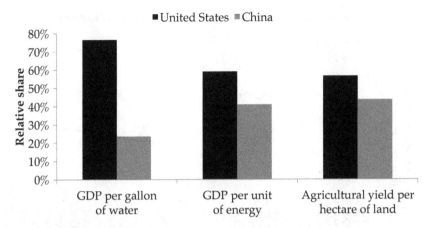

Figure 3.18. Efficiency of use of natural resources.

Source: World Bank 2016.

recycled, compared to 85 percent in the United States.[149] Geography further drags down the efficiency of China's water use: more than 80 percent of China's water is located in the south, but half of China's people and two-thirds of its farms are in the North, so China is spending tens of billions of dollars to divert water from the Yangtze River in the south to the Yellow River in the north.[150]

The United States generates roughly 40 percent more wealth per unit of energy than China (figure 3.18). China's energy efficiency has risen steadily since the 1970s, but it still lags behind that of the United States because China's economy is dominated by heavy industries and manufacturing plants that consume vast amounts of energy to make low-profit products.[151]

Finally, American farmers produce 30 percent more food per hectare than Chinese farmers. Part of the U.S. agricultural advantage stems from better soil and more plentiful water. Another reason is that most of China's farmers are poor peasants, roughly 40 percent of whom lack motorized equipment of any kind and have to plow and seed their fields using animals or their own muscle.[152]

WELFARE COSTS

With four times the population of the United States, China unsurprisingly consumes more water, energy, and land. In fact, China is the world's most voracious consumer of all three resources.[153] Figure 3.14, presented earlier, showed that China's food consumption is increasing rapidly and has overtaken that of the United States. Figure 3.19 shows the same is true for water and energy.

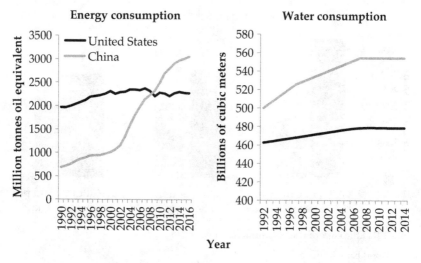

Figure 3.19. Resource consumption.

Source: Data for energy from BP 2016. Data for water from World Bank 2016.

China's resource consumption strains its limited supplies. China's per capita availability of water is less than one-quarter of the United States' and less than one-third the world's average. The World Bank defines water scarcity as less than 1,000 cubic meters of fresh water per person per year. By that standard, roughly one-third of China's provinces and two-thirds of its major cities suffer from water scarcity.[154] Beijing, for example, has roughly the same amount of water per person (145 cubic meters) as Saudi Arabia. Dealing with this scarcity, costs China roughly $140 billion per year in government expenditures and reduced productivity versus $12 billion for the United States.[155]

China already consumes 10 percent more energy than the United States and is expected to consume twice as much as America by 2040.[156] China currently depletes $400 billion of its energy resources per year and pays foreign countries another $500 billion in energy imports. U.S. annual depletion and net import costs, by contrast, are currently $140 billion and $120 billion respectively.

Finally, China's food consumption is outstripping the agricultural capacity of its land. In 2008, China became a net importer of grain, breaking its traditional policy of self-sufficiency, and in 2011 China became the world's largest importer of agricultural products.[157] Since then, China has increased its reliance on food imports, especially from the United States, which is China's top supplier of agricultural products and earns roughly $25 billion per year by selling food to China.[158] China is trying to regain food self-sufficiency by heavily subsidizing farmers. As a consequence, however,

China is rapidly depleting its supply of agricultural land; according to an analysis by Xinhua, more than 40 percent of China's arable land is suffering some form of "degradation" from overuse, including reduced fertility, erosion, changes in acidity, pollution, or all of the above.[159]

China's economic growth over the past three decades has been spectacular, even miraculous. Yet the veneer of double-digit growth rates has masked gaping liabilities that impede China's ability to close the wealth gap with the United States. China's rapid growth in economic output can be explained almost entirely by rapid growth of inputs: hiring workers and spending money. China has achieved high growth at high costs, and the trends show that the costs are rising while growth is slowing. Accounting for these costs and trends reveals that the United States is several times wealthier than China, and the absolute gap is growing by trillions of dollars each year.

Nevertheless, wealth is only one pillar of global power. The other is military capability. History shows that China could threaten the United States militarily even as it lags behind economically. The Soviet Union, for example, never matched the United States in terms of aggregate wealth, yet it still managed to threaten U.S. primacy by raising a huge military that loomed over Central Europe. Could China do the same in East Asia? The next chapter considers this question.

Military Trends

Is China poised to dominate East Asia militarily? Will China eventually challenge the United States for global military supremacy?

Many studies address these questions, but most tally military assets (e.g. military spending, personnel, and weapons systems) while neglecting liabilities. This is a serious shortcoming, because the amount of military power a country can project abroad depends crucially on the strength and security of its home base. Two nations with identical militaries may, nevertheless, wield vastly different levels of military power if one country is surrounded by enemies and wracked by domestic instability whereas the other is stable and surrounded by allies. Assessments of the U.S.-China military balance, therefore, need to consider not only the assets each military has at its disposal but also the burdens each military is forced to bear.

This chapter provides such an assessment. The first half examines each country's net military resources. The second half assesses how each side would fare in the most likely scenarios for a U.S.-China war. My main finding is that the United States has five to ten times the net military assets of China and maintains a formidable containment barrier against Chinese expansion in East Asia.

Defense Spending

The United States currently outspends China militarily three to one. Many analysts, however, expect that gap to shrink in the years ahead and some organizations, including *The Economist* and the International Institute for Strategic Studies, have projected that China's defense budget will overtake America's by the 2030s.[1]

There are many reasons to doubt such projections, not the least of which is that China's economic growth is slowing dramatically, as shown in the previous chapter. Even if China's defense spending eventually exceeds America's, however, it would not necessarily mean that China has more military resources. Defense spending statistics are gross flow measures that ignore accumulated stocks of military spending and fail to deduct welfare or security costs. As a result, such statistics vastly understate the U.S.-China military gap. Below, I elaborate on these points.

STOCKS VERSUS FLOWS

Since the 1950s, the United States has spent roughly half a trillion dollars every year on its military.[2] As a result, the United States has amassed an arsenal of thousands of ships, aircraft, vehicles, satellites, R&D labs, radar installations, ammunition stockpiles, testing and training facilities, and bases.[3] Many U.S. platforms built in the 1980s remain in service today, including hundreds of ships and thousands of aircraft that are as capable as China's most advanced platforms.

Even discounting these Cold War-era assets, the U.S.-China gap in military stocks is large and growing, because the United States outspends China every year. Figure 4.1 shows U.S. and Chinese accumulated defense spending since 2000 (not including U.S. appropriations for the wars in Iraq and Afghanistan) and makes clear that China would need to outspend the United States by substantial margins in the decades ahead just to start closing the gap in recently accumulated military capital.

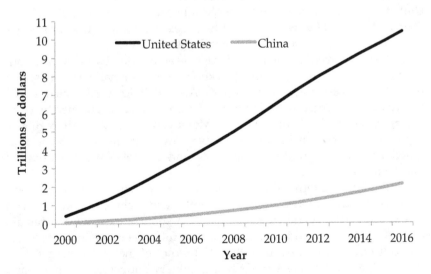

Figure 4.1. Stocks of accumulated defense spending since 2000 (constant 2015 dollars).

Source: SIPRI 2017a.

WELFARE COSTS

A second reason military spending data understate the U.S.-China gap is that welfare costs consume at least 34 percent of China's military budget versus 27 percent of the United States'. Chinese troops are cheaper than U.S. personnel on a per soldier basis—because they receive less equipment, lower wages, and fewer benefits than their U.S. counterparts[4]—but China employs 1.2 million more troops than the United States and thus has many more pensions and salaries to pay and food, medical care, training and housing to provide.[5]

The figures above probably understate China's true military welfare costs, because China's numbers only include personnel costs whereas the U.S. figures include personnel costs plus military construction costs.[6] Moreover, China's numbers do not include spending on the 8 million troops in the People's Liberation Army's (PLA) Militia, which handles the PLA's logistics and rear area security missions.[7] Nor do China's numbers account for the dramatic rise in Chinese wages over the past two decades. In 2006, for example, the PLA doubled troops' salaries, but the Chinese government reported, incredibly, that personnel costs did not increase. Independent estimates suggest that rising personnel costs actually are "an enormous burden on [China's] defense budget" and have consumed more than half of the increases in China's military budget since 2005.[8]

SECURITY COSTS

As noted in chapter 3, China suffers from more domestic unrest than the United States and is surrounded by hostile countries whereas the United States is bordered by two allies and two oceans. As a result, security costs drain more of China's military budget than America's.

At least 20 percent of the PLA's budget—as reported by the most popular public source of data, the Stockholm International Peace Research Institute—actually funds the People's Armed Police (PAP), an internal security force charged with domestic missions that are performed by civilian agencies in the United States.[9] Moreover, the PLA itself regularly expends resources on internal security.[10] For example, in 2008 the PLA rolled into Tibet to put down mass riots, and in 2009 PLA forces imposed martial law in Xinjiang.

In addition to internal security, the PLA must secure China's land borders, which stretch fourteen thousand miles and include boundaries with fifteen countries.[11] As described in chapter 3, some of these borders remain conflict zones today, and all of them require full-time border defense forces that collectively consume more than 15 percent of the PLA's budget.[12] All told, then, at least 35 percent of China's military budget goes to homeland security operations: 20 percent for the PAP and an additional 15 percent for border defense troops (figure 4.2).[13]

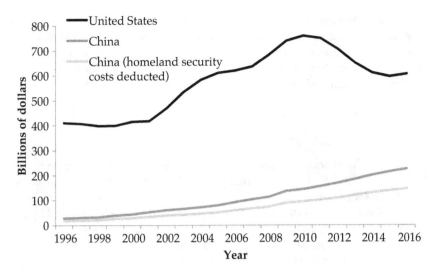

Figure 4.2. Annual military spending (constant 2015 dollars).

Source: SIPRI 2017a.

Whereas the PLA is bogged down at home, the U.S. military focuses on power projection abroad. The U.S. military does not maintain a paramilitary force equivalent to the PAP and is barred by law (the Posse Comitatus Act of 1878) from conducting internal security missions. State governments occasionally call on the National Guard—a military reserve of part-time "citizen-soldiers"—to help local police contain protests, secure infrastructure (e.g., airports), or provide disaster relief. But these homeland deployments are funded by state budgets, not the U.S. military budget. They therefore do not need to be deducted from U.S. military spending statistics the way PAP funding should be deducted from Chinese military spending data.

Border defense missions also take little financial toll on the U.S. military. No country claims any U.S. territory, and civilian agencies (mainly the Department of Homeland Security, the Federal Bureau of Investigation, and the National Security Agency) run and fund border patrol and domestic counterterrorism operations. In addition, the Department of Energy pays most of the costs of maintaining the U.S. nuclear arsenal, so the only homeland security mission funded primarily by the U.S. military is national missile defense, which consumes less than 1 percent of the U.S. military budget.

The U.S. military conducts expensive counterterrorism missions abroad, but the direct costs of these missions, which include the wars in Iraq and Afghanistan, have been paid out of a separate congressional slush fund called the Overseas Contingency Operations budget.[14] The long-term costs (e.g., the cost of medical care and disability compensation for veterans and their families) have been paid primarily by the Department of Veterans

Affairs and private charities.[15] Obviously the wars in Iraq and Afghanistan have taken an enormous economic and social toll on the United States—the wars cost $5 trillion and killed nearly seven thousand U.S. soldiers and wounded more than fifty thousand—but they are not hidden costs that need to be subtracted from U.S. military spending statistics.[16]

Personnel

China has the world's largest military and fields 1.2 million more troops than the United States. Extra manpower, however, does not necessarily give China a military advantage. As explained earlier, employing millions of troops generates welfare costs that deplete funds for weapons and operations. Moreover, as I will show below, PLA personnel are less skilled than U.S. military personnel on average, and nearly half of the PLA's personnel are tied down by homeland security missions.

PRODUCTION COSTS

To survive on a modern battlefield, military units need to be stealthy and nimble, attributes that require tremendous skill.[17] In previous centuries, populous countries could win wars by sending hordes of untrained conscripts to overwhelm opponents. Today, however, mass armies are sitting ducks, because a single precision-guided missile can wipe out a whole company of troops or sink a large warship. A country's military power, therefore, depends not just on the size of its ranks, but also on the skill of its soldiers, which can be assessed by four main factors: education, combat experience, training, and leadership.

Education. The PLA has nearly caught up to the United States in terms of the educational attainment of its personnel.[18] In 2000, half of the PLA had only a middle school education. By 2010, however, 88 percent of China's troops had attended high school and 20 percent had a four-year college degree—a percentage not far below that of U.S. military personnel (28 percent).

Combat Experience. The PLA, however, lacks combat experience. Whereas the United States has been the most militarily active country in the world since 1945, China has not fought a war since 1979 (a short border war against Vietnam involving only the army) and has conducted only one joint combat campaign in its history (the 1955 amphibious landing to capture Yijiangshan Island from Kuomintang forces). Both operations resulted in heavy PLA casualties. At present, essentially none of China's troops has ever been in combat. Chinese analysts call this problem "peace disease" and fret that PLA troops lack the valor (*xuexing*) necessary to win a war.[19]

China has sent roughly sixteen thousand troops on UN peacekeeping missions, and Chinese forces participate in multinational antipiracy missions in the western Indian Ocean. These deployments, however, have involved less than 1 percent of China's military and are a poor substitute for actual combat experience.[20]

Training. PLA training has improved dramatically since the 1990s, when most exercises were simple drills conducted under benign conditions. Today, Chinese units train against dynamic enemy "blue teams" on unfamiliar terrain, at night, in bad weather, and under hostile electronic warfare and cyber warfare conditions.[21]

Yet PLA exercises remain heavily scripted (the red team almost always wins) and most focus on nonwar operations, such as border control, counterterrorism, and counterpiracy, rather than high-intensity combat.[22] Most exercises involve a single service or branch, so troops lack the ability to conduct joint operations, and assessments are often nothing more than "subjective judgments based on visual observation rather than on detailed quantitative data" and are scored "based simply on whether a training program has been implemented rather than on whether the goals of the program have been achieved."[23]

PLA exercises also tend to be infrequent and small in scale. The PLA's Rocket Force, for example, has never fired more than ten ballistic missiles simultaneously during an exercise.[24] In wartime, however, the Rocket Force might need to fire hundreds or even thousands of missiles rapidly, a much more daunting task. Chinese pilots fly 100 to 150 fewer hours than U.S. pilots[25] and only began training on aircraft carriers in 2012 whereas the U.S. military has operated carriers since the 1920s.[26] Chinese troops spend 20 to 30 percent of their time studying communist ideology and attending political meetings, and some units at the brigade and regimental level farm to feed themselves.[27] Ninety percent of recent PLA air defense exercises were scripted while only 6 percent involved combined-arms and less than 1 percent involved joint exercises with another service.[28] And a recent study of China's submarine force finds that "only a small percentage of China's submariners benefit from deployments in which they might encounter a future adversary. The overall force's ability to find and destroy warships in the open ocean with torpedoes remains an open question."[29]

American military training methods, by contrast, are widely considered the best in the world. For example, a major study comparing U.S. training programs to those of China, Israel, France, the United Kingdom, and India finds that "the U.S. training system is the envy of the countries we examined, and they attempt to emulate many U.S. best practices."[30] The same study concludes that the "PLA undoubtedly falls well short of U.S. standards" in all aspects of training, including jointness, realism, complexity, and evaluation.[31]

Leadership. Successfully coordinating, supplying, and transporting forces in battle requires not just trained soldiers but also talented officers and brainy analysts.[32] Basic training for a typical soldier takes months, but grooming officers to lead them takes years and requires a system of military academies to disseminate know-how and breed trust within the ranks. An effective military administration also requires a robust network of research institutions and scholars to staff them.

The PLA lags behind the U.S. military in all of these areas. Chinese military academies are poorly staffed—only 15 percent of instructors have advanced degrees versus 90 percent of instructors in U.S. military academies[33]—and China has only three of the world's top one hundred military research institutes whereas the United States has twenty-five.[34]

More important, recent internal investigations found that the PLA "is riddled with corruption and professional decay, compromised by ties of patronage, and asphyxiated by the ever-greater effort required to impose political control."[35] According to U.S. intelligence assessments, "the level of corruption in the PLA at least equals, and probably far exceeds, the level of corruption in the civilian economy."[36] If the same is true for the United States, then the PLA is at least twice as corrupt as the U.S. military.[37] Hundreds of senior PLA officers have reportedly purchased their positions by paying bribes to superiors, and more than four thousand officers at the rank of lieutenant colonel or above, including eighty-two generals, have been investigated for corruption since 2010.[38]

The PLA is not just corrupt but also intensely political. From company level to the top brass, decision making is split between military officers and political commissars, the latter of whom enforce loyalty to the Communist Party by obliging troops to engage in fifteen hours of "political work" each week.[39] The U.S. military, by contrast, stresses "unity of command" in which all forces operate under a single leader, and for good reason: political commissars not only drain valuable resources, but also impede quick decision making in battle.[40]

SECURITY COSTS

As noted earlier, China suffers from a high level of domestic unrest and is surrounded by hostile neighbors. Dealing with these threats is labor intensive. Consequently, the PLA devotes more than 1 million troops (roughly 45 percent of the active-duty force) to internal security and border defense: 660,000 troops in the PAP, 128,000 troops in border defense units, and 239,500 ground troops based near major cities in border regions.[41] Thus nearly half of China's military personnel are focused on missions at home rather than abroad.[42]

American military personnel, by contrast, focus on missions abroad, because civilian agencies handle border patrol and internal security. Despite employing 1.2 million more personnel than the U.S. military, therefore, the PLA has around the same number of personnel available for a war with the United States: the PLA Air Force has 398,000 personnel whereas the U.S. Air Force has 312,453; the PLA navy has 235,000 personnel versus 321,599 in the U.S. Navy; and the PLA Army has 572,500 troops outside of its border defense units versus 504,330 troops in the U.S. Army and 187,891 in the Marines.[43]

Platforms and Munitions

The United States remains the only country with the bases, long-range platforms, and global intelligence and surveillance systems necessary to be a decisive military player in any region. China is nowhere close to achieving this capability. Figure 4.3 makes this point clear and actually understates the U.S.-China power-projection gap, because many U.S. platforms are two to three times as capable as China's.

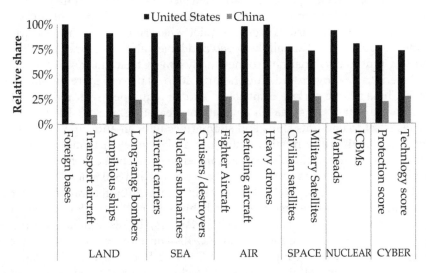

Figure 4.3. American and Chinese arsenals at a glance.

Note: Relative shares of power-projection platforms, nuclear weapons, and cyber warfare capabilities.

Source: Data on platforms from IISS 2016. Data on cyber capabilities from the Economist Intelligence Unit 2011. "Protection score" is an index of five indicators: cyber protection policies, intellectual property protection, government commitment to cyber development, cyber censorship, and political efficacy. "Technology score" is an index of five indicators: spending on information and communications technology (ICT), number of secure servers, quality of ICT, access to ICT, and cost of ICT.

For example, U.S. aircraft carriers are 50 percent faster and hold twice as many aircraft as China's carriers, and fighters launched from U.S. carriers can carry 40 percent more ammunition and fuel than fighters taking off from China's, because U.S. carriers hurl aircraft into the sky with catapults whereas China's carriers require aircraft to propel themselves off a ramp at the bow of the ship.[44] Furthermore, the endurance of China's carriers is limited by their steam-powered engines, which need to be refueled and refurbished many times a year. American carriers, by contrast, are powered by nuclear reactors that only need to be replaced once during a carrier's fifty-year service life. For all these reasons, military experts generally agree that China's carriers are incapable of high-intensity combat, even within waters close to China's shores.[45]

China's nine nuclear-powered submarines (four strategic, five tactical) carry less than half the munitions of current U.S. submarines and are louder than U.S. submarines from the 1960s.[46] Consequently, the U.S. Navy, which operates a sound surveillance system in the waters of East Asia, can track China's nuclear-powered submarines at long ranges.[47] China is developing its own sound surveillance system, but even when it becomes operational (the United States spent forty years developing its system) the PLA will have difficulty tracking U.S. submarines, which are so quiet that they sometimes reduce background noise as they pass by a target.[48] China's fifty-seven diesel-powered submarines are very quiet when running on their electric batteries, but they sail at half the speed and have half the endurance of U.S. nuclear-powered submarines, so they rarely leave China's near seas.[49]

American destroyers and cruisers carry 40 to 60 percent more munitions than China's large surface combatants and are equipped with radars and data systems that are at least a generation ahead of China's.[50] The United States is set to equip its ships and submarines with an antiship version of the Tomahawk cruise missile, which can strike targets a thousand miles away.[51] By contrast, China's most advanced sea-launched antiship missile, the YJ-18, is rumored to have a range between 130 and 330 miles.[52]

The United States operates hundreds of stealth fifth-generation fighter aircraft; China operates none and probably will not do so for at least a decade.[53] China's new aerial refueling tankers, IL-78s purchased from Ukraine, deliver half the fuel of U.S. KC-10s and have 30 percent shorter range. China's latest heavy drone, the Caihong 5, resembles U.S. Reaper drones, but carries half the payload and lacks the sophisticated sensors on U.S. drones.[54]

China's largest transport aircraft, the Y-20, carries half as much weight and has half the range of American C-5 aircraft. China's most advanced amphibious ship, the Type 071, carries 30 percent as many troops, vehicles, and aircraft as U.S. Wasp-class amphibious assault ships and is armed only with machine guns whereas U.S. amphibious ships have guns, cannons, missiles, and missile defense systems. China's new long-range bomber, the

H-6K, has only 40 percent of the unrefueled range and 30 percent of the payload capacity of American B-52 bombers; only 20 percent of the range and 30 percent of the payload of U.S. B-1 bombers; and half the range and payload and none of the stealth of American B-2 bombers.

China has an active cyber warfare unit, but data gathered by the Economist Intelligence Unit, some of which is aggregated in figure 4.3, suggest that the United States leads China by every indicator of cyber power, including the level of government commitment to cyber security and cyber warfare, the number and depth of public/private partnerships (e.g. cooperation between government security services and private companies), the number of secure servers, the level of funding for cyber warfare and security, the technical skills of the cyber security workforce, and the overall quality of information and communications technology.[55] Qualitative studies reach similar conclusions.[56]

Area-Denial within 500 Miles of China

The United States dominates China militarily at the global level. Within East Asia, however, the military balance is more evenly matched for two main reasons.

First, geography limits U.S. combat power.[57] American forces are scattered around the globe, and the U.S. military is vulnerable when it operates near enemy coastlines, where it is within range of enemy antiship missiles and tactical aircraft; in air operations below fifteen thousand feet, where enemy antiaircraft weaponry becomes more lethal; and in naval operations in shallow waters, where enemy ships are harder to detect.[58] A U.S.-China war would probably take place in such a "contested zone." In fact, the PLA is counting on it.

Second, the current state of technology bolsters China's home-field advantage. In past eras, China would have had to fight the U.S. military symmetrically by sending battleships to blast away at America's fleet, a head-to-head contest that China would almost surely lose. Today, by contrast, China can fend off the U.S. military asymmetrically, by conducting cyber attacks and launching precision-guided munitions from a variety of cheap platforms (e.g. trucks and small ships) based on or near China's territory.

The average cost of these so-called antiaccess/area-denial (A2/AD) capabilities is about one-fiftieth of the cost of the power-projection capabilities they could destroy in war.[59] Thus, even though the United States has outspent China militarily by more than $7 trillion since 2000 (not including spending on the wars in Iraq and Afghanistan), many defense analysts believe that China can now temporarily deny the U.S. military air and sea control near Chinese territory, something China was previously incapable of doing.[60] Below, I elaborate on these points.

AIR DENIAL

China would enjoy several advantages over the U.S. military in an air war within several hundred miles of China's coastline. First, China would be able to commit its entire air force to the battle, including more than one thousand fourth-generation fighter aircraft operating from more than two hundred air bases on mainland China. The United States, by contrast, only has nine air bases in East Asia and might have only a few hundred aircraft available on the first day of a war there.

Second, China's air forces would be protected by covering fire from ground-based air defenses.[61] American aircraft, by contrast, would have to fend for themselves, and might not even make it off the ground, because China has several hundred medium-range ballistic missiles (DH-21Cs) and land-attack cruise missiles that could strike U.S. air bases in Japan, South Korea, and the Philippines.[62] China also is developing an antiship ballistic missile that could potentially strike U.S. aircraft carriers thousands of miles away, though it is not clear the PLA can master the targeting capabilities needed to guide such a missile to a moving ship.[63]

To counter China's capabilities, the United States has deployed hundreds of stealth aircraft and dozens of submarines armed with "standoff" missiles that can be fired from beyond the range of China's air defenses,[64] acquired new electronic warfare capabilities to help nonstealth aircraft evade and degrade Chinese air defenses,[65] and dispersed its base structure in Asia by gaining access to two bases in Australia and five in the Philippines and allocating funds to build new airstrips on several small Pacific islands.[66]

China conceivably could disable U.S. air bases in Japan, South Korea, and the northern Philippines with a surprise air and missile attack. Should China pull off such an attack, U.S. air forces would have to operate from aircraft carriers and runways on and around Guam, which is 1,800 miles from China, and be refueled enroute to the combat zone. This extra distance would cut the number of U.S. air sorties in half and potentially enable China to establish air superiority over a concentrated area near its territory, such as over the Taiwan Strait.[67]

The United States could fight its way back into the combat theater, but doing so would be costly. The RAND Corporation calculates that in a worst-case scenario—a war over Taiwan in which the PLA destroys U.S. air bases in Japan in a surprise attack, and Taiwan does nothing in its own defense— the United States could lose seventy-eight aircraft in the process of winning back command of the skies over Taiwan.[68]

The above scenario, however, assumes not only that Taiwan does not defend itself but also that the United States refrains from attacking Chinese air bases. In reality, if China attacked U.S. bases, the U.S. military would almost certainly retaliate by cratering the runways at Chinese air bases. Computer simulations show that one week of U.S. air attacks, supplemented by 200

Tomahawk missiles launched from two Ohio-class submarines, could disable 30 to 45 percent of China's air bases near Taiwan or all of the air bases near the South China Sea, and destroy 90 percent of the aircraft parked at these bases, while losing few if any U.S. aircraft and no ships or submarines.[69]

Thus, the United States can still "win" an air war against China with no help from allies, but it might lose dozens of aircraft in air-to-air combat and potentially many more on the ground if China attacks U.S. air bases. For most countries, losing a few air bases and less than 1 percent of its combat aircraft (the U.S. military has roughly three thousand fighter aircraft) would be a small price to pay to win an air war against a major power. For the United States in the post–Cold War period, however, such losses would be unprecedented.

SEA DENIAL

Since the 1990s, China has signficantly increased its ability to attack U.S. surface ships within five hundred miles of Chinese territory. Most notable, China has upgraded its attack submarine fleet, adding four new nuclear-powered submarines and dozens of diesel-powered submarines with air-independent propulsion systems that can stay submerged for a week at a time (other diesel-powered submarines have to surface every few days to take in oxygen and recharge their batteries).[70] China soon will equip most of its attack submarines with the YJ-18 cruise missile, which may be able to strike targets up to 330 miles away.

China also has twenty-one destroyers, fifty-four frigates, and dozens of coastal patrol craft armed with advanced antiship missiles.[71] China's frigates and patrol craft lack the missile defense systems and endurance of U.S. destroyers and cruisers, but China could send swarms of them to overwhelm U.S. surface combatants.[72] China's destroyers carry roughly half the armaments of U.S. destroyers, and less than half the arms of U.S. cruisers, but in combat near China they could return to base frequently to reload whereas U.S. ships would have to do so at vulnerable bases in Japan or in faraway Guam or Hawaii (currently, the U.S. Navy cannot reload its ships at sea).

In addition, China can fire antiship missiles from shore-based batteries and from its 50 H-6K bombers, each of which has a combat radius of 2,000 miles and can carry 6 YJ-12 antiship cruise missiles with a range of 250 miles. China also has 100 older H-6H/M and H-6G bombers, each of which can carry 2 to 4 long-range antiship cruise missiles.

Finally, China has fifty thousand sea mines.[73] Although the PLA only has one dedicated mine-laying ship, which can lay three hundred mines at a time, China's ships, submarines, and bomber aircraft can each lay several dozen mines.[74] In a war over Taiwan, China would probably mine the entrances to the Taiwan Strait, and in any conflict involving the United States, the PLA might try to mine U.S. naval bases in Japan and Guam.[75] Historically, mine warfare has been a highly effective tactic: in the Korean War, North Korea sunk several U.S. ships and prevented U.S. forces from landing efficiently at Wonsan by mining its own waters; and during the Persian Gulf War, Iraqi mines knocked two U.S. ships out of the war and forced the U.S. military to abort an amphibious assault.[76] The PLA has studied these cases carefully and made mine warfare a core tenet of its naval doctrine.[77]

In sum, China's ability to attack the U.S. surface fleet has improved dramatically since 1990s, when U.S. ships could approach China's coast with virtual impunity. Computer simulations suggest that China's submarines would have a 50 percent chance of finding a U.S. aircraft carrier in waters within a thousand nautical miles of Taiwan in a seven-day campaign; and if China develops the radar and satellite infrastructure necessary to guide antiship ballistic missile to targets, it will be able to hold at risk any U.S. ship within nine hundred miles of China's coast.[78]

The U.S. military, however, can sink Chinese ships and submarines virtually anywhere in East Asia. The main reason is that the United States has dozens of missile-armed submarines that are almost invulnerable to China's notoriously weak antisubmarine capabilities.[79] In wartime, U.S. submarines, with the aid of America's vast undersea surveillance network in East Asia,[80] could set up picket lines near the combat theater, or near China's ports, and sink China's ships and submarines with torpedoes, missiles, and mines. According to estimates by the RAND Corporation, in a PLA invasion of Taiwan, eight U.S. submarines could destroy almost 40 percent of China's amphibious ships as they attempt to cross the Taiwan Strait while losing perhaps one submarine.[81] The same study estimates that in a conflict in the South China Sea—where the sea is deeper and provides U.S. submarines with better acoustics and more room to operate, and where most of the PLA's meager antisubmarine warfare forces cannot reach—U.S. submarines could destroy Chinese ships at almost no risk of being attacked themselves.[82]

In addition to upgrading its submarine force,[83] the United States has outfitted its surface ships with the advanced Undersea Warfare Combat System (the AN/SQQ-89), which tracks enemy submarines with active and passive sonar data collected from hull-mounted and towed arrays and sonobuoys.[84] The U.S. military also is replacing most of its P-3C Orion submarine hunter aircraft with the P-8A Poseidon—a Boeing 737 packed with missiles, torpedoes, mines, drones, and depth charges—which can sweep an area of 1,400 miles for enemy submarines. The navy will soon equip its 30 P-8As with the High-Altitude Antisubmarine Warfare Weapon, a powerful torpedo attached to a miniature jet and glider that can be fired from altitudes of thirty thousand feet at targets nearly a hundred miles away.[85] The navy also will soon deploy MC-4C high-altitude drones that can scan seas for enemy submarines for thirty hours at a time and direct the P-8As to targets.[86]

The U.S. Navy remains vulnerable to Chinese mines; the current U.S. mine countermeasures force consists of 13 wooden Avenger-class minesweepers,

28 MH-53E helicopters, and a small team of divers and mine-sniffing dolphins and sea lions. These forces clear mines one-by-one by attaching explosives to mines or shooting them with sniper rifles and would obviously be overwhelmed by a serious mine warfare campaign. To upgrade these forces, the U.S. Navy has procured 40 Littoral Combat Ships (stealthy surface combatants that can sail at 45 knots), 32 of which will carry a modern Mine Countermeasures Mission Package that detects mines with sonar and lasers and destroys them with torpedo-firing drones. In 2016, the United States procured additional Archerfish drones that can detect and detonate sea mines and be deployed by aircraft, ships, and submarines.[87]

Meanwhile, the United States has revived its own mine warfare capabilities by developing Quickstrike mines that can be deployed rapidly from a variety of combat aircraft and glide toward target areas forty-five miles away.[88] Given that China has no mine countermeasures aircraft and only four large mine countermeasures ships (China has forty-four small harbor craft based on 1950s Soviet designs), a U.S. mine warfare campaign would wreak havoc on Chinese naval operations.[89] The U.S. military could mine China's naval bases at Zhanjiang, Ningbo, and Qingdao as well as the PLA submarine base on Hainan Island. And if China tries to invade Taiwan, U.S. aircraft could mine the origin and landing points of PLA amphibious transports.

NET ASSESSMENT

The seas and skies within 500 miles of China constitute a contested zone where both the United States and China can threaten to sink each other's surface ships and shoot down each other's nonstealth aircraft.[90] This situation is a major change from the 1990s when the U.S. military could cruise along China's coastline virtually risk free.

Many American analysts fear that China could use its burgeoning A2/AD capabilities to hold the U.S. military at bay while conquering parts of East Asia.[91] Left unchecked, some analysts fear, China will eventually become the hegemon of East Asia and start projecting military power into other regions, including the Western Hemisphere.[92]

Below, however, I argue that China cannot impose regional hegemony nor achieve more limited aims, like conquering Taiwan or enforcing territorial claims in the East and South China Seas. One reason, as described above, is that the U.S. military maintains a massive arsenal in East Asia. Another reason is that China's neighbors have developed their own A2/AD capabilities, which can deny China sea and air control throughout most of its near seas—even without U.S. assistance. In other words, China's neighbors have imposed security costs on China that have partially offset China's military enhancements over the past two decades.[93] Below, I describe this East Asian balance of power and explain how the United States can reinforce it.

Regional Maritime Hegemony

Is China poised to take over East Asia militarily? In the past 150 years, only two nations have succeeded in establishing regional maritime hegemony: Japan in the 1930s and early 1940s, and the United States from the 1890s to the present. The U.S. and Japanese cases suggest that China would need two things to enforce its own version of the Monroe Doctrine in East Asia: a regional monopoly of naval power and a military presence on the landmasses surrounding the East and South China Seas. China, however, is nowhere close to achieving either of those objectives.

First, when the United States and Imperial Japan took control of their near seas, their navies accounted for 80 to 99 percent of the naval tonnage in their respective regions.[94] China's navy today, by contrast, accounts for less than 30 percent of Asia's naval tonnage and, as figure 4.4 shows, China's maritime neighbors have collectively matched China's procurement of modern submarines, ships, and aircraft over the past two decades. China's navy may be the most powerful in Asia, but it is no police power.

Second, the United States and Imperial Japan occupied the landmasses around their near seas and barred neighboring states from building

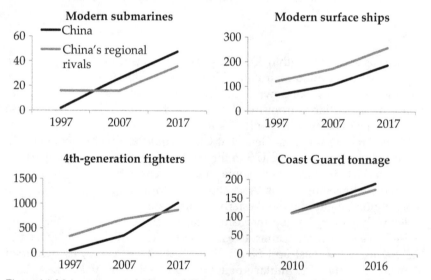

Figure 4.4. Major weapons platforms of China and countries around the East and South China Seas that have territorial disputes with China, 1997–2017.

Note: China's rivals are defined as those states with an ongoing maritime dispute with China and include Brunei, Indonesia, Japan, Malaysia, the Philippines, South Korea, Taiwan, and Vietnam. For chart on coast guard tonnage, data were available only for Japan, Vietnam, Philippines, Malaysia, and Indonesia. Modern ships and submarines are defined as those that are armed with antiship cruise missiles.

Source: IISS 2017; Morris 2017.

independent navies. At the turn of the twentieth century, the United States annexed Puerto Rico; turned Cuba, Haiti, the Dominican Republic, Panama, and Nicaragua into U.S. protectorates; and periodically occupied Veracruz, Mexico's only port on the Gulf of Mexico.[95] Today, the U.S. military operates from facilities in Cuba, Colombia, El Salvador, Honduras, Curacao, Aruba, Antigua, the Bahamas, Panama, and Puerto Rico.[96] Imperial Japan's coastal empire was even more extensive, including present-day Korea, Taiwan, the Philippines, Indonesia, Malaysia, Vietnam, Laos, Thailand, Cambodia, Burma, most of China's east coast, and numerous islands in the Pacific Ocean.[97]

China today has no prospect of controlling the coasts of East Asia. China's maritime neighbors are densely populated and possess modern militaries, and amphibious invasions have become extremely difficult, if not impossible, in an age of precision-guided munitions, a point I elaborate on later (figure 4.5).

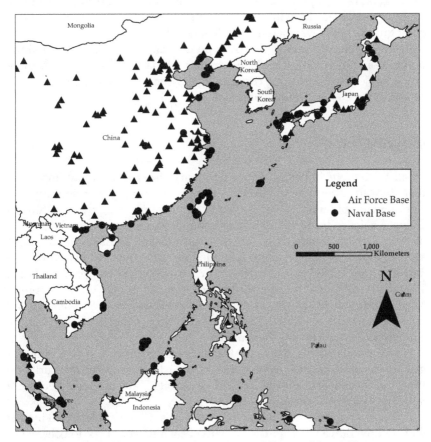

Figure 4.5. Rough neighborhood: Air and naval bases of China and its neighbors.

Source: Jane's Information Group 2017.

Given these obstacles to outright conquest, China has sought to expand on the sly via a "cabbage strategy," in which it wraps disputed waters in layers of coast guard, maritime militia, and fishing vessels—all backed by warships loitering just over the horizon.[98] This tactic, however, is unlikely to enable China to command maritime East Asia.

One reason is that China's neighbors have bolstered their own coast guard forces (figure 4.4). China's fleet remains the largest in Asia, but it is spread thin defending China's expansive claims, which encompass an area of nearly 2 million square miles. China's neighbors, by contrast, concentrate their fleets around their more limited claims.

More important, China's neighbors have shown that they are willing to use military force against China's civilian vessels. Indonesia and Malaysia, for example, announced in 2016 that they would sink foreign vessels that fish or drill in their claimed waters in the South China Sea, and Indonesia made good on this promise at least three times in 2016, firing on Chinese fishing vessels and blowing them up on national TV—all while Chinese coast guard cutters watched from a distance.[99]

In sum, China is not poised to overrun maritime East Asia. In the following sections, therefore, I analyze whether China could accomplish more limited objectives, including conquering Taiwan or enforcing its territorial claims in the East or South China Seas.

Conquering Taiwan

Of all the nations impeding China's military rise, none is more important than Taiwan. Conquering Taiwan is the PLA's primary war-fighting mission, and preparations for this campaign consume roughly one-third of China's defense budget.[100] If China conquered Taiwan, it would free up dozens of ships, hundreds of missile launchers and combat aircraft, thousands of personnel, and billions of dollars. Moreover, China could use Taiwan as an "unsinkable aircraft carrier" to project military power into the Western Pacific and to impose blockades on Japan and the Philippines. Most important, China would end the Chinese civil war once and for all and eliminate the world's only Chinese democracy, thereby bolstering the Chinese Communist Party's legitimacy.

For all these reasons, many strategists consider Taiwan to be a center of gravity in East Asia: in Taiwanese hands, the island is a defensive cork bottling up Chinese expansion; in Chinese hands, Taiwan could become a launching pad for Chinese aggression.[101]

A war over Taiwan could take several forms. China could try to invade and occupy Taiwan outright. Alternatively, China could try to coerce Taiwan into submission by strangling Taiwan's economy with a blockade or bombing Taiwan's cities. Later, I discuss all three options.

First, however, I discuss whether China could destroy Taiwan's air, naval, and missile forces in a surprise attack. Such an attack would enable China to establish air superiority over and sea control around Taiwan—two crucial ingredients, if not outright prerequisites, for a successful invasion, blockade, or strategic bombing campaign.

SURPRISE AIR AND MISSILE STRIKES

According to PLA strategy documents, China would initiate a war with Taiwan by bombarding its air and naval bases, missile batteries, and command centers with salvos of ground- and air-launched missiles.[102] The goal would be to destroy most of Taiwan's air defenses and offensive forces before they have a chance to fight back.

This tactic would constitute China's only hope of establishing air and sea command in the Taiwan Strait, which in turn would be vital to a successful invasion, blockade, or strategic bombing campaign. If Taiwan retained substantial missile forces, a Chinese amphibious invasion would be impossible, because Taiwan could pick off PLA landing craft as they motored across the Taiwan Strait. Similarly, a sustained bombing campaign would be impossible, because Taiwan's air force and air defenses could decimate China's bombers. A submarine blockade might be possible even without air and sea dominance, but it would be difficult to sustain if Taiwan can attack the blockade force. The bottom line is that conquering a developed island nation is difficult, so China would probably need to destroy most of Taiwan's military in the first few days of a war to prevail.

What are China's prospects? In 2000, the PLA had only a few hundred inaccurate missiles and a few dozen advanced aircraft and clearly could not carry out a disarming first strike.[103] Today, however, China has fifteen hundred accurate missiles pointed at Taiwan and more than a thousand advanced fighter aircraft.[104] If China catches Taiwan off-guard—with its missile batteries, aircraft, and ships parked in the open—China potentially could wipe out Taiwan's long-range air defenses, temporarily ground Taiwan's air force, and sink Taiwan's large naval ships.[105]

The above scenario presupposes Taiwan had no advanced knowledge of the Chinese attack. In reality, Taiwan probably would have some notice, because it has one of the best early warning systems in the world, consisting of at least twenty fixed early warning radars; ten ground-mobile radars; six E-2 Hawkeye aircraft; thousands of spies embedded on the mainland; and satellite and aircraft intelligence provided by the United States.[106] Historically, Taiwanese intelligence has provided advanced warning of PLA actions. For example, in 2013 spies forewarned the Taiwanese government about China's decision to announce an air defense identification zone in the East China Sea.[107] If China planned an all-out assault on Taiwan—an operation that would involve tens of thousands of personnel—the Taiwanese military would probably catch wind of it.

If Taiwan detected an impending PLA attack, it would quickly deploy its navy and disperse its combat aircraft among thirty-six airfields scattered around the island. Some of these locations have aircraft hangars built inside of mountains. Others have aircraft shelters with six-foot thick concrete walls.[108] If PLA missiles cratered the runways at Taiwan's air bases, Taiwanese aircraft could operate from ten civilian airstrips and five highways that double as emergency air bases, all of which have fuel and supplies prepositioned for the air force.[109] Meanwhile Taiwan's runway repair teams, which currently hold the world speed record for runway repair (three hours), would start patching the tarmac at the main air bases.[110]

Taiwan also would try to shoot down Chinese missiles and aircraft and perhaps strike Chinese bases and missile batteries. For air defense, Taiwan has 524 long-range surface-to-air missile launchers, 80 percent of which are road-mobile; thousands of short-range surface-to-air missile launchers mounted to vehicles or carried by ground troops; and 400 road-mobile anti-aircraft guns.[111] For offensive strike, Taiwan has at least 12 road-mobile cruise missile launchers; 50 short-range ballistic missile launchers in underground silos; 300 howitzers located on offshore islands (Jinmen, Mazu) just a few miles from the Chinese mainland; roughly 400 fighter aircraft, 73 ships, and 2 submarines that can fire long-range cruise missiles; and several thousand special operations troops embedded on the mainland that could blitz Chinese bases.[112]

History suggests that some of Taiwan's major weapons systems would survive a Chinese surprise attack. In the Gulf War, for example, the U.S.-led coalition pummeled Iraq with 88,500 tons of ordnance and shredded Iraq's airfields with cluster bombs, yet most of Iraq's air force and all of Iraq's road-mobile missile launchers survived and fought on.[113] In 1999, NATO pounded Serbian air defenses in Kosovo for 78 days with 7,000 tons of ordnance, but only destroyed 3 of Serbia's 22 mobile missile batteries.[114]

Given that China's short-range ballistic missiles could only deliver 700 total tons of ordnance on Taiwan—not to mention that Taiwan's air defenses and strike platforms are more numerous, mobile, and advanced than Iraq's or Serbia's were—China would have even more trouble than the United States did in Iraq and Kosovo in disarming its adversary with air and missile strikes alone.[115] Recent Chinese studies bolster this conclusion. For example, computer simulations in a 2013 PLA study found that China's missile inventory could knock out only a few Taiwanese air bases for a few hours.[116]

Assume nonetheless for the sake of conservatism that China could destroy most of Taiwan's air and naval forces in a surprise attack and quickly establish air and sea dominance. Would China then be able to conquer Taiwan via amphibious invasion or coerce it via a naval blockade or strategic bombing? Below, I consider each of these scenarios.

AMPHIBIOUS INVASION

An amphibious invasion is the most difficult mission in warfare and requires three vital elements.[117] An attacker must achieve air superiority. The attacker must land forces in a place where they outnumber the defender. The attacker must surge reinforcements to the landing zone faster than the defender. In the successful amphibious invasions of World War II and the Korean War, the United States and its allies enjoyed all three advantages— and still suffered huge losses.

Assuming that China already has air superiority, could it land enough troops on Taiwan's shores to secure a beachhead and then reinforce that position faster than Taiwan's defenders could converge on the landing site? China currently has 89 amphibious ships.[118] If all of them survived the eight-hour trip across the Taiwan Strait, the PLA could land a maximum of 26,000 troops and 640 armored vehicles on Taiwan's shores.[119] Taiwan has 150,000 active-duty troops and 1.5 million reservists.[120] With that force, Taiwan theoretically could station 2,000 defenders per mile along its shores and have more troops over any stretch of thirteen miles as China could deploy using its entire amphibious fleet.

In reality, Taiwan will have many more troops at the point of attack, because only 10 percent of Taiwan's coastline is suitable for an amphibious landing.[121] The east coast is off limits, because it consists of steep cliffs, and PLA landing craft would have to sail an extra day around Taiwan to reach it, a journey during which they might encounter rough seas—twenty-foot waves and torrential rain are common in Taiwan's waters—and attacks from any surviving Taiwanese ships, aircraft, or shore-based missile batteries.[122] The west coast, on the other hand, consists mostly of mud flats that extend two to five miles out to sea and are buffeted by severe tides. To avoid getting stuck in the mud, PLA units would have to land at high tide at one of a few suitable locations. Taiwan's military leaders know these locations well and would concentrate defenders at them.

In addition, Taiwanese intelligence would see the PLA armada approaching and tell the army where to mass. Even if these intelligence systems failed, Taiwanese soldiers would see the PLA armada at least thirty minutes before it reached the shoreline, providing time for Taiwan's army to mass at the landing site.[123] For all these reasons, China could not achieve even a temporary numerical advantage at the landing zone. China therefore would lack the second necessary element of a successful amphibious invasion.

China also lacks the third crucial element of a successful invasion—the ability to reinforce the initial assault faster than Taiwan can strengthen its defenses at the point of attack. The PLA could ferry a maximum of 18,000 troops per day to the landing zone, assuming that none of its amphibious ships are destroyed or break down.[124] Taiwan, by contrast, could surge at least 50,000 troops per day to battlefield via roads, railways, and aircraft.[125]

After forty-eight hours, therefore, at least 100,000 Taiwanese troops would face, at most, 44,000 PLA attackers—and from there the military balance would shift increasingly in Taiwan's favor.

China could transport additional troops across the strait using fishing boats and coast guard ships. These vessels, however, cannot hold large numbers of personnel or armored vehicles and, crucially, cannot carry landing craft, so troops ferried by them would have to swim or trudge through mud to get ashore at the landing site. Moreover, with no heavy armor and few or no weapons, civilian ships would be vulnerable to attack from Taiwanese coastal artillery.

China could supplement its invasion with an airlift of two brigades (roughly 6,000 troops and some light vehicles).[126] Even if all 6,000 paratroopers landed safely on Taiwan, however, they would be isolated and outnumbered. More important, China probably could not get anywhere close to 6,000 paratroopers on Taiwan, because PLA transport aircraft would encounter heavy fire from Taiwan's air defenses. Modern surface-to-air missiles are extremely effective against large, low-flying transport aircraft. As noted earlier, Taiwan has thousands of surface-to-air missile launchers and four hundred antiaircraft guns. Even if Chinese air and missile strikes eliminated half of these, attrition rates of Chinese transport aircraft flying over Taiwan could exceed 50 percent per sortie.[127]

In sum, the PLA could land a maximum of 26,000 troops on Taiwan's shores on the first day of a war and 18,000 troops each day thereafter. These numbers, however, do not account for attrition to PLA forces, which would be enormous.

For starters, unless China destroyed all of Taiwan's antiship missile launchers, Taiwan could "thin the herd" of PLA amphibious ships as they load in Chinese ports or transit the Taiwan Strait. Computer simulations suggest that Taiwan would only need to fire fifty precision-guided missiles to destroy a dozen Chinese amphibious ships, losses that would end all hopes of a successful invasion.[128] Taiwan also could bombard PLA landing craft with short-range artillery fire as they made their final twenty-minute run into the beach.[129]

Past invasions suggest that the PLA would lose many ships. During the 1982 Falklands War, when the United Kingdom carried out the only major amphibious assault in the past forty years, an Argentine military with only ninety-five combat aircraft, five antiship cruise missiles, and some World War II era "dumb" bombs (half of which failed to explode) sank 15 percent of Britain's naval task force (five ships out of thirty-three), and damaged an additional 35 percent, even though British ships never came within four hundred miles of the Argentine mainland.[130] Chinese naval losses would almost certainly be greater than 15 percent, as China's ships would be operating within a hundred miles of Taiwan from the moment they left Chinese ports and would spend substantial time within the range of Taiwan's artillery.

If PLA ships somehow landed on Taiwan's shores, Chinese troops would then need to run up the beaches and attack Taiwanese defenses—actions that essentially guarantee mass casualties. During the D-Day assault of 1944, the United States lost roughly 10 percent of its troops on the beaches while attacking a severely overstretched German army (most German units, including all of Germany's most highly-trained units, were fighting the Soviet Union in Eastern Europe) defending thin positions on foreign soil with small arms and mortars.[131] If the PLA invaded Taiwan today, it would be attacking massed forces defending home soil with precision-guided munitions, helicopter gunships, tanks, and smart mines. PLA losses during each wave of attack, therefore, would likely be much higher than 10 percent.

Adding the most conservative loss rates together suggests that China would lose at least 25 percent of its forces each time its amphibious fleet approached Taiwan. China therefore could not hope to land more than 20,000 troops in its initial assault and 15,000 troops the day after—assuming the initial wave of troops could hold the beachhead in the first place.

China, therefore, probably could not conquer Taiwan, even in the absence of U.S. intervention. Even if China's prospects are better than I have suggested, the PLA clearly would have its hands full just dealing with Taiwan's defenders. Consequently, the United States would only need to tip the scales of the battle to foil a Chinese invasion, a mission that could be accomplished in numerous ways without exposing U.S. surface ships or non-stealth aircraft to China's A2/AD forces.

Specifically, American defense planners estimate that it would take ten thousand to twenty thousand pounds of ordnance to decimate a PLA invasion force on the beaches of Taiwan.[132] The U.S. military could deliver that payload many times over with a single B-2 bomber or an Ohio-class submarine firing cruise missiles from an underwater location hundreds of miles away. Alternatively, the United States could unleash its attack submarines on the PLA invasion fleet; computer simulations show that eight U.S. submarines could sink 40 percent of the PLA's amphibious ships during any given transit across the strait while losing perhaps one submarine.[133]

BLOCKADE

If China cannot invade Taiwan, could it coerce Taiwan into submission instead? China's most promising coercive tactic is a blockade in which the PLA tries to strangle Taiwan's economy by preventing commercial ships from reaching Taiwan's ports. Taiwan is vulnerable to a blockade: it imports 60 percent of its food and 98 percent of its energy resources; maintains only a ninety-day supply of oil; and has a small coastline that forces large container ships to take predictable paths to seven major ports, four of which are located on Taiwan's west coast facing China.[134]

China could blockade Taiwan in several ways. The most aggressive approach would be for China to destroy Taiwan's air and naval forces, commercial port facilities, and offshore oil terminals in a surprise attack and then send PLA submarines to sink cargo ships and deploy mines near Taiwan's harbors. If China's surprise attack destroyed all of Taiwan's offensive forces and port infrastructure—an unlikely outcome, as explained earlier—Taiwan's economy would grind to a halt, because Taiwan would have no way to unload large cargo containers or oil tankers.[135] Given such dire circumstances, would life on Taiwan become so unbearable that Taipei would submit to Beijing's authority?

The answer would depend on two main factors: China's ability to choke Taiwan off from basic survival levels of food and energy resources; and the resolve of the Taiwanese people to endure hardship.

Regarding the first factor, China probably could not cut Taiwan off entirely from critical supplies, because Taiwan could ferry limited amounts of cargo to small harbors using shuttle tankers and barges.[136] China would try to sink merchant ships supplying Taiwan, but rigorous research suggests that the PLA could sink only 1 to 6 percent of Taiwan's shipping, and these results are based on assumptions that heavily favor China: specifically, these results assume a Chinese submarine force of sixty-three boats (China currently only has fifty-three attack submarines) and that Chinese submarines always find targets to attack, achieve historically high kill rates, experience no maintenance problems, and encounter no enemy resistance.[137]

China might hope that sinking a few merchant ships would deter others from supplying Taiwan. Historically, however, shipping companies and privateers have operated in wartime; in fact, many have volunteered to enter dangerous areas so that they could charge higher premiums. For example, the lure of profits kept seaborne commerce going throughout both world wars and the 1980–88 Iran-Iraq War, wars in which shipping losses were several times greater than what China could hope to inflict on Taiwan.[138] If money failed to motivate merchants to dock in Taiwan, the Taiwanese government could commandeer some of the 23 oil tankers and 326 large cargo ships registered under the Taiwanese flag and compel them to keep operating.[139]

Assume for the sake of conservatism, however, that China succeeds in completely cutting Taiwan off from external supplies. Would China then be able to conquer Taiwan?

The first thing to note is that no blockade in the past two hundred years has coerced a country into surrendering its sovereignty.[140] The reason is that modern states can adapt to supply shortages and civilian populations are usually willing to endure enormous punishment to defy foreign enemies. The most comprehensive blockade in history was the U.S. blockade of Japan in the early 1940s (codenamed Operation Starvation), which slashed Japan's imports by 97 percent. Japan, however, surrendered only after the

United States decimated Japan's military, leveled most of its major cities, dropped atomic bombs on Hiroshima and Nagasaki, and got the Soviet Union to declare war on Japan in 1945.[141]

For China to buck this historical trend, the Taiwanese people would need to be abnormally weak-willed or strongly predisposed toward reunification with the mainland. Given Taiwan's Chinese heritage, the latter possibility can never be discounted. At present, however, the Taiwanese people do not seem like they would cave quickly to Chinese coercion: 60 percent of Taiwan's population (and 85 percent of the twenty to thirty-year-old population) identifies solely as Taiwanese whereas only 3 percent identify solely as Chinese;[142] the Democratic Progressive Party, which leans toward Taiwanese independence, won both the presidency and a majority in the legislature in the 2016 elections, in part because voters felt that the previous Kuomintang regime was getting too cozy with China; and the Taiwanese government maintains a massive network of underground shelters stocked with food, fuel, and medical supplies.[143]

Therefore, if China blockaded Taiwan, and the United States decided to intervene, the United States would probably have several weeks, if not months, to rally an international coalition and explore options, some of which would pose little or no risk to the U.S. military. For example, the United States could impose financial sanctions on China or cut China off from 80 percent of its oil imports by blockading the Strait of Malacca, near Singapore, beyond the range of most of China's military forces.[144]

Alternatively, U.S. antisubmarine warfare forces could attack China's submarines and escort merchant ships to Taiwan. Such attacks obviously would entail risks for American sailors and pilots, but they also would capitalize on considerable U.S. advantages: U.S. attack submarines are faster, quieter, and have far greater endurance than Chinese submarines; the United States has a robust underwater sensor array in the waters east of Taiwan; the United States has recently developed drones that can hunt for Chinese submarines for seventy days straight and travel ten thousand miles; China's antisubmarine forces are weak (its diesel-powered submarines lack the speed and endurance necessary to sweep large areas; it only has a dozen surface ships with towed sonar arrays and seven fixed-wing antisubmarine warfare aircraft; and has few ships that can accommodate antisubmarine warfare helicopters, so most of China's rotary force can only patrol limited areas near China's coasts);[145] and whereas U.S. submarines could loiter silently in the waters near Taiwan, Chinese submarines would have to expose their positions to enforce the blockade (as soon as a Chinese submarine fires on a merchant ship, U.S. sensors can pinpoint its location).[146]

Historically, antisubmarine warfare forces have been able to disrupt blockades.[147] Germany's attempted blockade of Allied shipping in World War II, for example, collapsed in two months once the Allies launched a dedicated antisubmarine warfare campaign, and attempts by Iran and Iraq to blockade each other in the 1980s floundered because neither side could maintain sea control.[148] The U.S. blockade of Japan in World War II, by contrast, was enforced only after the United States won command of the seas around Japan—and even in this extreme case, it remains unclear if the blockade played a decisive role in the outcome of the war.

In sum, a PLA blockade of Taiwan would be a protracted operation with a low probability of success. Should the United States choose to intervene, it would have time to consider an array of options, the most aggressive of which would play to U.S. strengths. A submarine blockade might be China's best option for forcing Taiwan's reunification with the mainland, but it is hardly a reliable option.

STRATEGIC BOMBING

An alternative coercive tactic would be a strategic bombing campaign, in which the PLA tries to force cross-strait reunification by leveling Taiwan's cities and infrastructure. The historical record, however, suggests that this tactic would be even less effective than a blockade.

There have been only fourteen strategic bombing campaigns in history, and none decisively affected the outcome of the wars in which they were used (see this endnote for the list of cases).[149] The best that can be said of any of these campaigns is that they hastened the surrender of states that were already going down to defeat. In short, no state has ever conquered another with air power alone, largely for the same reasons that no country has ever conquered another with a blockade in the past two hundred years: modern states can adapt to the loss of critical infrastructure, and civilian populations usually react to foreign bombing by digging in and rallying around their home government.[150] As noted above, Taiwan does not give the impression that it will be the first nation to break the historical pattern.

China might be able to use strategic bombing to reinforce the political status quo in Taiwan. Opinion polls show that most Taiwanese are willing to court conflict with China to maintain Taiwan's de facto independence, but not to achieve de jure independence.[151] Thus China could potentially deter Taiwan from officially declaring independence by threatening to bomb it (arguably, China has already done so for decades) and perhaps even force Taiwan's government to retract a hasty declaration of independence by carrying out a partial bombing campaign.

China, however, probably cannot compel Taiwan to give up its de facto sovereignty by raining hell on Taiwan's cities. Strategic bombing is not only historically ineffective, it also does not neatly serve China's ultimate political objectives. In most of the past bombing campaigns cited above, the attacker simply wanted the defender to desist from some action, a goal that conceivably could be achieved by bombing the defender into oblivion. China, by contrast, wants to reincorporate Taiwan as a prosperous Chinese province and turn Taiwan's people into loyal Chinese citizens. Reducing Taipei to a smoldering ruin and incinerating hundreds of thousands of Taiwanese civilians would not achieve that end.

Sea Control in the East China Sea

Roughly a hundred miles northeast of Taiwan, China is in a showdown with Japan over eight islets, which the Japanese call the Senkakus and the Chinese call the Diaoyutai. The islets themselves are insignificant—none are inhabited or larger than two square miles—but they are the symbolic epicenter of a broader struggle between China and Japan for control of the East China Sea.

This conflict is rooted in geography. China and Japan are two great powers packed into a small space and sit astride each other's vital sea-lanes. The Japanese home islands are only five hundred miles across the East China Sea from Shanghai, a distance that could be traversed in a day by a ship, in half an hour by a fighter plane, and in minutes by a missile. Japan also controls the Ryukyus, a chain of more than a hundred islands that stretch from the Japanese home islands to within seventy miles of Taiwan. All of China's most direct routes to the Pacific Ocean run through choke points between these islands.

China claims sovereignty over the Senkakus and exclusive rights, including the right to control military traffic, throughout most of the East China Sea.[152] China also maintains an air defense identification zone (ADIZ) over most of the sea and describes the skies in this zone as "Chinese airspace," a claim that implies that China has sovereignty over the waters and land below.[153]

If China could somehow enforce these claims, it would gain direct access to the Pacific, a secure coastline stretching from Beijing to Shanghai to Fuzhou, lucrative fishing grounds and oil deposits, and a staging area for blockades of Japan and Taiwan. Given these stakes, not to mention the historical grievances generated by Japan's brutal occupation of China in the 1930s, it is understandable why China is determined to dominate the East China Sea—and why Japan is equally determined to defend its own claims in the East China Sea, which include sovereignty over the Senkakus and exclusive rights and an ADIZ over roughly half of the sea.

In theory, China could enforce its East China Sea claims nonviolently using economic coercion and the cabbage strategy described earlier. In practice, however, China will probably have to decimate Japan's air and naval forces, because Japan has made clear it will fight to defend its East China Sea claims. Since 2010, China has conducted regular patrols around the Senkakus with hundreds of coast guard cutters, fishing vessels, and military aircraft.[154] Japan, however, has responded in kind, maintaining a sizable coast guard and naval presence in contested waters and scrambling fighters to the Senkakus hundreds of times per year.[155]

What are China's prospects of destroying Japan's air and naval forces? In the 1990s, the Japanese Self-Defense Force enjoyed insurmountable qualitative superiority over the PLA and could essentially command the East China Sea. Today, however, China has numerous surface ships, submarines, shore-based missile batteries, and combat aircraft all armed with advanced missiles and backed by a defense budget that is nearly four times larger than Japan's.[156] Japan currently has almost twice as many advanced destroyers as China (thirty-five versus twenty-one), but some analysts predict that by 2030 China will have thirty-four destroyers and a five hundred-ship navy.[157]

The balance of naval tonnage, therefore, is clearly shifting in China's favor. Nevertheless, Japan retains enduring geographic and technological advantages that will allow it to deny China sea and air control throughout much of the East China Sea for the foreseeable future.

First, Japan has announced plans to string a line of missile launchers along the Ryukyu Islands that can target all naval and air traffic across a two hundred mile band stretching north to south between mainland Japan and Taiwan, an area that includes the Senkaku Islands.[158] As discussed earlier, it is extremely difficult to destroy mobile missile launchers with air and missile strikes or amphibious assaults. Thus Japan will soon have a resilient missile force running the length of the East China Sea.

Japan is also expanding its submarine fleet from seventeen to twenty-two boats and maintains an extensive network of underwater sensors in the Yellow and East China Seas that is integrated with the U.S. undersea surveillance system and can track Chinese ships and submarines as they leave port.[159] During the Cold War, Japan's diesel-electric boats helped contain Soviet submarines in the Sea of Japan. Today, Japan can do the same to China's navy by attacking Chinese ships as they pass through the narrow seas along the Ryukyus.[160] And whereas Japanese submarines could attack Chinese surface ships largely unmolested by China's weak antisubmarine forces, Chinese submarines would have to contend with Japan's world-class antisubmarine warfare forces, which include seventy-five fixed-wing aircraft and eighty-five helicopters that can operate from bases on the Ryukyus or from the decks of dozens of Japanese surface ships.[161]

Japan retains robust mine warfare capabilities, including mines that can target specific ships and be laid by surface ships, submarines, and aircraft.[162] China's navy has almost no mine-clearing capabilities, so Japan could mine China's harbors or block the path of Chinese ships through the Ryukyus. To clear these minefields, Chinese minesweepers and their escorts would need to cross several hundred miles of contested waters and airspace, a journey many of them would not likely survive.

Finally, if the shore-based missiles, submarines, and mines discussed above failed to deny China control of the East China Sea, Japan could commit its surface fleet and air force to the battle. China has a larger surface fleet overall than Japan, but 75 percent of China's ships are small coastal

patrol craft and another 15 percent are frigates with limited range, endurance, and armaments.[163] As noted, Japan currently has nearly twice as many
large surface combatants as China, and Japan's fifteen smaller coastal patrol
craft and frigates, though outnumbered by China's fifty-seven frigates,
would be able to refuel and reload at ports along the Ryukyus and thus
maintain a higher tempo of operations than China's missile boats and frigates, which would have to transit hundreds of miles between the Ryukyus
and the Chinese mainland to refuel and reload.[164] Japan also has more than
two hundred fourth-generation fighter aircraft and will soon receive forty-
two F-35A aircraft from the United States, making Japan only the second
country in the world with operational fifth-generation fighters.[165] These
stealth aircraft could approach Chinese naval armadas in the East China
Sea undetected and launch missiles at Chinese ships.

China could try to knock Japan's air and naval forces out of a war by
striking Japanese ports and airfields. Japan, however, has 20 air bases, 11
naval bases, and 14 naval aviation bases dispersed across more than 2,000
miles of territory.[166] China currently has only 100 to 300 ballistic missiles,
500 cruise missiles, and 100 aircraft (slow, nonstealthy H-6 bombers) that
could reach these bases. Given Japan's advanced missile and air defense
systems, it is unlikely that China could disable many of Japan's bases for
long, if at all.

In sum, although the balance of naval tonnage is shifting in China's favor,
geographic and technological factors give Japan an enduring A2/AD capability that can plausibly deny China sea and air control in the East China Sea.

Sea Control in the South China Sea

China claims ownership of more than 80 percent of the South China Sea
based on a nine-dash line sketched on a 1947 Republic of China map. This
claim has no international standing—in July 2016, an international tribunal
in The Hague explicitly rejected China's historical claims to the South China
Sea—but it appears on all Chinese maps and passports. The nine-dash line
encloses waters through which roughly 40 percent of the world's trade and
90 percent of China's imported oil passes.

If China could enforce its claims in the South China Sea, it would achieve
the greatest territorial expansion by any power since Imperial Japan.[167]
China would gain greater security for its supply lines, exclusive access to
rich fishing areas and undersea oil deposits, and unfettered access to the
Western Pacific. Most important, China would effectively become the maritime hegemon of Southeast Asia, as other countries around the sea would
be confined to narrow bands of water along their coastlines.

China, however, cannot enforce its South China Sea claims.[168] The sea is a
hotly contested zone, with five other countries laying claims to portions of

it.[169] China has a more powerful military than these Southeast Asian states, but they are closer than China to the areas of the sea that they claim. In a war, Chinese forces would need to cycle between the combat theater and a few bases hundreds of miles away in southern China to refuel and reload, a commute that would severely limit the amount of combat power China could sustain on the battlefield. Southeast Asian forces, by contrast, could operate from home bases bordering the combat theater and would have their full arsenals at their disposal.

Some Southeast Asian nations have capitalized on these geographic advantages by developing A2/AD capabilities, including shore-based missile batteries, diesel-powered attack submarines, swarms of small surface combatants and fighter aircraft armed with antiship missiles and mines. As a result, the western and southern sections of the South China Sea are now bordered by forces capable of denying China sea and air command. Only in the northeastern quarter of the sea, near the Philippines, could China easily defeat local opposition and establish sea control.

WEST

The west side of the South China Sea is claimed by Vietnam, which can credibly threaten to destroy ships and aircraft within two hundred miles of the Vietnamese coast—an area that encompasses the western third of the South China Sea and China's military base on Hainan Island, where China stations roughly one-third of its navy.[170]

Most notable, Vietnam has purchased from Russia at least two mobile shore-based antiship cruise missile batteries that can target ships two hundred miles away.[171] China could try to destroy these batteries with air or missile strikes, but such strikes would have a low probability of success, even if China enjoyed air superiority over Vietnam—as noted earlier, the United States dominated the skies above Iraq and Kosovo in the 1990s but still failed to eliminate most of Iraq and Yugoslavia's missile batteries.

More important, China probably could not establish air superiority over Vietnam in the first place. Vietnamese air defenses have a reputation as "giant killers," having shot down more than 1,700 U.S. aircraft between 1961 and 1968 with simple antiaircraft artillery and no early warning radar.[172] Today, Vietnam fields some of the most advanced early warning radars and surface-to-air missile batteries in the world, having purchased the SPYDER system from Israel and S-300 batteries from Russia that can shoot down aircraft ninety miles away. Vietnam is currently in negotiations with Russia to purchase four S-400 batteries, which have a range of 250 miles and would enable Vietnam to target Chinese aircraft over mainland China.[173]

Even if China somehow destroyed Vietnam's shore-based cruise missile batteries, however, Vietnam would retain many platforms that could deny China sea control in the western third of the South China Sea. The

Vietnamese air force has more than a hundred fighters, including thirty-five Su-30MK2Vs that are as advanced as any aircraft currently operational in China's air force.[174] These aircraft can be armed with multiple Kh-31 supersonic antiship cruise missiles that could overwhelm the limited missile defense systems on China's ships.

China could try to nullify this threat by engaging Vietnam in an all-out air war. With more than 1,000 fighters, China's air force vastly outnumbers Vietnam's. Vietnam's air force, however, would be backed by ground-based air defenses and would operate from eighteen air bases on home soil, whereas Chinese aircraft would have to contend with antiaircraft fire and commute several hundred miles from nine air bases in southern China.[175] China could operate a few aircraft from an airfield on Woody Island, which is two hundred miles east of Vietnam in the Paracel archipelago. This airfield, however, would not last long in a war; the island is less than one-square mile in size, so personnel and platforms there have nowhere to hide from enemy missiles. In sum, China could potentially destroy Vietnam's air force in a protracted air war, but only at great cost.

Even if China destroyed Vietnam's air force, Vietnam's navy could still contest Chinese sea control using six Kilo-class diesel-powered submarines that have better range, endurance, sensors, and acoustics than China's diesel submarines and carry torpedoes, mines, and Klub-S submerged-launch cruise missiles that accelerate to supersonic speeds and perform evasive maneuvers as they approach their targets, making them extremely difficult to shoot down.[176] Vietnam lacks experience with submarine operations and maintenance, so it is doubtful that it could maintain more than two submarines ready for operations at any given time.[177] However, even a single Vietnamese submarine operated by a mediocre crew could pose a persistent threat to a Chinese naval armada. During the Falklands War, for example, a lone Argentinian midget submarine operated by a crew of junior petty officers evaded the British fleet throughout the war—even though the British navy expended nearly all of its antisubmarine ordinance trying to destroy the submarine—and successfully tracked and targeted several British warships. Only a torpedo malfunction saved the targeted British ships from destruction.[178]

Vietnam also has twenty-six warships armed with antiship missiles, including six new stealthy Gepard-class frigates, purchased from Russia, twelve corvettes, and eight smaller missile boats.[179] These surface ships are not nearly as capable as China's modern destroyers and frigates, but they carry advanced missiles with ranges between 70 to 100 miles and may soon carry the BrahMos missile, jointly developed by Russia and India, which is the most lethal cruise missile in the world: the BrahMos has a range of 190 miles; skims just above the sea; performs evasive S-maneuvers shortly before impact; and is four times faster (2,300 miles per hour) and several times heavier (6,000 pounds) than U.S. Tomahawk missiles. In tests, the BrahMos obliterated large ships even when its warhead failed to explode.[180]

In sum, Vietnam has developed a credible A2/AD force. Vietnam cannot enforce its own claims in the South China Sea, but it can threaten to destroy Chinese ships and aircraft operating in the western third of the South China Sea. Given the bloody history between the two countries—the 1974 naval battle over the Paracels; the 1979 border war that killed tens of thousands of troops on both sides; the 1988 naval battle in the Spratlys in which Chinese forces killed seventy Vietnamese sailors; and the deadly anti-Chinese riots in Vietnam in 2014—Vietnam seems unlikely to allow China to command the western South China Sea without a fight.[181]

SOUTH

China also has little hope of establishing sea control anywhere in the southern portions of the South China Sea, by which I mean the waters south of Vietnam on one side and the Spratly Islands on the other.

The countries that claim this area—Indonesia and Malaysia—are much weaker than China militarily, but they border contested areas, whereas China is more than a thousand miles away. In a conflict there, China's navy would have to transit several days each way between the combat theater and China's naval base on Hainan. Consequently, China probably could not maintain more than a dozen ships and submarines in the combat theater at any given time, even if China redeployed vessels from the East China Sea and the Yellow Sea, an unlikely proposition given that China has to keep tabs on Japan and Taiwan.

China also probably could not sustain major air operations in the southern portion of the South China Sea, because China only has thirteen mid-air refueling tankers and sixteen airborne early warning and control aircraft, which Chinese combat aircraft would need for targeting, and its two aircraft carriers only carry twenty-four fighters each, and these aircraft have to fly with half their normal capacity of fuel and armaments due to the carriers' ski-jump takeoff systems.[182]

The nature of a war in the southern South China Sea would depend on where China made its stand. If China tried to establish sea control in the center of the area, it might find itself in a war with Indonesia, which occupies the Natuna Islands and claims territorial waters and a 200-nautical-mile exclusive economic zone around them. If China tried to control the waters to the east or west of Indonesia's exclusive economic zone, it would come into conflict with Malaysia, whose exclusive economic zone and territorial seas begin where Indonesia's end.

Indonesia and Malaysia could plausibly deny sea and air control to a restricted Chinese task force. Indonesia's navy has twelve frigates, twenty corvettes, and thirty fast-attack patrol boats all armed with antiship missiles.[183] In addition, Indonesia operates two submarines armed with torpedoes and has procured three stealthy diesel-powered submarines made in

South Korea that will carry antiship missiles and cutting-edge electronic defense and radar signal detection systems.[184] The first of these new submarines began sea trials in 2016 and all three are expected to be operational by 2020. Indonesia's submarine crews have never been tested in wartime, so it is unclear how proficient they would be at targeting Chinese ships. That said, Indonesia has operated submarines for more than thirty-five years and thus has more experience than most countries in basic submarine operations and maintenance.[185]

Indonesia has declared it will have a "green-water" navy by 2024 with a minimum operational force of 110 warships, 66 patrol ships, 98 support ships, and 12 submarines.[186] This goal is unrealistic, but even with a quarter of this fleet, Indonesia's navy would enjoy numerical superiority over a Chinese task force near the Natunas, because Indonesia's ships could operate from two bases within three hundred miles of the combat theater and from a new base on the Natunas themselves and another at Mempawah less than two hundred miles away.[187]

For similar reasons, Indonesia also would probably enjoy a local superiority in fighter aircraft. Indonesia's air force has 49 fourth-generation fighters, including 33 F-16s, 11 Su-30s, and 5 Su-27s, and is in negotiations with Russia to buy 10 Su-35S fighters, which feature fifth-generation avionics and radar technologies and thrust-vectoring engines.[188] In a conflict with China, Indonesia's fighters could operate without aerial refueling from four air bases within 500 miles of the Natunas and an expanded air base on the islands themselves.[189]

Malaysia has fewer platforms than Indonesia, but its sailors and pilots are generally better trained. Thus its A2/AD forces are more capable than they may seem on paper. For example, Malaysia only has two submarines, but both of these boats are advanced diesel-powered submarines made in France, Malaysian maintenance crews have shown that they can keep one submarine operational at any given time, and Malaysian submarine crews collectively spent more than 9,000 hours in submerged training exercises between 2009 and 2017, making them one of the most experienced crews in Southeast Asia.[190]

Malaysia also has ten frigates, and twelve patrol boats all armed with French- and Italian-made antiship cruise missiles.[191] Malaysia's frigates also carry sixteen surface-to-air missiles, torpedoes, and cannons, and have deck space for antisubmarine warfare helicopters. In 2019, Malaysia will add six stealth frigates with similar armaments and towed sonar arrays.[192] In a conflict with China, these ships could operate from at least twelve bases around the southern shore of the South China Sea.

Malaysia's air force enjoys similar proximity to potential combat theaters, with at least eight airfields within the unrefueled range of the southern South China Sea. Malaysia has 36 fourth-generation fighters, including 18 Su-30s that can launch Kh-31 supersonic antiship missiles from beyond the range of the air defenses of China's ships.[193]

EAST

The east side of the South China Sea is the most-contested area, with six countries laying claims to various portions of it. Territorial disputes center on the Spratly Islands, an archipelago of a hundred small features spread across 160,000 square miles of sea. These features collectively have less than two square miles of natural land above the water, but China is reclaiming land and placing airstrips and docks on the seven features in the Spratlys that it currently occupies.

China hopes to take over the Spratlys without firing a shot by creating facts on the ground—that is, by flooding the zone with Chinese ships and steadily occupying and turning tiny features into habitable islands that ultimately gain international acceptance, if not recognition, as Chinese territory.

China's plan, however, faces two obstacles: the 2016 ruling by the tribunal in The Hague dashed China's legal claims to the area;[194] and four other countries militarily occupy features in the Spratlys and are unlikely to budge unless China uses force. Vietnam occupies twenty-one features and has built airstrips on two of them, reclaimed land on at least ten others, and placed mobile rocket launchers on at least five features that can target ships and installations within ninety miles—an area that includes all of China's outposts in the Spratlys.[195] Taiwan occupies and maintains an airstrip on the largest natural feature in the Spratlys, Itu Aba, which accounts for roughly half of the natural land above the water in the archipelago. Malaysia occupies five features and has placed military outposts on three of them, one of which has an airstrip. And the Philippines occupies nine features and maintains small military outposts on eight of them and a community of about three hundred civilians and forty military personnel on the remaining feature.

In short, China's neighbors are firmly ensconced in the Spratlys and are backed by international law. To enforce its claims to the area, therefore, China would need to use military force. What are its prospects?

To control the Spratlys, China first would need to establish air superiority over them. The Spratlys, however, are nearly seven hundred miles away from China's nearest air base on Hainan and more than eight hundred miles from its air bases in southern China. China only has five hundred combat aircraft capable of making this journey, and these aircraft would only be able to spend a few minutes near the Spratlys before returning home to refuel.[196] As a result, China would have, at most, a few dozen combat aircraft near the Spratlys at any given time.[197] Vietnam and Malaysia, by contrast, have numerous air bases within the unrefueled range of the archipelago and thus would have the full strength of their combat air fleets available for an air war.

China could fly a few fighters from airstrips on Fiery Cross, Subi, and Mischief Reefs and forty-eight additional fighters from its two aircraft carriers.[198] China also could conduct mid-air refueling operations using its thirteen tanker aircraft. These assets, however, have limited defenses and probably would not last long in a major war. Vietnam and Malaysia have several submarines and dozens of aircraft and naval ships armed with advanced missiles, and Vietnam has highly accurate rocket launchers installed within range of China's airstrips in the Spratlys.

Given these obstacles, China is unlikely to try to take the Spratlys all at once and incur the wrath of the whole region. Instead, China is more likely to pick off its rivals one-by-one and carve out a limited section of the sea. The easiest target for such limited expansion is the northeast quarter of the sea, which is claimed by the Philippines, a country with no missile-armed ships or aircraft. If China imposed itself in this area, there is little the Philippine military could do in response, and other Southeast Asian countries would probably stay out of the fight as long as China did not try to take over the areas that they claim. Given that the Philippines has signed a defense pact with the United States, these waters also are the most likely site of a U.S-China war in the South China Sea.

Fortunately for the United States, the area is far from China. Unlike in a Taiwan scenario, China's shore-based surface-to-air missiles cannot target aircraft near the Philippines, so China would have to rely on its combat aircraft and sea-based air defenses to establish air superiority. As noted, however, China only has about five hundred combat aircraft capable of reaching the east side of the sea, and these aircraft could only loiter for a few minutes near the Spratlys before returning to China to refuel.[199]

The United States, by contrast, could keep hundreds of aircraft over the islands at all times, because U.S. forces could operate from air bases in the southern Philippines beyond the range of all but a hundred to two hundred of China's conventional ballistic missiles.[200] China could try to attack these bases with H-6 bombers armed with long-range cruise missiles, but the slow speed of these bombers and missiles expose them to intercepts by U.S. fighters and air and missile defense systems.[201]

The Philippines, of course, might deny the U.S. military access to its bases, but such an outcome is unlikely: since 1945, more than 90 percent of U.S. requests for contingency base access have been granted, and in many of these cases the United States had no preexisting bases in the country in question (unlike in the Philippines today) and the host country was not under attack or otherwise involved in the conflict. Given this sterling record of U.S. base access, it seems unlikely that the Philippines would respond to Chinese annexation of Filipino waters by denying the U.S. military access to Filipino airfields.[202] Yes, the Filipino president, Rodrigo Duterte, has repeatedly threatened to downgrade the U.S.-Filipino alliance, but he also has authorized the United States to upgrade its military facilities in the Philippines, ordered further reclamation on Philippine-held islands in the Spratlys, instructed Filipino troops to "fight to the death" to defend these islands against China, and threatened to raise the Philippine flag himself on Thitu Island and to ride out to other Chinese-claimed features on his jet ski and plant Philippine flags on them too.[203] Furthermore, recent polls show that more than 80 percent of Filipinos favor defending Philippine-held features in the Spratlys from Chinese annexation, and recent Filipino government and military elites (most notably the defense minister) have publicly pressured Duterte to confront China's navy and coast guard.[204]

Even if the Philippines does expel the U.S. military, the U.S. military could still mass airpower over the Spratlys from carriers east of the Philippines, beyond the range of most of China's A2/AD forces. Alternatively, U.S. aircraft could operate with the help of aerial refueling from U.S. bases in Guam, Australia, and Japan and from additional airfields in the Marianas. Or the United States could request contingency access at some of the hundred airfields maintained by other Southeast Asian states that have maritime disputes with China.[205]

Computer simulations show that a single U.S. air wing operating only from bases in Guam and Japan could destroy more than half of China's strike aircraft in three weeks in a Spratly Islands scenario, and two U.S. air wings could do the same in less than a week.[206] If China attacked these bases, the U.S. military could respond in kind by cratering the runways at China's nine air bases within range of the Spratlys, actions that would knock China's air force out of a Spratly Islands war within hours.[207]

Without air cover, China's 19 destroyers and 57 frigates would be vulnerable to U.S. missiles launched by aircraft as well as ships and submarines. China's cruise missiles currently outrange America's, but by 2019 the U.S. military will regain the upper hand: new U.S. sea-launched antiship cruise missiles will have a range of 1,000 miles and new U.S. air-launched antiship cruise missiles will have a range of 570 miles; China's newest sea- and air-launched cruise missiles, by contrast, have ranges of 330 miles and 250 miles respectively.[208]

China could escort its surface ships with submarines. But China's five nuclear-powered attack submarines are noisier than U.S. submarines from the 1960s; and China's diesel-powered submarines would need to deploy their snorkels during the long journey to the combat theater (making the submarines easily detectable) and would only be able to operate in the area for a few weeks before returning to China's naval base on Hainan Island to refuel—assuming that the United States did not disable this base with missile strikes. American submarines, by contrast, could remain in the combat theater for months.[209] Moreover, if the United States had air superiority, it could deploy hundreds of antisubmarine warfare aircraft to hunt for Chinese submarines throughout the area.[210] Even without air superiority, the U.S. navy could attack China's fleet with submarines and its emerging fleet of drones armed with torpedoes.[211] In such a contested environment, China's submarines and surface ships would do well to survive for more than a few weeks.[212]

In sum, local actors can plausibly deny China sea and air control in the western and southern portions of the South China Sea, and the United States could deny China control of the northeast quarter of the sea at moderate risk to U.S. forces. China therefore faces a robust containment barrier and cannot command major portions of its near seas—at least for now.

The United States has multiple times the net stocks of military assets of China and maintains a daunting containment barrier against Chinese expansion in East Asia. These results, combined with the discussion of China's economic problems in chapter 3, show that the United States retains a preponderance of power over China. For China or any other nation to catch up to the United States, they will need to grow their power base much faster than they currently are. How likely is that?

CHAPTER 5

Future Prospects

This chapter analyzes the future prospects of the great powers and shows that the United States has the best foundation for continued growth.

I begin by addressing a fundamental question: what drives the rise and fall of the great powers? International relations scholars have used two main theories to answer to this question: balance-of-power theory and convergence theory.[1] Balance-of-power theory holds that weak states gang up on strong states and force a redistribution of power in the international system. Convergence theory, on the other hand, holds that poor countries grow faster than rich countries, thus rising challengers inevitably overtake established hegemons.

I argue that neither theory applies today. Balance-of-power dynamics are muted, because weaker states lack the wealth and military capabilities necessary to mount a sustained challenge to U.S. primacy. Convergence theory, on the other hand, is underspecified. Sometimes poor countries grow faster than rich countries, and sometimes they fall further behind. Knowing which scenario is more likely in the coming decades requires identifying the drivers of economic growth and assessing the prospects of today's major powers in light of these factors.

This chapter does exactly that. Drawing on research in the field of economics, I show that there are three main drivers of long-run economic growth: geography, institutions, and demography. I then use indicators of each to assess the prospects of the eight most powerful countries: the United States, China, Russia, Japan, Germany, the United Kingdom, France, and India. The United States does not rank first in all sources of strength, but it scores highly across the board whereas the other countries suffer from critical weaknesses. The United States thus has the best prospects to amass wealth and military power in the decades ahead.

Balance-of-Power Theory: Muted

The logic of balance-of-power theory is intuitive: states want power for them-selves and fear it in the hands of others, so when one nation starts to become more powerful than the rest, weaker countries usually react by building up their militaries and banding together to strangle the emerging hegemon.[2]

This instinctive fear of concentrated power stems from the anarchical nature of the international system. With no world government to shelter the weak from the strong, countries have to protect themselves by acquir-ing arms, forming alliances, and doing whatever else they can to prevent rivals from amassing preponderant power. The violent reactions of other countries to the rise of Habsburg Spain, Napoleonic France, and Imperial Germany illustrate the point.

Balance-of-power theory helps explain why bids for hegemony usually fail. But what happens when one succeeds? On the rare occasion when one nation becomes much more powerful than the rest, balancing dynamics may become muted.[3]

The reason is that in a unipolar system, no country is strong enough to balance the leader singlehandedly, so balancing requires cooperation among many countries, each of which has incentives to free ride on the efforts of its partners. This collective action dilemma allows the leader to play divide-and-conquer, punishing adversaries while rewarding allies.

Given the high costs of balancing, and the low likelihood of success, many weaker states will simply bandwagon with the sole superpower, or at least avoid provoking it.[4] Weaker nations may gripe about the hegemon's power and try to maximize their influence within the unipolar system, but such "soft balancing" will not fundamentally challenge the hegemon.[5] Con-sequently, the leader of a unipolar system will encounter less overt opposi-tion than a rising potential hegemon in a multipolar system.

Counterhegemonic balancing is especially unlikely if the most powerful nation is located further away from the other great powers than they are from one another.[6] In such a scenario, "regional balancing dynamics are likely to kick in against the local major power much more reliably than the global counterbalance works against the [hegemon]."[7] Regional powers may even compete with each other for the hegemon's support, because geography makes the distant hegemon "the perfect ally"—one that is powerful enough to be of help, but remote enough not to constitute an overriding threat.[8]

The United States today possesses both of these characteristics: prepon-derant power and a remote geographic location. It is several times wealth-ier and more militarily powerful than any other state, and it is the only great power located in the Western Hemisphere whereas all of the other great powers are clumped together in Eurasia.

The United States is also an "extant" hegemon; it did not overturn the preexisting international order, instead the previous order collapsed around it. When the Soviet Union imploded in 1991, the United States was suddenly left standing atop a Western liberal alliance system that already included most of the world's strongest nations, many of whom had spent decades linking their militaries, economies, and foreign policy bureaucracies with those of the United States.

Since 1991, the United States has expanded the size and scope of the key institutions of this liberal order—most notably, NATO, the WTO, the World Bank, the IMF, and the UN—and prevented rival orders from emerging by squelching regional initiatives—for example, by making sure the EU does not replace NATO as Europe's main defense organization—and maintaining a dominant military presence around the globe.[9]

For any nation, therefore, balancing against the United States would be a costly endeavor that would risk exclusion from the international community and require, at minimum, higher taxes to finance greater military spending. At a time of slow global growth, it is hard to imagine many foreign leaders being willing to stomach such costs.

Below, I illustrate this point by showing that balancing against the United States has been minimal since 1991 whereas bandwagoning has been widespread. I define balancing broadly as actions taken by states that increase their power relative to that of the United States. This expansive definition includes a variety of behaviors that come in three general forms: internal balancing, external balancing, and soft balancing. Internal balancing occurs when U.S. rivals build up their military capabilities. External balancing occurs when countries form alliances against the United States. Soft balancing involves the use of non-military tools (e.g. economic statecraft, diplomacy, cyber attacks) to undermine U.S. power.

INTERNAL BALANCING

Countries can engage in internal balancing in three main ways. The most extreme method would be for a country to try to become a military peer competitor of the United States and usher in a bipolar world order. The Soviet Union, for example, engaged in global balancing against the United States during the Cold War. Second, there is local balancing, in which a U.S. rival incrementally extends its defensive perimeter within its home region. Local balancing does not immediately alter the global distribution of power, but it lays the groundwork for future global balancing by helping a state carve out a sphere of influence near its homeland. Third, there is nuclear balancing, in which a state acquires nuclear weapons to blunt U.S. military superiority and deter the United States from attacking it. Below, I scour the empirical record for all three types of internal balancing.

Global Balancing. According to MIT military expert Barry Posen, the foundation of U.S. hegemony is the U.S. "command of the global commons." By "commons," Posen is referring to international waters, outer space, and airspace above 15,000 feet. The United States "commands" these areas in the sense that the U.S. military enjoys almost total freedom of action there and can deny such freedom to other nations. Command of the commons allows the United States to project military power worldwide and coerce adversaries by threatening to cut them off from international shipping routes and communications networks.

Global balancing involves challenging U.S. command of the commons. To achieve this goal, Posen explains, a country would need to develop a large suite of power-projection platforms, including aircraft carriers; nuclear-powered attack submarines; guided-missile destroyers and cruisers; overseas military bases; fighter, heavy-lift, and airborne early warning and control (AEW&C) aircraft; and satellites and anti-satellite weapons. These platforms are expensive, so the clearest sign of global balancing would be a significant increase in military spending.

Are countries engaging in global balancing against the United States? Since the 1990s, only two major powers—China and Russia—have significantly increased their military spending, yet their defense budgets and power-projection arsenals still pale in comparison to those of the United States (figure 5.1 and figure 5.2).

This persistent gap in military capabilities is historically unprecedented. In the nineteenth century, France, Russia, and Austria-Hungary quickly

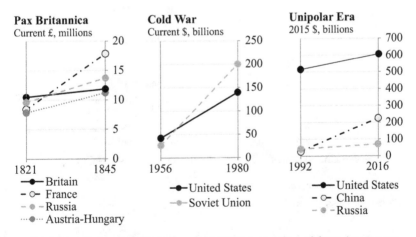

Figure 5.1. Internal balancing efforts compared: Military spending of the major powers: 1821–45, 1956–80, and 1991–2013.

Source: Singer, Bremer, and Stuckey 1972; SIPRI 2017a.

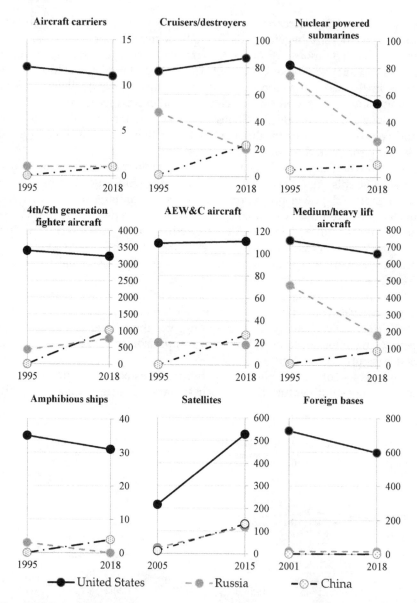

Figure 5.2. Power-projection platforms.

Source: IISS 1995; IISS 2018.

balanced Britain, the hegemon of the era, by outspending it militarily. Simi-larly, the Soviet Union ramped up military spending and raised a huge army to balance the United States during the Cold War. The military invest-ments of China and Russia today are consequential for security dynamics near their homelands, but they do not compare to these past cases of global balancing (figure 5.1).

Local Balancing. The U.S. dominates militarily at the global level, but China and Russia are working hard to shift the local military balances in their home regions. China's local balancing efforts were discussed at length in chapter 4. What about Russia's efforts?

Between 2007 and 2017, Russia doubled its military spending, invaded Georgia, annexed Crimea, incited an insurgency in eastern Ukraine, intervened militarily in Syria, harassed NATO warplanes, and threatened to use nuclear weapons if attacked by NATO. Some analysts portray these actions as savvy local balancing by a resurgent power.[10] On closer inspection, however, they look more like damage control by a declining power.

First, Russia's recent hike in defense spending looks impressive only because it followed the two steepest peacetime declines in history: when the Soviet Union collapsed, Russia's military spending dropped 75 percent (from $195 billion in 1990 to $42 billion in 1992); and then Russia cut military spending by an additional 65 percent between 1992 and 2000 (from $42 billion to $15 billion).[11] Russian military spending did not return to 1992 levels until 2009.

Although Russia's defense spending surged to $70 billion in 2016, a quarter of these funds were used to pay outstanding debts to defense contractors, and another 20 percent was stolen by corrupt officials, so Russia's actual military spending in recent years has hovered closer to early 1990s levels (roughly $40 billion), which is fifteen times less than what the United States spends.[12] Now that Russia's economy is in free fall—between 2013 and 2016, Russia's GDP shrank by 40 percent—the Russian government is slashing defense spending again, cutting the budget by 7 percent in 2017 (or 30 percent if the one-off payment to defense contractors is included in the 2016 budget) and another 5 percent in 2018.[13] The Russian government says it expects to make more cuts in the years ahead.[14]

Second, Russia's strategic gains in Georgia, Ukraine, and Syria are mitigated by the fact that Russia intervened in each country in response to a strategic setback. Russia invaded Georgia after Georgian President Mikheil Saakashvili, who was fervently committed to getting his country into NATO, sent the Georgian army to reincorporate two majority-Russian regions, Abkhazia and South Ossetia. Russia invaded Ukraine after Ukraine's pro-Russian president was ousted in a coup. And Russia intervened in Syria when the civil war there threatened to topple the regime of Bashar al-Assad, the caretaker of Russia's main naval base on the Mediterranean.

Third, Russia is paying a price for its local balancing. After Russia invaded Ukraine in 2014, the United States, the EU, Japan, Canada, Australia, Switzerland, and several Eastern European countries imposed sanctions on Russia that reduced its GDP by 1.5 percent that year and an additional 9 percent in subsequent years.[15] Furthermore, by annexing Crimea, Russia removed the largest pro-Russian voting bloc from Ukraine's electorate, thereby making it all but impossible for a pro-Russian leader to win a Ukrainian presidential election ever again. Russia also has to rebuild Crimea, a task that has already cost Russia more than $10 billion since 2014.[16]

Most important, Russia's actions have reinvigorated NATO, which responded to Russian aggression by increasing defense spending 4.3 percent, sending four multinational combat battalions to Poland and the Baltic states, establishing two new military commands to coordinate operations in the event of a war with Russia, increasing the number of exercises it carries out in central and eastern Europe, building infrastructure to surge reinforcements to eastern Europe, and ramping up its naval and air presence in the Baltic and Black Seas.[17] The United States has bolstered these efforts by sending 4,000 additional U.S. troops to Europe—the largest new American deployment there since the Cold War—and authorizing the sale of lethal weapons to Ukraine, including anti-tank missiles.[18]

In sum, Russia has engaged in local balancing against the United States, but its efforts have been offset by fiscal constraints, strategic setbacks, and counterbalancing by NATO and the United States.

In the years ahead, however, Russia could pose serious problems for the United States in the Baltics, where Russia enjoys a local superiority of military force over three NATO members: Estonia, Latvia, and Lithuania. Collectively these tiny countries have 20,000 soldiers, 158 pieces of artillery, a few tanks and patrol vessels, and no aircraft. Their combined territory is roughly the size of Missouri and, to make matters worse, they are wedged between the Russian heartland and Kaliningrad, a fortified Russian exclave.[19] Vladimir Putin has boasted that Russian forces could conquer the Baltic capitals in two days, and analyses by Western defense experts suggest that he was not embellishing by much.[20] Even if Russia never tries to conquer the Baltics, it could challenge NATO's credibility by seizing a small plot of land in one of the Baltic States, thereby forcing NATO to choose between attacking ensconced Russian forces or abandoning a NATO member.[21]

Russia has not yet carried out such an incursion—probably because it worries that NATO would honor its security guarantees to the Baltics and strike Russia with overwhelming force.[22] Russia also probably worries that the Baltic States would wage guerilla warfare in the event of a Russian invasion, replicating on a grand scale the punishment that a few thousand Chechen insurgents inflicted on Russian forces in Grozny, Chechnya's capital, in 1994 and 1999.[23] In short, Russia is currently deterred from attacking the Baltics. The situation, however, is precarious and fraught with risks of inadvertent escalation. In chapter 6, I propose ways to minimize them.

Nuclear Balancing. Only one country, North Korea, has developed a nuclear weapon since 1991. Meanwhile, four countries (Belarus, Kazakhstan, South Africa, and Ukraine) have dismantled their nuclear arsenals, and three other countries (Algeria, Romania, and Libya) have abandoned their nuclear weapons development programs.[24] The only other countries to pursue nuclear weapons since 1991 are Iran and Syria, and Iran agreed to suspend its program in 2016, and Syria has descended into civil war.[25] In short, there has only been one successful case of nuclear balancing in the unipolar era.

From an American perspective, of course, one new nuclear weapons state in thirty years is one too many. The United States has long been determined to prevent nuclear proliferation, and rightly so. The crisis currently brewing over North Korea's nuclear arsenal poses the gravest threat to American security since the Cold War. No geopolitical issue scares me more.

As I discuss in chapter 6, however, there may be ways to defuse this crisis without going to war or sacrificing core U.S. interests. Moreover, North Korea's nuclear success should not obscure the "great proliferation slow-down" that has occurred since 1991.[26] During the Cold War, nine countries acquired nuclear weapons in quick succession, and U.S. intelligence agencies predicted that dozens more would go nuclear.[27] Those predictions did not come to pass, partly because nuclear weapons are difficult to build and partly because the United States imposes severe costs on nuclear aspirants—in the last two decades alone, it has invaded Iraq, orchestrated multinational embargos on Iran and North Korea, and bombed Libya.[28] The U.S. government shows no sign of abandoning its aggressive counterproliferation policies. As a result, nuclear balancing will likely remain rare.

EXTERNAL BALANCING

The same can be said for external balancing. No countries have formed an alliance against the United States, while sixty-eight countries have formally allied with the United States, and dozens more have formed defense partnerships with it. The U.S. alliance network encompasses 25 percent of the earth's population and accounts for 75 percent of world GDP and defense spending.[29] No major power in history has had so many partners. Russia today maintains only a few defense agreements with some former Soviet states, and China's only ally is North Korea (figure 5.3).

The absence of anti-American alliances is especially remarkable, because the United States has gone out of its way to antagonize other nations. It stations dominant military forces in every region and uses force frequently, engaging in more than sixty militarized conflicts between 1991 and 2018.[30] The 2003 invasion of Iraq was particularly galling to other nations, and many scholars predicted it would spark serious balancing against the United States.[31] Yet no countries abrogated their alliances with the United States or formed alliances against it. Instead, thirty-nine

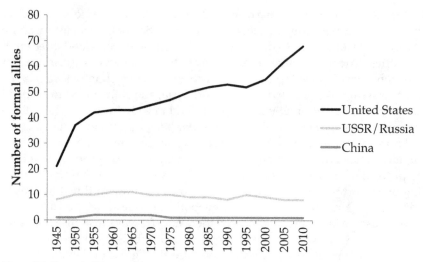

Figure 5.3. Formal alliances, 1945–2010.

Source: ATOP dataset.

countries joined the U.S. coalition against Iraq, contributing 50,000 troops for the invasion and 20,000 troops and $15 billion for postconflict stabilization operations.[32] Russia and China blocked UN authorization for the invasion, but did not challenge U.S. operations once underway.[33] Notably, thirty-five of Russia and China's forty-one neighbors contributed to the U.S. war effort.[34]

Looking ahead, there are only two coalitions that could muster the strength to challenge American primacy: a central Eurasian alliance anchored by Russia and China; or a Western European superstate built on the bones of the EU. Neither coalition, however, is likely to emerge. A central Eurasian coalition would require Russia and China to put aside their long-standing rivalry and subdue Japan in the east, NATO in the west, and India in the south. A Western European coalition on the other hand would require Britain to rejoin the EU, France and Britain to share their nuclear forces with Germany, and Russia to accept an EU superarmy on its doorstep.

Russia and China currently maintain a "strategic partnership," but this relationship is unlikely to become a genuine alliance, because the two countries share a 2,600-mile border and a desire to dominate Eurasia—a goal that one side can accomplish only by subjugating the other. Perhaps a shared hatred of the United States will bring Russia and China together, but history suggests otherwise.[35] At the start of the Cold War, China initially aligned with the Soviet Union, but by the 1960s the two Communist powers were literally at war with each other, and in the 1970s China officially switched sides and aligned with the United States.[36]

Today, many Russian and Chinese strategists warn their respective governments not to place too much faith in a sustainable partnership.[37] Foreign analysts come to similar conclusions. As one study explains: "[Sino-Russian] cooperation is limited to areas where their interests already overlap, like bolstering trade. In the parts of the world that matter most to them, Russia and China are more rivals than allies."[38]

For every example of Sino-Russian cooperation, there is a counterexample of competition. For instance, Russia sells weapons to China, but it recently reduced sales to China while increasing sales to China's rivals, most notably India and Vietnam.[39] Russia and China conduct joint military exercises, but they also train with each other's enemies and conduct unilateral exercises simulating a Sino-Russian war.[40] The two countries share an interest in developing Central Asia, but Russia wants to tether the region to Moscow via the Eurasian Economic Union whereas China wants to reconstitute the Silk Road and link China to the Middle East and Europe while bypassing Russia.[41] Collectively, these conflicting interests have placed Russia and China "on a trajectory toward intensifying competition from latent to emergent rivalry."[42]

What of the EU, the other potential anti-U.S. coalition? Since 1998, EU member states have developed a Common European Security and Defense Policy (CSDP) and raised a "rapid reaction force" of 60,000 troops and eighteen 1,500-troop "battle groups." Some scholars characterize these developments as balancing against the United States.[43] But EU nations have devoted less than 1 percent of their military manpower to the CSDP, far less than they contribute to the U.S-led NATO alliance; the EU battle groups have never been deployed; and all of the missions undertaken under the CSDP have been small peacekeeping missions involving an average of 3,000 troops.[44]

In 2017, the EU announced a new initiative—the Permanent Structured Cooperation (PESCO)—that committed members to increase defense spending and improve the bloc's ability to project power in hot spots near Europe. The initiative, however, is unlikely to offset the damage done by Britain's exit from the EU, given that Britain accounted for a quarter of EU defense spending and half of EU military R&D spending.[45]

SOFT BALANCING

Soft balancing—the use of non-military tools to shift the balance of power—comes in two main varieties: economic and political. Economic soft balancing entails the use of economic tools, such as sanctions, cyber attacks, espionage, and exclusionary economic blocs. Political soft balancing, on the other hand, occurs when foreign powers meddle in U.S. domestic politics or manipulate global public opinion to enhance their image or sully the reputation of the United States.

Economic Soft Balancing. The United States has almost never been sanctioned during the post–Cold War era, but it has sanctioned other countries forty-six times, accounting for nearly 60 percent of all cases of economic sanctions imposed since 1991.[46] According to a recent study, U.S. sanctions succeeded in coercing the target state to comply with American demands in more than 40 percent of these cases.[47]

The United States is uniquely empowered to impose economic sanctions because it plays a central role in global shipping and banking: the U.S. Navy can intercept shipping almost anywhere in international waters;[48] and the U.S. dollar is used in 80 percent of all financial transactions worldwide.[49] Most dollar-denominated transactions cross the American financial system, so the U.S. government has ample opportunities to manipulate or freeze the transactions and assets of hostile countries.[50]

Furthermore, when the United States imposes sanctions, it often gets its wealthy allies to help out. In some cases, therefore, the United States has been able to cut hostile regimes off from hard currency, financial credit, vital imports, and access to assets in North America, Western Europe, Oceania, and parts of East Asia.[51] For example, after Russia invaded Ukraine in 2014, the United States, the EU, Japan, Switzerland, Australia, and Canada froze Russian assets on their territory, prohibited their banks from conducting transactions with Russian entities, banned top Russian leaders and businesspeople from traveling to their countries, and cut Russia off from advanced technology imports. The multinational sanctions imposed on Iran from 2006 to 2016 were even more onerous, amounting to an almost total economic embargo on the country.

Instead of sanctioning the United States, and inviting economically devastating retaliation, rival powers have focused their economic ire on America's allies. Russia, for example, has manipulated oil and gas prices at least fifteen times since 1991 to coerce countries in central and eastern Europe.[52] On three of these occasions, Russia targeted NATO members: Lithuania in 2006, and Poland and Slovakia in 2014.[53]

China, too, has sanctioned several U.S. allies during the past decade, banning rare earth metal exports to Japan in 2010 during a dispute over the Diaoyu/Senkaku Islands; salmon imports from Norway after the Norwegian Nobel Committee awarded the Nobel Peace Prize to Chinese dissident Liu Xiaobo in 2010; banana imports from the Philippines during a standoff over Scarborough Shoal in 2012; and visas for some South Korean celebrities, businesspeople, and tourists after Seoul decided to deploy the Terminal High Altitude Area Defense (THAAD) missile defense system in 2017.[54]

Some of these sanctions arguably weakened the United States by cowing its allies into concessions. Norway, for example, released a statement in 2016 promising to "fully respect China's sovereignty . . . and core interests",[55] and the Philippines has downplayed the 2016 world court ruling it won against China's territorial claims, canceled some military exercises with the United States, and halted construction on a sandbar in a disputed area of the South China Sea.[56]

In most cases, however, China and Russia's sanctions have not significantly improved their strategic situations. The United States offset Russian gas sanctions by shipping American natural gas to allies in eastern Europe.[57] Japan responded to China's sanctions by reasserting its claims in the East China Sea, bolstering its military, and reducing its reliance on Chinese rare earths.[58] The Philippines still occupies Chinese-claimed portions of the South China Sea and is allowing the United States to expand and upgrade its military bases on Filipino territory.[59] And South Korea deployed THAAD in September 2017.[60]

Given their limited ability to impose sanctions, U.S. adversaries have sought other ways to chip away at American wealth and power. An increasingly common approach is cyber warfare. American organizations and businesses have been the targets in roughly 40 percent of all publicly known state-sponsored cyber attacks and intrusions worldwide since 2005.[61] The majority of these attacks were carried out by China, Russia, Iran, or North Korea and involved espionage, data destruction, service denials, or all of the above. It is difficult to calculate the costs these attacks have imposed on the United States, but estimates range from $8.5 billion per year to $400 billion per year if all of the potential long-term losses from espionage are included.[62]

America's rivals also are soft balancing against the United States by developing alternatives to the liberal economic order.[63] China and Russia, for example, are promoting an international basket of currencies to replace the dollar as the world's reserve currency and a new international financial transaction system to provide an alternative to the Society for Worldwide Interbank Financial Telecommunication (SWIFT) system, which the United States and its allies have used to cut foreign leaders and their cronies off from assets abroad.

Other examples of soft balancing include China's founding of the Asian Infrastructure Investment Bank (AIIB), which could dilute U.S. economic influence by providing poor countries with financial alternatives to the World Bank and IMF, where the United States controls three times the voting shares of any other country. China also is negotiating with at least sixteen countries to form a free-trade zone, the Regional Comprehensive Economic Partnership (RCEP), which would exclude the United States and create the world's largest trading bloc by population. Finally, China's Belt and Road initiative—which aims to provide $1 trillion in loans for infrastructure projects in sixty-nine countries, mostly in Central, South, and Southeast Asia—could create a Chinese-centric economic order in the center of Eurasia.

Time will tell whether these initiatives diminish American power. At present, each faces obstacles. The dollar has only become more dominant as a global currency since the 2008 financial crisis.[64] China and Russia have found few takers for their SWIFT alternatives. China's ability to direct the operations of the AIIB is limited, because other countries control 75 percent of the voting shares, the bank has to raise capital from international financial markets, and many of the bank's projects are co-sponsored by the World Bank.[65] RCEP negotiations are two years behind schedule and, as of early 2018, are being held up by India.[66] India also is boycotting China's Belt and Road initiative; Japan and Russia are pushing alternative schemes; and according to the Chinese government, roughly half of the participants in Belt and Road will not be able to repay the loans they plan to take from China, so when those loans come due next decade, China either will have to write off hundreds of billions of dollars in losses or try to seize assets in participating countries, as it recently did in Sri Lanka—hardly a great way to win friends or persuade countries to abandon the liberal order for a Chinese-dominated one.[67]

Political Soft Balancing. Some authoritarian nations—most notably China and Russia and, to a lesser extent, Iran—are spending billions of dollars on an "antidemocratic toolkit" of NGOs, media outlets, think tanks, hackers, and bribes.[68] Their main aim is not to win hearts and minds, but to reverse the international spread of democracy, destroy America's image abroad, and subvert American political institutions.[69]

Such political soft balancing, which the National Endowment for Democracy calls sharp power, comes in various forms.[70] The most direct approach involves meddling in the domestic politics of the United States and its allies. For example, Chinese agents have tried to bribe politicians in Australia, Germany, Britain, and the United States to get them to endorse China's positions on territorial disputes, trade, and human rights.[71] Russia has interfered in the elections of at least twenty-seven Western countries since 2004—most infamously in the 2016 U.S. presidential election—by stealing and releasing compromising emails, hacking voting machines, and spreading fake news using a network of social media trolls and bots.[72] In a nightmare scenario, such meddling could enable foreign powers to manipulate American policy by getting Manchurian candidates elected. In fact, some commentators think Russia already accomplished this goal by swinging the 2016 presidential election for Donald Trump.[73]

Americans are rightly concerned about foreign meddling, but they can take some solace in the fact that leaders installed by a foreign power rarely behave as loyal puppets; most get checked by other political actors or simply go rogue and brush off the demands of their foreign backer—a phenomenon the United States experienced first-hand during the Cold War when some of its proxies in Latin America, the Middle East, and Southeast

Asia gave American policymakers the cold shoulder.[74] The Trump case also illustrates the difficulty of coopting a democracy: even if President Trump is a Russian puppet, and Russian meddling won him the election—both of which are debatable points—the political backlash incited by Russia's actions has turned U.S. policy further against Russia, resulting in more sanctions on Russian elites and more NATO troops near Russia's borders.

A more likely harm of foreign meddling is that it undermines Americans' trust in their own government. In 2017, only 18 percent of Americans said they trusted their government to do what is right always or most of the time.[75] This lack of faith may have more to do with domestic failures than foreign meddling—public trust in government has hovered around 20 percent since the 2008 financial crisis, which occurred before Russian and Chinese influence activities kicked into high gear—but foreign meddling certainly has not helped and could prove devastating in the future. Imagine, for example, the pandemonium that might erupt in American society if foreign hackers successfully sabotaged voting machines during a close election.[76]

Even if such a dramatic outcome never occurs, countries can balance against the United States by waging what Chinese president Xi Jinping calls a "discourse war" (*huayu zhanzheng*). China, for example, is spending $10 billion a year to promote pro-China views abroad; by comparison, the U.S. government only spends $670 million on foreign outreach.[77] Some of China's image-building initiatives are harmless (e.g. sponsoring Chinese new year celebrations around the world), but others are blatant attempts to stifle Western criticism of China. For example, the Chinese government has pressured Western publishers to censor articles and books on sensitive subjects, such as the Tiananmen Square massacre and unrest in Hong Kong, Xinjiang, and Tibet. In 2017, two Western academic publishers, Springer and Cambridge University Press, caved to China's demands and removed objectionable content from their databases in China, though Cambridge eventually reinstated the content following furious criticism in the West.[78]

China also has tried to inject Chinese propaganda into Western public discourse. For example, in 2015, American reporters discovered that China Radio International, a state media company, had covertly sponsored at least thirty-three pro-China radio stations in fourteen countries, including the United States.[79] *China Daily*, the Chinese government's main English-language mouthpiece, floods the streets of American cities with free newspapers and pays for inserts in major American papers, such as the *Washington Post* and the *Wall Street Journal*.[80] Since 2004 China has established more than five hundred government-funded "Confucius Institutes" in 140 countries, including more than one hundred institutes in American universities. These institutes ostensibly teach Chinese language and culture, but some scholars accuse them of trying to censor research and teaching (full disclosure: my university hosts a Confucius Institute, but it has never contacted me about my research, much less pressured me to adopt certain views, and this book is hardly flattering to China).[81]

Russia has sponsored similar initiatives. In recent years, it has created a global television network called Russia Today (RT), established think tanks in Washington, D.C., hired journalists to submit content to American periodicals and websites, and created fake personas to post comments on social media.[82] These outlets relentlessly beat home a pro-Russian, anti-American, message. According to Liz Wahl, a former RT news anchor who left the station in protest over its biased coverage, the "basic principle" to which RT stories "must conform" is: "make the U.S. and the West look bad."[83]

Have these efforts eroded America's standing abroad? It is difficult to say. The share of the world's population that approves of the United States declined from 64 percent in 2016 to 49 percent in 2017, but this sudden drop probably had more to do with the election of Donald Trump, a historically unpopular president, than Chinese or Russian influence activities.[84] As of early 2018, America's foreign approval rating remains higher than it was under President George W. Bush and higher than China or Russia's.[85]

Perhaps China and Russia's machinations will eventually even the score, but this outcome is far from guaranteed, because the United States is fighting back. As Dartmouth scholars Stephen Brooks and William Wohlforth have shown, "the United States is clearly the world's number one soft balancer."[86] It hosts think tanks that promote an American world view and funds media and pro-democracy groups—such as the National Endowment for Democracy, Freedom House, the Ford Foundation, the Asia Foundation, Voice of America, and Radio Free Europe and Asia—that shelter Chinese and Russian dissidents and journalists, name and shame China and Russia's human rights violations, and support democratic movements in both countries' backyards. These actions build on a long American legacy of meddling in other countries' internal affairs.[87] During the Cold War, the United States launched at least seventy-two political operations to coopt or destabilize foreign regimes, sixty-six of which were carried out covertly.[88] It is unclear how many political operations the United States runs today, but investigative studies found evidence of covert programs in Libya in 2011 and Syria in 2012.[89]

Most important, America's civil society—everything from its highly successful companies and foundations to its world-class universities and trendsetting pop culture—radiates soft power and helps the United States attract foreign partners.[90] By contrast, China and Russia's stodgy state-directed charm offensives lack genuine appeal.[91] China's efforts have made it more popular in Africa, mainly because China has poured money into stadiums and other infrastructure there. But China and Russia have not been able to buy much love abroad. According to a widely cited international soft power index, the United States ranks third from the top whereas Russia and China rank fifth and sixth from the bottom respectively.[92]

Net Assessment. To sum up, balancing against the United States has been limited since the end of the Cold War. North Korea has acquired nuclear weapons, and Russia and China have engaged in local military balancing and soft balancing. Yet no countries have seriously challenged U.S. command of the global commons or formed anti-American alliances.

The United States thus operates in a relatively permissive international environment. This environment is not free of threats to U.S. security, but the United States faces fewer and smaller direct challenges to its hegemonic position than did past lead powers. These trends, along with a large body of international relations theory, suggest that full-blown balancing against the United States will not reemerge until other countries narrow the gap in power resources between themselves and the United States. The fate of unipolarity thus depends on the other major driver of international change: economic convergence.

Convergence Theory: Underspecified

As Yale Historian Paul Kennedy has shown, the rise and fall of the great powers is largely the result of "differentials in growth rates and technological change, leading to shifts in the global economic balances, which in turn gradually impinge upon the political and military balances."[93] The question is: Why do some countries, at some times, grow faster than others?

To answer this question, international relations scholars have borrowed an old idea from economics—convergence theory—that holds that poor countries tend to grow faster than rich countries.[94] The reason, according to the theory, is that poor countries enjoy the "advantages of backwardness": they can copy or steal the latest technologies from rich countries without paying the costs to invent them; and they can engage in "cost innovation," mass-producing advanced technologies at a fraction of the price of rich countries, because they have lower labor and input costs.[95]

Given these advantages, poor countries eventually move "from imitation to innovation" and "leap-frog" up the value chain by mastering and improving on foreign technologies.[96] Meanwhile, rich countries suffer declining rates of profits, rising wages, and the exhaustion of resources, all of which encourage investment to migrate to greener pastures in emerging markets. As two prominent economists conclude: "For poor countries with large young populations, growing fast should be easy: open up, create some form of market economy, invest in human and physical capital, don't be unlucky and don't blow it. Catch-up and convergence should do the rest."[97]

The main implication of convergence theory for world politics is that rising challengers inevitably overtake reigning hegemons. As Princeton political economist Robert Gilpin explains: "With lower costs and equivalent

technology, backward societies frequently can outcompete the more afflu-
ent advanced society economically and militarily" and thereby catalyze "a
fundamental redistribution of power in the system."[98]

Yet convergence theory is not an iron law of history. At best, it is a conditional hypothesis that confronts several inconvenient facts.

First, rich countries have grown faster than poor countries during seventeen of the past twenty decades.[99] In other words, *divergence* has been "the
dominant feature of modern economic history."[100] Poor countries have
grown faster than rich countries since the early 2000s, but the trends are
turning back the other way, and many economists now worry that poor
countries' recent growth spurts stemmed from ephemeral factors (cheap
capital, low interest rates, and high commodity prices) that are disappear-
ing, potentially for good.[101]

Second, the wealth gap separating rich and poor nations has expanded
steadily over the past two hundred years. The gap in ratios of per capita GDP
between rich and poor countries has narrowed slightly since 2000, but remains
as wide as it was in the 1970s and greater than during the height of the imperialist era in the nineteenth and early twentieth centuries. Few nations have
gone from rags to riches. Besides oil states and trading entrepôts, like Hong
Kong and Singapore, the only success stories are Japan, South Korea and
Taiwan—all three of which had the good fortune to develop during the
Cold War, when the United States lavished money, technology, and trade
privileges on its partners because it needed strong anticommunist allies.[102]

Third, the economic trajectories of less-developed countries have varied
tremendously: a few have converged rapidly with rich countries, others
have fallen further behind, and most have had a mixed experience of "take-
offs, stalls and nose dives."[103] Asian economies have been the main success
stories—Japan, South Korea, Taiwan, and Singapore have become rich; and
China and India have grown rapidly since the 1990s, albeit from a low
base—but bursts of growth in Latin America, Africa, and the Middle East
have fizzled.

Fourth, the trends highlighted above hold even if we focus solely on
great powers. For every case of great power convergence, there have been
many more cases of divergence.[104] For example, Germany, Japan, and the
United States rose relative to Britain in the late nineteenth century; but
Austria-Hungary, France, Russia, China, India, and the Ottoman Empire
fell further behind. During the second half of the twentieth century, Japan
rose relative to the United States; the Soviet Union, France, Britain, China,
and India not so much.

In sum, convergence is "anything but automatic."[105] Superpowers are not
doomed to decline, and developing countries are not destined to rise. There
may be advantages to backwardness, but there are also considerable disad-
vantages, including a lack of capital, skilled labor, know-how, market share,
and brand recognition.[106]

Convergence theory, therefore, is underspecified. The likelihood of catch-up growth depends on a set of factors that, so far, have not been incorporated into theories of international change. Fortunately, economists have been hard at work identifying these growth ingredients. The next section highlights the three most important factors.

Sources of Growth

Abraham Lincoln supposedly said that a nation's strength stems from its land, laws, and people.[107] It turns out Lincoln was right. According to a voluminous literature in economics, the three main factors driving long-term economic growth are geography, political institutions, and demography. None of these factors is necessary for growth; some countries have grown rapidly in spite of having bad geography, institutions, or demography. Moreover, economists do not agree about which factor matters most. Nevertheless, there is considerable evidence that each factor shapes the probability of economic growth over periods of several decades. Below, I discuss each in turn.

GEOGRAPHY

In international politics, as in real estate, location matters. The ideal location for wealth-creation is one with an abundance of exploitable energy resources, transport infrastructure, and protective buffers.[108]

Exploitable Energy Resources. There is substantial evidence linking the rise of great powers to exploitable energy resources.[109] Britain, for example, surged ahead of other countries in the early nineteenth century in part because its major cities happened to be located near massive coal deposits, a stroke of luck that spurred widespread adoption of machines that obliterated previous limits on transportation and industry.[110] By the 1800s, English coal was yielding as much energy as could be generated by 6 million horses, 11 million acres of firewood, or 40 million men (who would have eaten more than three times Britain's entire wheat output).[111] Similarly, the United States rose rapidly in the late nineteenth century by pioneering the exploitation of oil, which fueled the "American system" of mass manufacturing that made the United States the wealthiest nation in the world.[112]

Today, most natural resources are sold on global markets, and many countries are developing renewable sources of energy. Nevertheless, renewable energy only accounts for 3 percent of world energy consumption, and studies still find a significant positive relationship between exploitable fossil fuel reserves and wealth.[113] Among countries in the top three energy quintiles (as measured by energy reserves per capita) only 6 percent are poor; by contrast, 58 percent of the countries in the bottom two energy quintiles are poor.[114]

Of course, countries that depend heavily on resource exports for growth may suffer recurrent economic busts because of sudden drops in global commodity prices. Moreover, resources can cripple growth by fueling corruption, undermining the rule of law, or increasing the likelihood of civil war.[115]

Yet there is no guaranteed "resource curse."[116] Norway, a major oil producer, ranks near the top of the international tables for governance and economic performance; the most recent major study on the issue finds that resource wealth may actually facilitate democratic development;[117] and many other studies find that resources fuel growth, as long as a country has a diversified economy, consolidated democratic political institutions, or both.[118]

Transport Infrastructure. Countries with natural transport infrastructure, namely navigable rivers and deepwater harbors, enjoy an economic advantage over landlocked countries, because moving goods over land is forty to seventy times more expensive than over water.[119] For example, in the United States, semitrailer trucks transport goods for roughly $2.40 per mile whereas modern container ships transport goods for roughly 17 cents per mile;[120] and maintenance of U.S. highways costs $160 billion per year whereas maintenance for all U.S. waterways cost $2.7 billion.[121] Countries that have navigable rivers and natural harbors thus save vast sums of money that would otherwise have been spent lugging goods over land and building and maintaining roads, railways, and ports.

In addition, a country with many navigable rivers connected to ocean harbors is more likely to participate in world trade and have a flourishing domestic market.[122] When goods can easily reach many locations within a country, regions within the country can specialize and reap the gains of trade. The result is a large and diversified consumer market. The political philosopher Adam Smith made this point centuries ago: "As by means of water-carriage a more extensive market is opened to every sort of industry than what land-carriage alone can afford it, so it is upon sea-coast, and along the banks of navigable rivers, that industry of every kind naturally begins to subdivide and improve itself, and it is frequently not till a long time after that those improvements extend themselves to the inland part of the country."[123]

The correlation between waterways and wealth is striking. The four most prosperous economic zones in the world—Western Europe, northeast Asia (coastal China, Japan, and the Republic of Korea), and the eastern and western seaboards of the United States and Canada—contain most of the world's natural harbors and navigable rivers.[124] By contrast, nearly all of the world's dry and landlocked countries are poor.[125] This pattern repeats itself within countries: the most prosperous regions in most nations are located near waterways.[126] The pattern also holds for the great powers; for instance, detailed case studies have linked the economic dynamism and outsized international influence of the Dutch Republic, Britain, the United States, and Germany to their waterway networks.[127]

Buffers. A good location is a secure location. Countries that are surrounded by powerful enemies tend to fight more wars and maintain larger armies.[128] Such militarization drains resources and scares off investment.[129] Countries that have natural buffers (e.g., bodies of water, mountains, or weak neighbors) separating them from powerful rivals not only have more money to invest in their economies, but also enjoy cheaper access to finance because lenders view them as safe havens.[130] The ideal buffer is a body of water, because it provides protection from enemies in wartime but facilitates international trade in peacetime.[131]

INSTITUTIONS

Just as a computer needs a sleek operating system to run efficiently, an economy needs to be governed by clean and capable institutions to prosper. A good government is strong but limited; it enforces laws and provides public services, but is constrained by rules that ensure that it acts in the interests of the community.[132] A state without constraints is a tyranny, and a nation without a state is anarchical. The ideal government therefore strikes a balance between order and accountability; it has the *capacity* to enforce laws and get things done, but it remains *accountable* to society and treats people equally on the basis of citizenship rather than on their political connections.

Capacity. The idea that state capacity is vital for economic development has a long lineage dating back at least to the writings of Thomas Hobbes and Max Weber. The argument attracted significant attention in the 1980s and 1990s as a consequence of the "East Asian Miracle," when scholars noticed that the Asian countries that became rich—Japan, Taiwan, South Korea Taiwan, Hong Kong, and Singapore—were run by strong "developmental states."[133] Conversely, other studies have linked the economic failure of African and Latin American nations to state weakness.[134] Cross-national and subnational studies bolster these findings, showing that countries and regions with higher per capita tax revenues (a crude proxy for state capacity) and better scores on indexes of state capacity tend to be wealthier.[135] In sum, there is a large literature supporting the rather intuitive argument that nations need governments with the capacity to maintain order, regulate economic activity, and provide public services in order to grow economically.

Accountability. Dictatorships may be able to engineer growth during early stages of development—the Soviet Union, for example, achieved some of the highest growth rates in the world in the 1950s by shoving peasants into factories and channeling investment into strategic industries[136]—but in the long-run, checks on executive power are vital to sustain growth.[137] Such constraints not only reduce corruption, but also help secure private property rights. Property rights, in turn, foster entrepreneurship and innovation, because people are more likely to start new businesses and engage in R&D if they believe that the fruits of their labor will be protected and respected by the state.[138]

It may seem logical to equate democracy with accountability, and authoritarianism with corruption, but some authoritarian regimes have become rich (e.g., Singapore today or Imperial Germany in the early twentieth century), and many democracies are economic basket cases. Most countries in Latin America, for example, are nominally democratic, yet the region's average per capita income is less than $8,000 in real terms. Similarly, there are sixteen democracies in Africa, but their average per capita income is $2,500.[139]

The large number of poor democracies shows that the key to growth is not elections per se, but rather constraints on government elites. These constraints can be imposed by a variety of political counterweights, including noble lords, local governments, business groups, religious movements, or cultural norms. Regular elections might be the most reliable means of checking tyranny and corruption, but they are no guarantee. Voters may fail to hold leaders accountable due to ignorance, ethnic ties, or elite manipulation; and leaders may run for office not to pursue a vision of the public good, but to enrich themselves.[140]

Given these limitations of democracy, most economists measure accountability in terms of the number of constraints on the executive, the level of expropriation risk faced by private investors, or the degree of voice and accountability in countries.[141] These indicators are not perfect; most are based on surveys of "experts" at international organizations and political risk firms, many of whom may be biased in favor of liberal democratic institutions.[142] Nevertheless, there is a clear correlation between these measures and wealth: the countries with the most constraints on the executive, the lowest expropriation risk for private investors, and the highest scores on governance indexes are, with few exceptions, the richest countries in the world.[143]

Such correlations, of course, do not prove that accountable institutions cause economic growth. There could be reverse causation—perhaps as countries become wealthy they develop checks on executive power.[144]

Another possibility is that unobserved factors, such as geography or culture, determine both a country's level of economic development and the nature of its political institutions.

Rigorous studies, however, have addressed these issues by using natural experiments (for example, comparing the institutional and economic experiences of North and South Korea or East and West Germany),[145] instrumental variables,[146] and subnational variation.[147] This literature has produced a massive body of evidence showing that accountable institutions dramatically improve a country's prospects for sustaining long-term economic growth. For example, the most recent study in this line of work shows that when a country democratizes, its GDP per capita rises by an additional 20 percent over the following thirty years.[148]

DEMOGRAPHY

Countries with populations that are big, young, and educated are primed for economic growth.[149] Big populations support large labor forces and domestic markets, young populations can work hard, and educated populations can work efficiently and invent new technologies.

Size. Population surges do not always spur economic growth, but they often do. Germany and the United States, for example, grew rapidly in the late nineteenth century in part because of rapid population growth, which Germany achieved by unifying several smaller states and the United States achieved through immigration.[150]

Age. As noted in earlier chapters, a large population can be a burden if it is not productive. To grow, countries need young workers, not geriatrics. Not surprisingly, there is considerable evidence linking so-called demographic dividends, in which the working-age population grows faster than the population of retirees, to economic growth. For example, demographic dividends accounted for roughly one-third of the Soviet Union's rapid growth in the 1950s, the East Asian tigers' growth in the 1960s and 1970s, and China and India's growth in the 1990s and 2000s.[151]

These are not isolated examples. Among the fifty-six cases since 1960 of a country growing its economy 6 percent annually for a decade or more, the working-age population grew on average at 2.7 percent, a finding that suggests that the rise in number of workers did much of the heavy lifting to produce these economic miracles.[152] By contrast, countries with declining working-age populations have found it nearly impossible to sustain economic growth. On average, for every 1-percentage-point decline in a country's population growth rate, the country loses a percentage point of GDP growth.[153] Among the thirty-eight of cases since 1960 of countries with declining working-age populations, the average GDP growth rate was

1.5 percent.[154] Only three of these countries grew their economies at or above 6 percent annually, and all of them were small countries recovering from domestic instability: Portugal in the 1960s and Belarus and Georgia between 2000 and 2010.[155]

Education. Productivity depends not only on youth but also on smarts. Countries with weak education systems can purchase or steal advanced technologies and methods from abroad, but they may lack the knowledge or "absorptive capacity" necessary to use them.[156] For that reason, studies suggest that differences in educational attainment and quality account for 20 to 35 percent of the variation in per capita wealth among countries and across regions within countries.[157] Similarly, historical studies suggest that the expansion of education systems in Germany in the late nineteenth century and in the United States in the twentieth century added roughly a third of a percentage point to GDP growth annually in each case.[158]

Future Prospects of Today's Great Powers

Having identified the main drivers of long-term growth, I now use indicators of each to assess the future prospects of the eight most powerful countries in the world, by which I mean the countries that currently possess the largest stocks of economic and military resources: the United States, China, Russia, Japan, Germany, the United Kingdom, France, and India.

GEOGRAPHY

Exploitable Energy Resources. The United States recently became the world's largest producer of oil and natural gas, bringing up more oil than Saudi Arabia and more natural gas than Russia.[159] According to the three most widely cited projections of world energy production, the United States will become a net energy exporter by 2030 and perhaps as early as 2022.[160] This development is due to the fact that the United States is the only nation exploiting large quantities of shale oil and natural gas.[161]

China remains the world's largest coal producer, but coal is not as valuable as oil and gas because it is harder to transport, releases more particulate matter, and cannot be used to power most vehicles. For those reasons, the United States does not produce as much coal as China despite having more than twice the reserves.

Russia has larger natural gas reserves than the United States, but the Russian economy is overly dependent on resource rents—hydrocarbons contribute 60 to 70 percent of Russia's federal budget and two-thirds of its exports.[162] Whereas the United States has large energy reserves and a diversified economy, Russia suffers from what economists call "Dutch disease," meaning an overreliance on commodity exports that fuels corruption and starves other sectors of investment.[163] Russia's overreliance on hydrocarbon exports also generates boom-bust cycles that wreak havoc on the economy. For example, when the oil price plunged from $147 to $50 per barrel between 2008 and 2009, Russia's economy shrank 20 percent.[164]

China, Russia, and France have large shale reserves, but they are unlikely to tap them in large quantities soon, if ever.[165] The International Energy Agency predicts that China will extract less than 0.1 million barrels of shale oil and one-quarter of a million barrels of oil per day from coal in 2035—an amount equal to just 3 percent of China's current oil consumption.[166] France has banned fracking entirely, partly because its best shale field lies directly under Paris. And Russia's decrepit energy giant Rosneft lacks the technology to tap the country's vast reserves.[167]

The main reason the shale revolution has been an American phenomenon, besides the fact that U.S. shale fields happen to be located near major refining centers, is that the United States, unlike other countries, has a legal system that enshrines private ownership of land and the resources below it.[168] In America, any company can strike a deal with a landowner to lease the rights to the resources beneath his or her land. Consequently, the United States has more than 22,000 independent oil and gas companies competing vigorously for drilling rights, market share, and technological breakthroughs.[169] In the rest of the world, by contrast, mineral rights are owned or controlled by the government, and energy resources are managed by state-owned monopolies, which face no competitive pressure to explore new sources or adopt new technologies. In Russia, for example, ten companies produce 90 percent of the oil output, and a single company, Gazprom, controls 80 percent of the country's natural gas.[170]

The result of the United States' unique energy market is that U.S. drilling capacity and intensity dwarf that of other countries. Since the dawn of the oil and gas age in the nineteenth century, nearly 4 million wells have been drilled in the United States versus only 1.5 million in the rest of the world combined.[171] At present, the United States owns 60 percent of all the rigs in the world, and 95 percent of American rigs can perform horizontal drilling, unlike those of other countries.[172] Since 2010, 99 percent of the horizontal wells drilled globally have been drilled in the United States.[173]

In sum, for geologic, technological, and institutional reasons, the United States will reap disproportionate benefits from its energy resources for the foreseeable future.[174] Already, shale production has slashed oil and gas prices in the United States, created more than one million new jobs, and added $400 billion—roughly 2.5 percent of GDP or $1,400 for every American—to the U.S. economy every year since 2010.[175]

Energy independence might also help the United States accumulate wealth and power in indirect ways.[176] For example, some analysts expect the United States to shift to a cheaper "over-the-horizon" military posture in the Persian Gulf.[177] The U.S. decision not to get too deeply involved in the Libyan and Syrian civil wars might be the new normal. China, by contrast, is headed in the opposite direction. By 2035, it will be the world's largest petroleum consumer and will import 85 percent of its oil from the Middle East.[178] Chinese strategists fear that China will have to take over the burden of stabilizing the Middle East as the United States becomes less involved there.[179]

American energy exports also might reduce China and Russia's ability to coerce U.S. allies in Asia and Europe. Currently, many U.S. allies in Europe depend on natural gas from Russia; and U.S. allies in Asia depend on oil and gas shipped through the South China Sea, where China's navy lurks.[180] American energy exports, however, could "unshackle" U.S. allies from reliance on Russian gas and reduce China's ability to blockade allies in East Asia by opening up secure energy supply routes across the Pacific.[181]

Transport Infrastructure. America is primed for cheap internal transportation.[182] The continental United States has 14,650 miles of navigable rivers (rivers that can handle drafts of nine feet for at least nine months of the year), which is more than the rest of the world combined.[183] The United States also has a "bonus" three-thousand-mile waterway along its eastern coast, where thousands of barrier islands turn exposed coastline into a series of connected bays stretching from the Chesapeake to the Texas-Mexican border. Consequently, 90 percent of the population of the continental United States lives within 150 miles of a navigable waterway.[184]

This unique waterway network saves the United States hundreds of billions of dollars in infrastructure costs each year and stitches together a giant national market.[185] Americans living almost anywhere in the lower forty-eight states can enjoy goods produced in other regions without paying exorbitant shipping costs. For this reason, the U.S. consumer market has been the largest in the world since the Civil War and is equal to the consumer markets of the next five nations—China, Japan, Germany, Britain, and France—combined.[186]

In addition, the United States has more natural deepwater ports than the rest of the world combined.[187] Puget Sound, San Francisco Bay, and Chesapeake Bay are the world's three largest and best natural harbors. Chesapeake Bay alone has more deepwater port area than the entire coastline of Asia, from northeastern Russia to the southern tip of India. New York Harbor, Mobile Bay, and the thirteen deepwater ports in Texas are "merely world class."[188]

These ports enable the United States to exploit its unique location between the world's two great trading zones in Europe and Asia; when one of those regions is in recession, the United States can shift trade and investment flows to the other.[189] The advantage of this swing capacity is illustrated by a simple fact: in the post–World War II era, no recession in Europe or Asia has caused a recession in the United States, but every American recession has triggered recessions in Europe and Asia.[190]

Buffers. The United States is the only great power that does not share a land or sea border with another great power. Its two land neighbors, Canada and Mexico, are weak and separated from the United States by rugged borders. Neither poses a conventional military threat to the U.S. homeland, nor do any of the great powers of Eurasia. As discussed earlier, China, the most militarily powerful of the second-rank powers, cannot maintain sea or air control in its near seas; doing so in the Pacific Ocean or near the American coast is out of the question.

Whereas the United States is bordered by allies and oceans, the other great powers are packed together in Eurasia and encircled by rivals. Figure 5.4 compares the U.S. security environment with that of the other great powers by charting the combined defense spending of each country's neighbors. The United States is clearly in the safest location.

Whereas the United States is immune to a Eurasian invasion, the U.S. military has numerous launching pads from which to impose itself on Eurasia. The United States has 587 military bases scattered across every continent except Antarctica and on islands in every ocean.[191] This global military presence not only enhances U.S. power, but also underscores the fact that forty-two countries, including most of the great powers, have

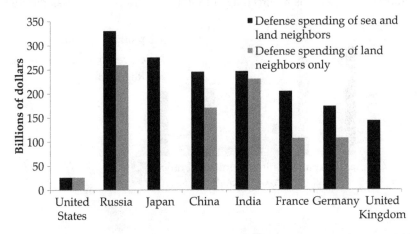

Figure 5.4. Combined defense spending of each great power's neighbors (constant 2015 $).

Note: Totals only include countries bordering each great power's homeland (e.g., the lower forty-eight states for the United States), not outlying territories.

Source: SIPRI 2017a.

invited the U.S. military to operate from their territory—in many cases because they fear their neighbors more than they fear the United States.

INSTITUTIONS

The most widely used measures of government capacity and accountability are the World Bank's six Worldwide Governance Indicators, which aggregate data from more than thirty international institutions, media outlets, think tanks, survey institutes, and private firms.[192] Three of these indicators measure aspects of state capacity: government effectiveness, regulatory quality, and political stability and the absence of violence. The other three indicators measure accountability: voice and accountability, rule of law, and control of corruption. Below, I use these indicators to provide a first look at each great power's institutions. Then I supplement the indicators with data from country-specific studies. The results suggest that the United States has much more capable and accountable institutions than Russia, China, or India; slightly more capable and accountable institutions than France; and slightly less capable and accountable institutions than Japan, Germany, and the United Kingdom.

Capacity. The United States scores slightly lower in terms of state capacity than Germany, Japan, and the United Kingdom (figure 5.5) mainly because it has a smaller and more divided state. The U.S. system has more "veto points" (aka checks and balances spread across the courts, Congress, presidency, and the states) than the parliamentary systems common in other developed democracies;[193] and as a percentage of GDP, the United States has the third

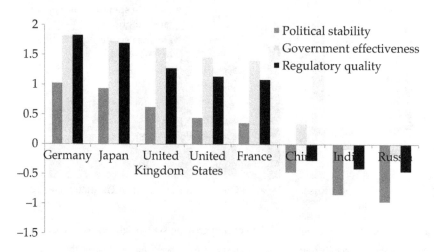

Figure 5.5. State capacity.

Source: World Bank 2016.

lowest levels of government spending and tax revenues among the thirty-four countries in the OECD. American fiscal capacity is only 80 percent that of Japan, 75 percent that of the United Kingdom, 67 percent that of Germany, and half that of Denmark, which tops the World Bank's state capacity rankings.[194]

History helps explain why the U.S. government is smaller and more divided than that of other developed countries. In Western Europe and Japan, law and a modern state came first, followed later by democracy.[195] The United States, by contrast, was born a democracy and only began developing a modern bureaucracy in the 1880s.[196] For most of U.S. history, a vast western frontier, the relative absence of foreign threats, and a liberal ideology limited state building. The U.S. government expanded during the World Wars and the Cold War, but less so than the governments of other major powers.[197] The American constitutional system, designed to minimize government and maximize liberty, facilitates commerce but constrains state capacity.

The downside is that the U.S. government provides fewer services to its citizens. Consequently, the percentage of Americans living in poverty is 60 to 100 percent greater than that in Western Europe and Japan.[198] Although Social Security and Medicare help the elderly, working-age Americans basically have to pull themselves up by their bootstraps: as a share of GDP, the United States spends six times less than the OECD average on so-called active labor-market policies, such as job training programs, job-search assistance, and hiring subsidies; and three times less on family benefits, such as childcare support and early education programs.[199] As of 2018, some Republican lawmakers are clamoring to cut these benefits further to help pay for the 2017 tax cuts, which reduced U.S. government revenues by $1.5 trillion.[200]

The payoff of the weak U.S. state is that it facilitates entrepreneurship and private investment.[201] In the United States, it takes half as many steps, and less than half the time, to start a business, obtain construction permits, register property, and enforce contracts as it does in Europe and Japan.[202] As a result, Americans are 50 to 300 percent more likely than Europeans and Japanese to start new businesses;[203] and U.S. venture capital investment as a share of GDP is seven and a half to twelve times greater than that of Germany, France, the United Kingdom, and Japan.[204] Americans hire and fire each other more frequently than do Europeans and Japanese, work 5 to 30 percent longer, produce 10 to 50 percent more output per hour, and earn 50 to 65 percent higher wages.[205]

Limited government may have served the United States well for most of its history, but past performance is no guarantee of future success. The United States has the dubious distinction of being the only presidential democracy (i.e., a system with separate executive and legislative branches) with a long history of political stability.[206] Others, most of which are in Latin America, have tended to oscillate between authoritarianism and chaos. The reason is that presidential systems have an Achilles heel: they require contending branches of government to compromise and strike bargains. In parliamentary systems, by contrast, the prime minister usually heads a majority in the legislature, and political stalemates can be overcome on the spot by holding new elections. Without such safety valves, the American system is susceptible to political polarization, legislative gridlock, and capture by special interests. As I discuss in the next chapter, such problems are already infecting the American government and threaten to undermine U.S. state capacity in the decades ahead.

For the time being, however, U.S. state capacity is only slightly below that of Germany, Japan, and the United Kingdom, and far above that of Russia, China, and India.

Russia's personalist regime gives the president, Vladimir Putin, immense power over the secret police, the media, and flows of cash, but not for providing services to citizens or enforcing laws across Russia's sprawling territory.[207] During his first two terms, more than 1,800 of Putin's decrees were ignored or circumvented,[208] and Putin himself estimates that only about 20 percent of his decisions get implemented unless he intervenes forcefully.[209] The former president, Dmitri Medvedev, has stated: "Without exaggeration, Russia is a country of legal nihilism. . . . No other European country can boast of such a level of disregard for law."[210] Rigorous studies corroborate this claim: nearly 30 percent of Russians admit to breaking the law on a regular basis, and Russian police earn more money from second jobs (roughly 40 percent of which involves illegal activity) than from their official salaries.[211]

China also has severe state capacity problems. While formal authority is concentrated in Beijing, much policy implementation is delegated to local governments that routinely evade central government mandates.[212] Local autonomy may have spurred growth during the reform years by allowing different regions to experiment with different policies (although this claim is debated among China scholars),[213] but now China's "decentralized authoritarianism" is undermining Beijing's efforts to "rebalance" the economy from investment to domestic consumption and innovation.[214] In November 2013, the Communist Party outlined sixty reform proposals affecting almost every aspect of the economy, but less than 10 percent were implemented.[215]

Many Chinese local government officials and bosses of state-owned firms siphon state funds on the sly. In a typical arrangement, a local government will seize land from peasants and transfer ownership to a shell company, which uses the land as collateral to borrow from state banks and shadow lenders.[216] Local rulers then use these funds to line their pockets, run patronage networks, and build extravagant infrastructure projects, reasonably assuming that Beijing will never dare call in its loans, which now total more than 40 percent of China's GDP.[217] In essence, local governments have become too big to fail, so the central government is unable to impose fiscal discipline.[218] The results for the country will be devastating over the long-term. As shown in chapter 3, China has racked up more debt and excess capacity than any developing country in history.[219]

India, too, lacks state capacity. Only 3 percent of India's population pays taxes (most people are too poor), so India's tax base is comparable to that of a small European country. India's government revenues are equal only to 20 percent of its GDP, whereas tax revenues in the other great powers are equal to 30 to 50 percent of GDP,[220] and India's urban per capita public spending is only $50, which is only 14 percent of China's $362 and 3 percent of the United Kingdom's $1,772.[221] These figures actually overstate India's fiscal capacity, because half of India's public spending is wasted or stolen.[222] For example, at least 30 percent of India's agricultural produce rots on the shelf, because the country lacks a basic food supply network.[223]

The result of India's state weakness is endemic poverty. More than half of India's population (roughly 680 million people) lacks consistent access to food, clean water, electricity, housing, toilets, healthcare, education, or paved roads.[224] The Indian government has drafted a series of pro-growth initiatives, but has failed to implement most of them, which may actually be a good thing given the government's long record of economic incompetence—a common saying is that "India's economy only grows at night while the government is asleep." The World Bank ranks India 130th out of 190 countries in terms of the ease of doing business, 178th for enforcing contracts, and 183rd for securing construction permits. On average, it takes the Indian government 3.8 years to settle a court case (versus one year in OECD countries) and 4.3 years to resolve a bankruptcy case, with an average recovery rate of only 26 cents on the dollar.[225] By contrast, bankruptcy cases in OECD countries are resolved in 1.7 years, on average, and recover 71 cents on the dollar.[226]

Accountability. Despite having a more open system, the United States ranks slightly lower than rich European nations and Japan in terms of government accountability (figure 5.6). Ironically, out of fear of empowering "big government," Americans have created a system that entrusts unelected courts, congressional committees, and interest groups to carry out government functions that in Western Europe and Japan are performed by professional bureaucracies.[227]

The power of courts and interest groups yields excessive litigation and gargantuan pieces of legislation filled with thousands of giveaways to special interests. For example, the 2010 Dodd-Frank bill, which regulates the financial industry, is 849 pages long, not counting several thousand pages of additional rules. The Affordable Care Act is 2,700 pages plus 20,000 additional pages of regulations.[228] The 2017 tax cut bill is nearly 500 pages

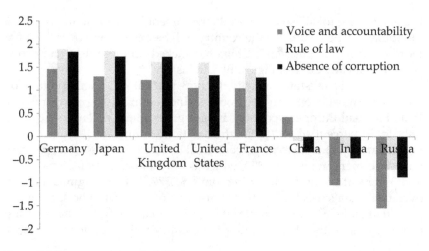

Figure 5.6. Government accountability.

Source: World Bank 2016.

long, received input from more than half of the 11,000 lobbyists living in Washington, D.C., and created a tax code that is nearly 4 million words long—roughly ten times as long as the tax codes of Germany and France.[229] These laws, and many others, are so long because they are dotted with loopholes, many of which have been put in place by the very industries they are supposed to regulate—a process that academics call "regulatory capture."[230]

Special interests are not necessarily bad. Alexis de Tocqueville famously praised American interest groups as "schools" for democracy, because they bring people together to solve common problems and resist tyranny.[231] According to "pluralist" theory, a cacophony of interest groups produces sound public policy, just as competition among self-interested firms in a free market boosts the aggregate wealth of society.[232]

Yet the actual practice of democracy in America bears little resemblance to this pluralist utopia. The interest groups that command the attention of Congress represent the most politically organized and engaged segments of American society, which in many cases means the wealthiest.[233] For this reason, some pundits now consider the United States a "kleptocracy."[234] That conclusion may be hyperbolic, but it captures more than a grain of truth and reflects the feelings of many Americans that the system is rigged by elites.[235]

No doubt, American democracy has serious problems. When analyzing the global balance of power, however, it is important to keep America's shortcomings in international perspective. The U.S. system is only slightly less accountable than that of Japan, Germany, and the United Kingdom;

and it is much more accountable than the governments of Russia, China, and India.

Russia has oscillated among shades of authoritarianism for the past century.[236] At present, the country is dominated by a single ruler, Vladimir Putin, who runs a "pyramid of patronage" over a small band of tycoons that collectively own the commanding heights of the economy.[237] Private property rights are nonexistent. According to *The Economist*, Russians are not so much property owners as "temporary holders," serving at the pleasure of "Tsar" Putin, his oligarch cronies, and his henchmen at the Federal Security Service (the successor to the KGB).[238] Under Putin, the state-owned share of the economy doubled from 35 percent in 2005 to 70 percent in 2015.[239] Putin himself seems to be the main beneficiary of this state expansion, having amassed a personal fortune estimated between $40 billion and $200 billion: the low estimate would make Putin the richest man in Europe; the high estimate would make Putin almost twice as wealthy as Jeff Bezos, the richest man in the world.[240]

China's government is becoming just as personalist and patrimonial as Russia's. Chinese president Xi Jinping has appointed himself "chairman of everything" and, by all accounts, rules as an "imperial president."[241] At the 2017 party congress, Xi amended the party constitution with a new guiding ideology, Xi Jinping Thought, and packed the highest levels of government with loyal followers: fifteen of the twenty-five members of the Politburo have long-term ties to Xi; and none of the seven members of the Politburo Standing Committee, the highest body in the Chinese government, is qualified by rank and age to succeed Xi.[242] In 2018, China's legislature abolished presidential term limits, paving the way for Xi to rule China until the day he dies.

Xi presides over the Chinese Communist Party, an oligarchy that owns almost all of China's land and roughly two-thirds of its assets.[243] The constitution states explicitly that the Chinese government can confiscate private property at any time; every company with more than fifty employees is required to have a Communist Party official on staff; and 70 percent of private companies in China (domestic and foreign) now have a party cell on site that monitors workers and operations.[244]

In addition, the Chinese government is carrying out "the most extensive effort to selectively censor human expression ever implemented."[245] It controls the media, employs hundreds of thousands of internet police to remove online content that might spur social mobilization; employs 2 million netizens to flood social media with fake posts celebrating the Communist Party and trolling its critics; and systematically deletes historical documents that challenge party orthodoxy.[246] In 2017, China ranked 186th out of 197 countries on a scale of press freedom.[247]

Most disturbing, the Chinese regime is developing a "social credit score" system that will determine each citizen's access to essential services— including education, bank loans, insurance, and transportation—and help the regime monitor and detain dissidents.[248] To build this system, the Chinese government is collecting blood and saliva samples and cell phone data from Chinese citizens and developing facial recognition technology that can identify any of China's 1.4 billion people within three seconds.[249] Chinese cities are already experimenting with the system. In Shenzhen, the local government deters jaywalkers by posting their names and pictures on a screen as they approach an intersection.[250] In Beijing, the government does the same in public restrooms to stop people from stealing toilet paper (the official limit is sixty centimeters per nine-minute period).[251] China already imprisons thousands of dissidents without trial.[252] Once the social credit system goes live nationwide in 2020, the ranks of Chinese political prisoners will probably swell.

In the meantime, the Chinese government has preemptively barred Chinese citizens from taking money out of the country, so most people have little choice but to place their life-savings in state-owned banks, where interest rates are set below the rate of inflation. This "financial repression" enables the party to run a massive patronage network and security apparatus, which in turn enables the party to function as "the dominant dispenser of commercial, business, professional, and even social opportunity" throughout the country.[253]

Crucially, the Communist Party holds the senior management positions of all of the major state-owned enterprises, which receive 75 percent of the country's bank loans and 95 percent of government stimulus spending.[254] Private firms, by contrast, are forced to take out high-interest loans from shadow banks and bribe party members for permits and protection from expropriation.[255] This "crony capitalist" system has been highly lucrative for China's ruling elite.[256] Among the 1,271 richest people in China, 203 are delegates to the National People's Congress, the nation's legislature.[257] In 2015, the delegates' combined net worth was $463.8 billion, which was more than the GDP of Austria that year.[258] Meanwhile, 40 percent of China's population still lives on less than $5.50 per day.[259]

India holds regular elections, but state-ownership and corruption limit government accountability. The state owns 70 percent of the banking system as well as major insurance companies, utilities, hotels, and an airline. India ranks seventy-sixth out of 168 countries in corruption perceptions, and India's political system is populated by "authoritarian" leaders—roughly 20 percent of whom have been charged with violent crimes—that use "money and muscle" to carve out fiefdoms for themselves and "run industries rather than regulate them."[260] In public surveys, more than half of Indian respondents report regularly paying bribes for basic public services, including police protection, utilities, education, and medical attention; and more than 80 percent of Indians say the government and political parties are infected with corruption.[261] Sadly, Salman Rushdie's aphorism remains as apt as ever: "Indian democracy: one man, one bribe."[262]

DEMOGRAPHY

Population Size. The United States is the only major power with a working-age population (people of ages fifteen to sixty-four) that is projected to grow throughout the century.[263] Whereas the United States will add 40 million working-age adults, China will lose 470 million—half of its current workforce. Labor forces in Western Europe will shrivel due to low birth rates. And Japan's population is already dying off rapidly, as evidenced by the fact that the country consumes more diapers for seniors than for babies.[264]

Russia's labor force will "implode," shrinking 30 percent by midcentury, because of high death rates.[265] From 1991 to 2009, Russia was a "mortality society" with three funerals for every two live births—the worst surfeit of peacetime deaths over births in modern history besides China's ratios during the Great Leap Forward, when 30 million people starved to death. Russia's high mortality rate is mainly due to rampant binge drinking and related traffic accidents, murders, and suicides.[266] The Russian government launched public health initiatives in 2006 to reduce these harms, but then reversed course and slashed public health budgets to save money during the 2008 financial crisis. At present, Russian death rates remain the tenth highest in the world and are on par with Somalia's.[267]

India's labor force will peak in 2035 and then decline steadily. Although India's working-age population will remain much larger than the United States', only 55 percent of India's working-age population has a job versus 73 percent of Americans of working age. India's labor force participation rate is low partly because of chronic poverty and partly because of systematic discrimination against women—only 28 percent of Indian working-age women are employed outside the home, a ratio that is one of the lowest in the world (only Pakistan and a few countries in the Middle East have lower shares).[268] Perhaps India's cultural norms will change in the decades ahead. At present, however, the trends are moving in the opposite direction: from 2005 to 2014, the share of Indian women in the workforce declined from 38 percent to 28 percent.[269]

Population Age. By 2040, the United States will have the second youngest population among the great powers (figure 5.7). More important, the U.S. median age will remain stable for the rest of the century whereas that of the other great powers will rise.

China's median age will surge from 35 to 50 between 2015 and 2050, and the number of Chinese older than 65 is expected to rise from roughly 130 million to 410 million—a population of geriatrics larger than the total U.S. population and nearly equivalent to the combined populations of Germany,

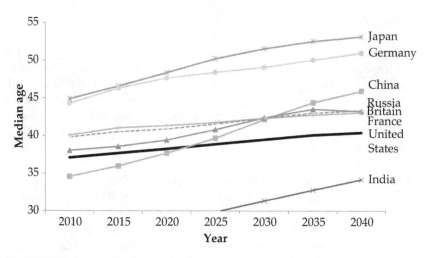

Figure 5.7. Median age (medium variant).

Source: UN population database 2017.

Japan, France, Britain, and Russia. China currently has eight workers for every retiree; by 2050, it will have two workers per retiree.

In 2015, China relaxed its one-child policy, allowing some parents to have two children. Despite this reform, however, China is guaranteed to suffer the most rapid aging process in human history, because China's huge population of future senior citizens and the tiny one-child generation that must support it have already been born. Moreover, many Chinese families now opt to have only one child, mostly for financial reasons, and 40 million Chinese men will not be able to start a family at all because a cultural preference for sons spurred widespread abortion of female fetuses over the past three decades.[270]

Education. The United States leads the other great powers in quantity of education, but lags behind some of them in quality. Americans receive, on average, one to three more years of schooling than people in Germany, the United Kingdom, Japan, Russia, and France; and roughly twice as many years of schooling as people in China and India.[271] On international tests, however, American teenagers score similarly to their peers in the other great powers in reading and science and score significantly worse in math.[272]

The most famous of these exams is the OECD's Programme for International Student Assessment (PISA) test. Every three years, half a million fifteen-year-olds in sixty-nine countries take the two-hour test, which asks them to solve problems, identify patterns, and write essays. American students have always scored in the middle of the pack among developed countries on these exams since they were instituted in 2000.

Scholars have criticized the PISA tests, because different countries draw test-takers from different socioeconomic backgrounds. China's results, for example, are based solely on scores from four of China's wealthiest locales (Beijing, Shanghai, Jiangsu, and Guangdong) and do not include the scores of the millions of migrant children living in these areas. If similar adjustments are made to U.S. scores (for example, by only using scores from students in Massachusetts), then the United States would rank first in the world in reading, second in science (after Singapore), and twelfth in math (ahead of all the major powers except Japan and Germany).[273]

Another factor may be that American students simply do not try very hard on international tests that have little to no effect on their social or educational standing at home—a situation that is not the case for students in some other countries. A 2017 study by American and Chinese economists found that introducing financial incentives for good performance, by allowing students to keep $1 for every correct answer, dramatically improved the performance of American students but not of Chinese students.[274]

Nevertheless, the PISA test remains the best cross-national metric of educational quality and reveals genuine flaws in the U.S. education system.[275] Most notable, the cross-national data suggest that the American system of teacher recruitment, training, and accountability has been put together backward: it draws teachers from the bottom half of college classes; gives them minimal training; and when teachers fail to improve student performance, the government imposes rigid standards, hoping to do on the back end what it failed to create on the front end.[276] By contrast, countries with top PISA scores, such as Japan, Singapore, and Finland, do the opposite: they select teachers from the top third of college classes, train them rigorously, and then give them the freedom and time to hone their skills and share best practices with other teachers.[277] As Harvard's Jal Mehta has shown, such methods largely obviate the need for external accountability, because "selection and preparation on the front end makes extensive monitoring on the back end unnecessary."[278]

Despite these shortcomings, however, the United States ranks first among the great powers by standard measures of human capital per capita and labor productivity.[279] These results are puzzling: how can the United States have the most productive workforce in the world when it has a mediocre primary and secondary education system?

Studies on this question have produced three main answers.[280] One is simply that the United States enjoys other economic advantages—most notably its excellent geography and business-friendly commitment to limited government—that compensate for its educational shortcomings. A second reason is that the United States makes up for a lack of educational quality with greater quantity: American teenagers may lag several years behind their foreign peers in cognitive skills, but they will receive several more years of education, on average, during their lifetimes. Third, the United States poaches human capital from other countries. As the home of 50 of the top 100 universities in the world, the United States is able to attract millions of smart, young people from other countries every year, including hundreds of thousands of doctoral candidates in science and engineering fields.[281] More than half of these students join the American workforce and stay for at least five years after they graduate, bolstering the U.S. stock of human capital while draining the stocks of other nations.[282]

The United States is far from perfect, but it has better growth prospects than the other great powers—as well as a huge economic and military lead. Unipolarity is not guaranteed to endure, but present trends strongly suggest that it will persist for many decades. The final chapter discusses what this development means for world politics and U.S. policy.

The Unipolar Era

"If Sparta and Rome perished," the philosopher Jean-Jacques Rousseau asked, "what State can hope to endure forever?"[1] The resounding answer given by history is "no state." In time, perhaps in another century or so, the American empire will crumble and new powers will rise. But we are not there yet, nor will we be for many decades. We are living in the unipolar era, and it will probably outlive us.

So what? The United States might be the most powerful country in history, but it has a limited presence in many corners of the globe, and weaker nations routinely trample on U.S. interests.[2] The United States failed to prevent the 9/11 terrorist attacks, the rise of the Islamic State, the Russian invasion of Crimea, Russian meddling in the 2016 U.S. presidential election, North Korean nuclear proliferation, and Chinese island-building in the South China Sea. Unipolarity, bipolarity, multipolarity: What difference does it make?

In this final chapter, I explain why this view is wrong by highlighting several ways that unipolarity transforms world politics. The good news is that unipolarity dramatically reduces the likelihood of great power war. The bad news is that it may increase the likelihood of asymmetric conflict and undermine American national unity and the liberal world order.

No Hegemonic Rivalry

The story of world politics is often told as a game of thrones in which a rotating cast of great powers battles for top-dog status. According to researchers led by Graham Allison at Harvard, there have been sixteen cases in the past five hundred years when a rising power challenged a ruling power.[3] Twelve of these cases ended in carnage. One can quibble with Allison's case selection, but the basic pattern is clear: hegemonic rivalry has sparked a catastrophic war every forty years on average for the past half millennium.

The emergence of unipolarity in 1991 has put this cycle of hegemonic competition on hold. Obviously wars and security competition still occur in today's unipolar world—in fact, as I explain later, unipolarity has made certain types of asymmetric conflict more likely—but none of these conflicts have the global scope or generational length of a hegemonic rivalry.

To appreciate this point, just consider the Cold War—one of the four "peaceful" cases of hegemonic rivalry identified by Allison's study. Although the two superpowers never went to war, they divided the world into rival camps, waged proxy wars that killed millions of people, and pushed each other to the brink of nuclear Armageddon. For forty-five years, World War III and human extinction were nontrivial possibilities.

Since the collapse of the Soviet Union, by contrast, the United States has not faced a hegemonic rival, and the world, though far from perfect, has been more peaceful and prosperous than ever before.

Just look at the numbers. From 1400 to 1991, the rate of war deaths worldwide hovered between 5 and 10 deaths per 100,000 people and spiked to 200 deaths per 100,000 during major wars.[4] After 1991, however, war death rates dropped to 0.5 deaths per 100,000 people and have stayed there ever since. Interstate wars have disappeared almost entirely, and the number of civil wars has declined by more than 30 percent.[5] Meanwhile, the global economy has quadrupled in size, creating more wealth between 1991 and 2018 than in all prior human history combined.[6]

What explains this unprecedented outbreak of peace and prosperity? Some scholars attribute it to advances in communications technology, from the printing press to the telegraph to the Internet, which supposedly spread empathy around the globe and caused entire nations to place a higher value on human life.[7]

Such explanations are appealing, because they play on our natural desire to believe in human progress, but are they convincing? Did humans suddenly become 10 to 20 times less violent and cruel in 1991? Are we orders of magnitude more noble and kind than our grandparents? Has social media made us more empathetic? Of course not, which is why the dramatic decline in warfare after 1991 is better explained by geopolitics than sociology.[8]

The collapse of the Soviet Union not only ended the Cold War and related proxy fighting, it also opened up large swathes of the world to democracy, international commerce, and peacekeeping forces—all of which surged after 1991 and further dampened conflict.[9] Faced with overwhelming U.S. economic and military might, most countries have decided to work within the American-led liberal order rather than fight to overturn it.[10] As of 2018, nearly seventy countries have joined the U.S. alliance network—a Kantian community in which war is unthinkable—and even the two main challengers to this community, China and Russia, begrudgingly participate in the institutions of the liberal order (e.g., the UN, the WTO, the IMF, World

Bank, and the G-20), engage in commerce with the United States and its allies, and contribute to international peacekeeping missions.[11] History may not have ended in 1991, but it clearly changed in profound ways—and mostly for the better.

Crisis Instability

Unfortunately, the unipolar era will not be totally free from conflict. Although unipolarity precludes hegemonic rivalry, it may increase the risk that crises between the United States and weaker nations will escalate to war.[12] The reason is that U.S. military superiority could embolden the United States to stand firm in a crisis while simultaneously inciting weaker opponents to shoot first, in a desperate attempt to stun the United States before the U.S. military wipes out their offensive forces.[13]

Under unipolarity, this dynamic looms over U.S. relations with all nations. It is most dangerous, however, with regard to North Korea, China, and Russia, because these countries can inflict apocalyptic damage on American cities and have ongoing disputes with the United States over territory (e.g., Taiwan, Crimea, the Korean Peninsula), the U.S. military presence abroad, freedom of navigation, and human rights. In the years ahead, many events can, and almost surely will, spark crises between the United States and these countries. A primary goal of U.S. security policy, therefore, must be to reduce the risk that such crises escalate to major wars. How?

NORTH KOREA

The North Korean case is the gravest, but also the simplest, because the United States has no good options and only one nonhorrible option: deterrence.[14] North Korea will never give up its nuclear arsenal, which is its main insurance policy against a U.S. or South Korean attack, and the U.S. military cannot reliably destroy North Korea's nuclear weapons or conventional artillery before it has a chance to use them.[15]

Deterrence may feel unsatisfying, because it places U.S. security at least partly in North Korea's hands. Like old age, however, deterrence only seems intolerable until one considers the alternative.[16] The U.S. Department of Defense estimates that a U.S.-North Korean war would kill 20,000 people per day in South Korea alone, even if no nuclear weapons were used. It also admits that the U.S. national missile defense system only has a 50 percent chance of intercepting a North Korean ballistic missile headed for the U.S. mainland.[17] Given these dire statistics, the United States should learn to live with a North Korean nuclear capability—just as it learned to live with the Soviet and Chinese nuclear arsenals.

Deterrence, however, does not mean doing nothing. The United States should continue to make clear that it will "totally destroy" North Korea if it attacks the United States or its allies or transfers nuclear materials to other states or groups.[18] To back up these threats, the United States should integrate additional terminal and midcourse interceptors to its national missile defense system and develop boost-phase interceptors.[19] It also should redouble efforts to improve civil defenses and counterforce capabilities.[20] These measures will enhance America's ability to emerge from a nuclear war relatively unscathed, and thereby hopefully deter North Korea from starting a war in the first place.[21]

At the same time, the United States should engage in diplomacy with North Korea and contingency planning with China. North Korea will never negotiate away its nuclear arsenal, but it might accept limits on that arsenal in exchange for U.S. security assurances. The United States therefore should offer to recognize North Korea as a nuclear weapons state, forswear military strikes, and lift economic sanctions so long as North Korea abides by "three no's": no additional nuclear weapons, no improved nuclear weapons or delivery vehicles, and no export of nuclear materials.[22]

To compel North Korea to accept this bargain, the United States needs to tighten sanctions on North Korea, which in turn requires making a side deal with China. Currently the Chinese government looks the other way when Chinese companies smuggle goods into North Korea. China could crack down on these violations, but will do so only if it feels assured that a North Korean collapse, which would be made more likely by tighter sanctions, would not result in U.S. forces swarming up the Korean Peninsula toward China's border. Recent research suggests that China is willing to abandon North Korea, but not if it means American troops on the banks of the Yalu.[23]

The United States, therefore, should offer China a deal: in return for full Chinese sanctions on North Korea, the United States will let China dictate the terms of a joint contingency plan for a North Korean collapse. As part of this plan, the United States would promise to keep its troops south of the 38th parallel and offer to withdraw its forces entirely from the Korean Peninsula once the dust has settled if China will accede to a U.S. alliance with a reunified Korea.

The U.S. military will probably hate this proposal, because it cedes control of North Korea's territory and nuclear sites to China without a fight. Allowing China to secure North Korea, however, would keep U.S. troops out of a potential nuclear hellhole and reduce the likelihood of a U.S.-China clash.[24] The geographic reality is that Chinese forces can occupy North Korea before U.S. reinforcements even mobilize for an attack—China has at least 150,000 troops perched on its border with North Korea, which is only sixty miles from North Korea's main nuclear sites and two-thirds of its missile sites.[25] Given that Chinese troops will be first on the scene, the U.S.

military should stay out of their way. Instead of going to war with China over North Korea's carcass, the United States should help China secure the area by providing intelligence on North Korea's nuclear sites and technical expertise to dismantle them.

CHINA AND RUSSIA

The situations with China and Russia are less dire than the North Korean case, but more complicated, because China and Russia have more ways to hurt the United States but also more to offer it. Even as the United States competes with these powers for influence, it cooperates with them in numerous areas. Adopting a policy of pure deterrence, therefore, would be shortsighted and dangerous.

Unfortunately, there is widespread disagreement among strategists about what the United States should do to enhance crisis stability with these two regional powers, aside from some fairly obvious confidence building measures, including codes of conduct for military forces and for civilian aircraft and ships, backchannels for diplomats to work out face-saving compromises, crisis hotlines linking the top leaderships, military-to-military exchanges, cyber and nuclear risk reduction centers, and joint peace and humanitarian operations.[26]

Some scholars argue that the United States should simply retrench from East Asia and Eastern Europe and grant China and Russia broad spheres of influence.[27] The most extreme of these proposals would have the United States abrogate its alliances in Asia and Europe and pull its forces out of both regions.

Retrenchment has its appeal.[28] Indeed, it seems the logical, God-given strategy for a self-sufficient superpower protected by two vast oceans. Yet large-scale retrenchment not only would sap U.S. influence in Asia and Europe, but also reduce crisis stability by undermining deterrence.[29] China or Russia might be emboldened by a U.S. withdrawal from their regions and ramp up coercive pressure on their demoralized neighbors. Successful security policy requires a balance of reassurance and deterrence.[30] Retrenchment is skewed too heavily toward the former.

A better way to enhance crisis stability while preserving the territorial status quo in Asia and Europe would be to combine economic and political engagement with an "active denial" military strategy.[31] The overarching goal of this strategy would be to create local "situations of strength" that raise the costs of military aggression for China and Russia, but without backing them into a corner.[32] Such a strategy would have three main elements.

First, the United States would bolster the antiaccess/area-denial (A2/AD) capabilities of China and Russia's neighbors by providing them with loans, arms, training, and intelligence. The objective would be to turn China and Russia's neighbors into prickly "porcupines," capable of denying territory to China and Russia but not to take and hold territory themselves.[33] In East Asia, this means helping China's maritime neighbors acquire advanced anti-air and anti-ship missiles plus the platforms and targeting capabilities to launch them. In Eastern Europe, it means prepping the Baltic States to wage guerilla warfare.[34]

Second, the United States would create buffers between U.S. forces on the one hand and Chinese and Russian forces on the other. American forces would remain in Asia and Europe and roam wherever international law allows, but they would be stationed in dispersed and hardened bases scattered around the periphery of each region, where they could be called on in the event of war but otherwise kept beyond the reach of Chinese and Russian forces. Decreasing the number of American soldiers based near China and Russia's borders would reduce the likelihood of incidents, help reassure China and Russia that the United States does not intend to launch massive strikes on their homelands at the outset of a crisis, and increase the resilience of U.S. forces in the region by reducing their exposure to Chinese or Russian preemptive attacks.

Third, the United States would backstop the local balances of power in Asia and Europe, but would plan to do so gradually. In minor conflicts, the United States would try to convince China or Russia to back down by using nonmilitary forms of coercion.[35] As described in chapter 5, the United States is uniquely empowered to impose painful sanctions and embargoes on hostile countries (and to deny enemies the ability to respond in kind) because of its central role in global banking, plentiful energy resources, and unparalleled ability to disrupt international shipping.[36] In the initial stages of a conflict, therefore, the United States could use financial sanctions, embargoes, or cyber operations to try to achieve "victory without violence," as it did in compelling Iran to negotiate curbs on its nuclear program and in deterring Russia from annexing eastern Ukraine.[37]

If the conflict escalated to war, the United States could initially "lead from behind," supporting local forces with logistics, intelligence, and if absolutely necessary, limited air and missile strikes on Chinese or Russian forces operating in the combat theater rather than those stationed on the Chinese or Russian mainlands. These strikes could be conducted from submarines, stealth-aircraft, or road-mobile missile batteries—all of which are far less vulnerable to Chinese and Russian A2/AD forces than surface ships, nonstealth aircraft, and ground forces. If the United States needed to ratchet up the pain, it could escalate horizontally before doing so vertically; that is, by opening up new geographic fronts rather than throwing U.S. forces into the cauldron of the main combat theater.

This strategy obviously sacrifices military effectiveness for crisis stability. The U.S. military could gain a major advantage over China or Russia if it simply unloaded on their bases, missile batteries, satellites, and radar installations at the outset of a war. The U.S. military generally favors this type of knockout punch strategy and for good reason: pinprick strikes and gradual escalation invite a grinding war of attrition.[38] Why give the enemy a chance to fight back?

Offensive doctrines make sense against weak states that do not have nuclear weapons. Against China or Russia, however, a military posture primed for rapid escalation could be a recipe for disaster. An offensive posture not only risks turning minor disputes into major wars, it also could turn conventional wars into nuclear wars. Some of the systems that support China and Russia's conventional military forces—missile batteries, radars, satellites, submarines—also support their nuclear arsenals, so Chinese or Russian leaders might mistake U.S. strikes on these systems as a preemptive U.S. attack on their nuclear deterrents. Moreover, China and Russia have declared that they would use nuclear weapons to retaliate against a conventional attack on their homelands. Perhaps these declarations are bluffs. But is it really so hard to imagine that, in the heat of battle and when facing the potential annihilation of their militaries, one of these nations might fire off a nuclear weapon in the hope of shocking the United States into a cease-fire? Such a scenario might sound alarmist, but Russia's military doctrine explicitly calls for using nuclear weapons to "deescalate" conventional wars, and Chinese leaders have suggested that the PLA is prepared to do likewise.[39]

In a multipolar or bipolar world, it might make sense for the United States to risk nuclear war to prevent a peer competitor from overrunning Asia or Europe. Better to nip the problem in the bud than repeat the mistakes of Munich and empower aggressors. In today's unipolar world, however, no rival power is capable of going on a Hitler-style rampage across Eurasia, so the stakes for the United States in a war there would be moderate, and the main danger would be in doing too much rather than too little. Instead of rushing into wars with China or Russia, therefore, the United States should pick its battles, escalate gradually, and let local actors do most of the heavy lifting.

Imperial Overstretch

The theory of imperial overstretch holds that superpowers tend to expand beyond their means and collapse as a result.[40] Such overexpansion is driven in part by hubris. As Christopher Layne explains: "A hegemon easily is lured into overexpansion. When it comes to hard power, hegemons have it, and seldom can resist flaunting it. . . . Thus, we should expect a unipolar hegemon to initiate many wars and to use its military power promiscuously."[41]

In addition to hubris, superpowers also tend to suffer from a pervasive sense of insecurity. As Robert Jervis explains:

> The very extent of the hegemon's influence means that all sorts of geographic and ideological disturbances can threaten it. Frontiers can be expanded, but doing so just recreates them. . . . Hegemony thus also ironically magnifies the sense of threat. The very fact that the United States has interests throughout the world leads to the fear that undesired changes in one area could undermine its interests elsewhere. . . . Disturbances that would be dismissed in a multipolar or bipolar world loom much larger for the hegemon because it is present in all corners of the globe and everything seems interconnected.[42]

In short, superpowers tend to become paranoid and militaristic, and these impulses, in turn, compel them to expand abroad—thereby creating more "turbulent frontiers" to defend, interests to pursue, and threats to address.[43] This self-perpetuating pattern of expansion ultimately exhausts the superpower's resources because "the costs of empire tend to rise geometrically as its size increases, whereas its resources increase only arithmetically."[44]

Is the United States doomed to follow this historical pattern and fritter away its resources on reckless adventures abroad? In the wake of the wars in Iraq and Afghanistan, it is hard to argue with the assessment that "the United States is becoming the poster child for strategic overextension."[45]

Yet, U.S. overextension is not inevitable. In fact, a clear-eyed recognition of the unipolar distribution of power could help the United States temper its imperial temptations.

As the world's only superpower, the United States is exceptionally secure and, therefore, can afford to play wait-and-see, allowing threats to emerge fully before responding. This situation stands in contrast to the Cold War, when anything that happened anywhere in the world seemingly had implications for the U.S.-Soviet power balance. Allies had to be wooed and coddled to keep them from joining the other side. Communist advances, even in peripheral areas, had to be countered to maintain U.S. prestige and credibility. Today, by contrast, there are no dominos that must be kept from falling, and America's survival does not hang in the balance of the crisis of the day. The U.S. military, therefore, can focus on first-order missions—deterring major powers and rogue states that brandish weapons of mass destruction—rather than playing globo-cop.

The virtues of strategic restraint might seem obvious, but they often are lost in U.S. foreign policy debates.[46] As Fareed Zakaria points out, the American media and some policymaking elites in Washington remain wedded to a Cold War mindset that mistakes "activity for achievement."[47] In this view, every crisis abroad and every move by a foreign rival must be countered with a robust assertion of American power. To do otherwise, some pundits and policymakers argue, would abdicate American leadership, embolden enemies, and demoralize allies. Better for the United States to shoot first and develop a strategy later, they argue, then fail to intervene at all.

This misguided mindset has kept the U.S. military at war for most of the past two decades—with little to show for it. Of the campaigns in Kosovo, Afghanistan, Iraq, and Libya, only the first could be considered a clear victory.[48] The combined costs of these conflicts—seven thousand American dead, fifty thousand wounded, and $6 trillion—hardly seem justified.

To regain strategic solvency, the United States should take three steps. First, American policymakers should resurrect the so-called Powell Doctrine and make it the cornerstone of debate before every major military intervention.[49] This doctrine, which was originally developed by Secretary of Defense Caspar Weinberger in the 1980s and then elaborated by chairman of the Joint Chiefs of Staff Colin Powell in the 1990s, consisted of a series of questions that had to be answered "yes" before sending American soldiers to fight and die abroad:

1. Is a vital national security interest threatened?
2. Do we have a clear attainable objective?
3. Have the risks and costs been fully and frankly analyzed?
4. Have all other nonviolent policy means been fully exhausted?
5. Is there a plausible exit strategy to avoid endless entanglement?
6. Have the consequences of our action been fully considered?
7. Is the action supported by the American people?
8. Do we have genuine broad international support?

The core assumption of the Powell Doctrine is that the United States rarely needs to rush into war to keep itself safe. It is a doctrine designed to conserve U.S. power, so that when vital interests are threatened, the U.S. military can respond vigorously with forces that have not been chewed up in wars of choice over trivial issues in peripheral areas.

In practice, the Powell Doctrine implies that the U.S. military should focus on preparing for wars against China and Russia, which are the only major powers not currently aligned with the United States, and against North Korea, which is the only minor power that currently has nuclear weapons and clear hostile intent toward the United States. The U.S. military also can allocate some resources to killing terrorists abroad, but this should be done primarily with special operations forces and drones rather than large-scale military occupations.

The doctrine further implies that the United States should avoid fighting wars where victory depends on controlling the politics of chaotic countries. As the wars in Iraq and Afghanistan have shown, local leaders will rarely do what the United States wants if doing so conflicts with their interests, and no reasonable amount of American blood or treasure can change that fundamental fact.[50] The United States can support local allies in troubled regions with tools short of military occupation, including diplomacy, aid, military training, intelligence, arms, special operations raids, and drone strikes. In general, however, the U.S. military should be allowed to focus on its core competency—destroying enemy militaries—rather than being asked to rebuild tattered nations.

Second, Congress should reassert its authority to regulate the use of force.[51] According to the U.S. Constitution, Congress is supposed to decide where and when the United States goes to war. The president can order short-term military interventions, but only when the nation's security is in imminent danger. The United States followed this Constitutional principle for most of its history.

Since the end of the Cold War, however, Congress has retreated from foreign policy. It allowed the Clinton administration to send U.S. forces to Haiti, Bosnia, and Kosovo without congressional authorization; rubber-stamped the invasions of Afghanistan and Iraq; and allowed the Obama administration to double U.S. forces in Afghanistan in 2009 without a vote and attack Libya in 2011 without a single hearing.

In the future, Congress should subject proposals for large-scale military interventions to public debate and a formal vote. The foreign affairs committees could lead the way by holding hearings before each intervention and soliciting testimony from a wide-range of experts. These hearings could be paired with trips to the region in question, where members of Congress could meet with political actors and journalists, researchers, and aid workers. These practices were standard operating procedure in the 1970s and 1980s and should become so again.

Congress also should pass legislation limiting the president's ability to launch a preventive or unprovoked nuclear strike.[52] The president should still be able to order retaliatory or preemptive strikes, but preventive or unprovoked strikes should require sober deliberation among multiple officials. President Trump's casual comments about nuclear war with North Korea underscore the risks of giving him unchecked authority to order an attack. To reduce these risks, Congress should require the unanimous consent of a small group of officials—including the vice president, the secretary of defense, the chairman of the Joint Chiefs of Staff, and the four leaders of the House and the Senate—for any preventive or unprovoked nuclear strike.

Third, the United States should institute a war tax for any military operations that require supplemental funding. For nearly 200 years, from 1812 to 2001, the United States paid for its wars in part by raising special taxes on individuals and corporations. These "pay as you fight" taxes ensured that all Americans sacrificed for the common cause. Since 9/11, however, the United States has paid for its wars by borrowing, adding trillions of dollars to the national debt. This practice of putting wars on the credit card is not just fiscally irresponsible, it is dangerous, because people are much more likely to support a stupid war if they do not have to pay higher taxes to finance it.[53] The flip side is that a mandatory war tax would make American leaders more judicious about when and where to send U.S. forces into battle.[54]

The three steps highlighted above would almost certainly reduce U.S. military involvement in the Middle East. That would be wonderful. The United States has three important interests in the region—oil, counterterrorism, and democracy—but none requires a large U.S. military commitment. Instead, the United States should adopt an offshore balancing strategy in the Middle East, limiting its peacetime presence to a skeletal base structure, and put boots on the ground only if a local power threatens to dominate or destroy the region.[55]

The U.S. military does not need to guard Middle Eastern oil reserves, because no state is powerful enough to seize them or seriously disrupt world oil markets: Iraq's military has already been neutered by the United States; Iran's military has been ground down by decades of conflict and sanctions; Iranian-backed Shiite militias lack the heavy forces and air defenses needed for large-scale conquest; and Saudi Arabia's military is geared for internal security and air superiority, not ground invasions.[56] Iran could try to blockade the Strait of Hormuz, where most of the oil flowing out of the Persian Gulf is shipped, but rigorous campaign analyses suggest that Iran could destroy only twenty oil tankers, a number far from sufficient to shock the oil market, and the U.S. military could break an Iranian blockade with air and missile strikes launched from over the horizon.[57]

A Saudi civil war could threaten the free flow of oil, given that most of the Kingdom's disgruntled Shia minority lives in the Eastern Province near the country's oil production facilities. A mass uprising, however, is unlikely, because Saudi Arabia's internal security forces are robust, roughly 90 percent of Saudi workers are government employees that depend on the monarchy for their livelihoods, and the Saudi government has huge cash reserves to keep the gravy train running during economic downturns.[58] Even if Saudi Arabia succumbs to civil war, sending U.S. Marines into Mecca and Medina would not pacify the situation.[59]

The United States also does not need a large military presence in the Middle East to contain Islamist terrorism. All of the deadly Islamist terrorist attacks committed on American soil since 9/11 have been carried out by U.S. citizens or legal residents, so bombing or occupying the Middle East for the umpteenth time is unlikely to reduce the risk of attacks further.[60] Moreover, that risk is already extremely low: since 1991, Americans have been four times more likely to drown in bathtubs than be killed by a jihadi.[61] The main battles in the war on terror should be fought by U.S. intelligence agencies and domestic law enforcement, not by the U.S. military. In this regard, the United States already does more than enough: it has more than a thousand government organizations and two thousand private companies engaged in counterterrorism, giving it two counterterrorism organizations for every Islamist terrorist suspect it has ever arrested.[62]

Finally, the United States should not use military force to promote democracy in the Middle East. If two decades of nation-building in Iraq and Afghanistan have taught us anything, it is that the U.S. military cannot install liberal democracy where powerful local actors do not want it.[63] The United States succeeded in democratizing Germany and Japan after World War II only because their populations were war-weary and desperate for U.S. protection from the Soviet Union.[64] In the Middle East today, by contrast, most people hate the United States and do not share a common enemy with it. They therefore tend to view U.S. troops stomping around their homelands the same way the Vietnamese did in the 1960s. If the United States is serious about promoting democracy in the Middle East, it should reduce its support for corrupt authoritarian regimes there— that is, by becoming less involved in the region—not by occupying more countries militarily.

Domestic Decay

According to a tradition of political thought going back to Plato and Aristotle, hegemons can become victims of their own success and collapse from within.[65] Having vanquished foreign rivals, various clans within the dominant nation may turn on each other, resulting in the weakening of national institutions and, in extreme cases, civil war.

This pattern—peace abroad fueling conflict at home—has been documented by numerous scholars, including Max Weber, Otto Hintze, Charles Tilly, and Michael Desch.[66] These scholars have shown that during periods of great power competition nations tend to develop strong bureaucracies and efficient systems of taxation and espouse a strong sense of patriotism and national unity. During periods of low external threat, however, nation-states sometimes tear apart.[67] For example, the relatively tranquil international environment in Europe from 1815 to 1853 (often called the Pax Britannica) witnessed an unprecedented breakdown in state cohesion and a series of revolutions in the late 1840s.[68] Similarly, the benign external threat environment enjoyed by the United States in the 1850s exacerbated internal tensions that culminated in the Civil War.[69] By contrast, during the World Wars and the first half of the Cold War, American national unity rose and government institutions expanded dramatically in scope and size.[70]

Recent trends in the United States fit this historical pattern: since the collapse of the Soviet Union in 1991, partisan divisions in the United States have surged to levels not seen since the Civil War, and gridlock has become America's political norm, with recent Congresses ranking among the most polarized and least productive in the post–World War II era (figure 6.1).[71]

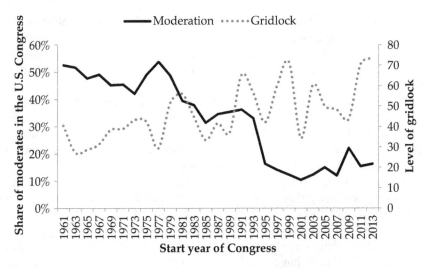

Figure 6.1. Historically dysfunctional: polarization and gridlock in the U.S. Congress, 1947–2013.

Note: "Moderation" measures the proportion of centrist legislators in the House and Senate (lawmakers whose floor votes place them closer ideologically to the center of the chamber than to their own party median), divided by the ideological gulf between party medians. "Gridlock" measures the ratio of failed measures to all salient issues on Washington's agenda. For an issue to be "salient," it needed to inspire at least four *New York Times* editorials in a given Congress.

Source: Binder 2003, 2014, 2015.

The 9/11 terrorist attacks briefly brought Americans together, but the camaraderie quickly evaporated, a fact that suggests that the threat of terrorism is not serious enough to mobilize the nation the way a genuine hegemonic rivalry does. If anything, the terrorist threat has probably exacerbated divisions within American society by inciting witch hunts for terrorist suspects and igniting vicious debates on immigration, torture, war, and privacy.

Without a unifying national mission, Americans have sorted themselves into clans based on social class and culture. Consequently, the two major political parties are divided not just by policy preferences, but also by identity. Rural whites now overwhelmingly vote Republican while most minorities and urban whites vote Democrat.[72] This crude tribalism leaves little room for compromise. If the partisan divide were merely about policy, the parties could split the difference. Now that American politics has become a clash of cultures, however, both parties view compromise with the other side as immoral and dangerous.

For this reason, policymaking in the unipolar era has lurched between gridlock and partisan overreach, and many of the problems highlighted in earlier chapters have festered, including spiraling entitlement costs; crumbling infrastructure; declining rates of upward mobility and entrepreneurship; racially and economically stratified systems of education and healthcare; a bloated and racially biased criminal justice system; a convoluted tax code that incentivizes tax evasion rather than domestic investment; and a crazy patchwork of federal, state, and local regulations that benefit big firms with armies of lawyers rather than small start-ups or public infrastructure projects.

If present trends are not reversed, the United States may slip into a vicious cycle in which partisan gridlock undermines public trust in government, which incentivizes politicians to starve the government of resources and authority, which leads to even poorer government performance, which leads to more defunding of the bureaucracy.

This downward spiral has already begun. Non-defense discretionary spending, a category that includes everything besides interest payments on the national debt and spending on entitlements and defense (e.g. spending on education, infrastructure, transportation, R&D, housing, energy, environmental protection, job training, food, agriculture, childcare, justice, and international affairs), has shrunk to just 11 percent of the federal budget, down from 25 percent in the 1960s and 1970s.[73] As journalist Ezra Klein has pointed out, the U.S. government is becoming nothing more than an insurance company with an army.[74] Such a weak state might be great for lobbyists and large corporations, but not for the average American.

The United States thus faces a challenge: how to tackle national problems without a foreign bogeyman to unite the country and galvanize collective action. To meet this challenge, the United States needs to empower a centrist American majority, and doing that requires structural change to U.S. political institutions. What changes?

First, the United States needs to increase voter turnout. Currently the United States has some of the lowest turnout rates of any developed democracy; in recent U.S. presidential elections, including the 2016 election, just over half of voting age citizens cast ballots. Low turnout polarizes American politics, because extreme partisans are more likely than moderates to show up at the polls. Consequently, each party focuses on firing up its base rather than appealing to centrists. If the United States had near-universal voting, by contrast, politicians might spend more time courting the political center and developing compromise solutions to the nation's problems.

The most straightforward way to boost turnout would be to make voting mandatory, a step that more than two dozen countries have taken to great effect. Unfortunately, a mandatory voting law is a political non-starter in the United States—taxes and jury duty are bad enough, the last thing Americans want is the government marching them to the polls.

More feasible would be a law that made voting easier by automatically registering people to vote when they receive a driver's license or state ID and by holding elections on weekends or, better yet, on a new national holiday. The current practice of holding elections on Tuesdays, when most people have to work, is based on an obsolete 1845 law: at the time, Congress reasoned that Tuesday was the best day for voting, because Sunday was the Sabbath, Wednesday was market day, and people needed Monday to travel to town by horse-and-buggy to vote. Needless to say, times have changed. The U.S. electoral system should too.

Second, states should hold open nonpartisan primaries for all elections.[75] Currently, most states hold separate closed primaries for each party in which only registered party members can vote. Most of these voters are zealous partisans and they often elect extremists to represent their party in the general election, forcing the general public to choose between two bad options. States should replace this perverse system with a single primary ballot for all candidates, regardless of their party affiliation, and allow all voters to participate in primaries, not just registered party members.

Third, states should institute ranked-choice voting in all elections with runoffs. The current system is a "winner-take-all" model, in which the candidate that receives the most votes wins, even if he or she failed to receive a majority of the votes. Under this system, voters have to worry about the "spoiler effect," in which they inadvertently help elect their least favorite candidate by casting a vote for an independent.

In ranked-choice voting, by contrast, voters would rank candidates in order of preference from first to last. If no candidate receives a majority in the first round, the candidate with the fewest first choice votes is eliminated, and voters who ranked that candidate first would have their second choices counted. This process repeats until one candidate reaches a majority and wins.

This system allows voters to support the candidate they like the best without worrying that their vote will help elect the candidate they like least. It also encourages candidates to avoid negative campaigning and seek broad public support to avoid alienating voters whose second- or third-place votes they may need to get elected.

Fourth, states should institute nonpartisan redistricting. Currently, most states allow the majority party to redraw districts to enhance its electoral prospects by "packing" voters from the other party into fewer districts. This practice, known as gerrymandering, fosters partisan extremism by creating "safe seats" for each party; when districts are packed with voters that overwhelmingly support one party, the winner of that party's primary is virtually guaranteed to win the general election. As a result, representatives from gerrymandered districts pander to partisans rather than the general electorate.

Gerrymandering is as old as the Republic—the practice is named after Massachusetts Governor Elbridge Gerry, who approved a district in 1812 that was so convoluted that a local newspaper said it looked like a salamander— but computer technology has made it easier for politicians to pick their voters, and gerrymandering has clearly gotten out of hand: in 2016, fewer than 10 percent of U.S. House races and only 28 percent of Senate general election races were competitive. The rest were in safe seats, and the winner was effectively decided in the primary.

To increase the number of mixed districts, states should hand over redistricting responsibility to independent nonpartisan or bipartisan commissions, an approach that Arizona, California, Idaho, and Washington have already instituted.

Finally, Congress should diminish the role of money in politics by requiring full transparency for all political donations. Currently, politicians spend more than half their workdays soliciting donations from shadowy donors, who are allowed to funnel unlimited funds to groups called political actions committees, which back particular candidates on the sly.[76] In recent elections, Congressional campaigns raised more than $1 billion.[77] This money obviously was not earned at bake sales. Instead, according to a large body of research, most of it came from the coffers of rich ideologues and single-issue interest groups.[78] The research further shows that these donations exacerbate polarization and corruption by incentivizing candidates to cater to private interests at the extremes of the ideological spectrum.[79] Requiring public disclosure of political donations, so that voters know who is backing which candidate, would help reduce these incentives and drain the swamp of corruption currently inundating American politics.

World Order

Since the end of World War II, the United States has led multinational movements to expand free trade and investment and promote democracy and human rights. These efforts have fostered a global system of international institutions, commerce, and democratic nations that many observers now refer to as the liberal order.[80]

This liberal system has unleashed an unprecedented period of freedom and prosperity.[81] Prior to 1945, there had never been more than a dozen democracies in the world. Today there are over a hundred. Before 1950, global GDP had never risen by more than 1 percent a year. Since 1950, it has risen by an average of 4 percent per year. The liberal order is often criticized for causing the 2008 financial crash. As my Tufts colleague Dan Drezner has shown, however, the institutions of the liberal order actually prevented the Great Recession from becoming another Great Depression.[82]

As the world's sole superpower, the United States remains vastly more capable of supporting this liberal order than any other nation. The problem, however, is that it may have less incentive to do so given its vast stocks of wealth and secure location. In the coming decades, the United States could become a "global power without global interests," turning inward while leaving others to pay the costs of maintaining the international system.[83]

The "America first" policy of the Donald Trump administration might be just a preview of what is to come.[84]

If the United States returns to its isolationist and protectionist roots, would the world revert to its traditional patterns of war, despotism, and poverty?

Some scholars think not. In their view, "the underlying foundations of the liberal international order will survive and thrive" even without U.S. support.[85] According to this logic, the institutions that constitute the liberal order have taken on a life of their own and will continue to regulate world politics; and other countries will pick up the slack and patrol the oceans, maintain open markets and borders, and champion liberal values even if the United States does not.[86] In short, the liberal order is self-sustaining. It succeeds because liberal ideas are so obviously the best organizing principles for world society.[87] It therefore does not require the support of a liberal hegemon.[88]

History, however, tells a different story.[89] Liberal order is extremely rare and has flourished under only one set of conditions—when a great power possesses both a globally dominant navy and a profound commitment to liberal values.[90] This situation has existed only twice in modern history—during the Pax Britannica in the nineteenth century and after World War II. The British liberal order did not survive the decline of British power.[91] Can we be so sure that today's liberal order would survive a collapse of American commitment?[92]

I would have more faith in such a rosy outcome if two of the most powerful countries in the world—China and Russia—did not espouse blatantly illiberal values. In just the past few years, these nations have murdered pro-democracy advocates, promoted a version of state capitalism that resembles sixteenth-century mercantilism, and used military force to seize foreign territory and close international waters. These actions provide a glimpse of a future "world in disarray" in which the United States no longer backs the liberal order.[93]

Americans are understandably frustrated with the current order, because the United States often pays more than other nations to sustain it. Allies sometimes free ride on U.S. protection. Trade partners sometimes pursue protectionist policies while tapping the American market and stealing U.S. technology. International institutions occasionally constrain U.S. freedom of action. Democracy promotion has produced mixed results, and nation-building has bogged the U.S. military down in costly quagmires. The burdens of hegemony have indeed taken a toll on the United States. Little wonder, then, that so many Americans voted for Trump and his promise to wall the United States off from global responsibilities.

The fundamental problem facing the United States is what scholars call the "hegemon's dilemma": the harder the United States tries to solve global problems, the more weaker nations can free ride on U.S. efforts, thus forcing the United States to choose between getting exploited and letting the world burn.[94]

Fortunately, there is a way out of this dilemma. The United States can be both "system-maker and privilege-taker."[95] It can pay a large share of system maintenance costs but take a disproportionate share of the benefits. It can practice "internationalism with a nationalist accent," maintaining U.S. engagement with the liberal order but doing so on terms that more forcefully assert American interests.[96] How?

First and foremost, the United States can use the active denial strategy described earlier to orchestrate stable balances of power in Asia and Europe. As Brookings scholar Thomas Wright has shown, a peaceful global order depends on healthy regional orders.[97] An active denial strategy promotes such orders while husbanding U.S. resources and offloading some of the costs and risks to local actors.

Second, the United States can aggressively punish unfair trade practices, but do so through the WTO rather than by unilaterally slapping tariffs on foreign goods. The unilateral approach favored by the Trump administration is akin to slashing a rival's tires instead of suing him in court. Yes, the judicial process takes longer and may be less emotionally satisfying, but it prevents tit-for-tat escalation. The 1930s showed how unbridled trade wars can destroy the world economy and trigger violent conflict. The United States does not need to revive such a world just to "win" on trade, given that it already wins roughly 80 percent of the cases it brings before the WTO and 40 percent of the cases other countries bring against it.[98] By contrast, China only wins 41 percent of the cases it brings and 23 percent of cases brought against it.

The Trump administration says tariffs are crucial to protect American workers. Working-class families, however, bear the brunt of trade wars, because they depend most on cheap imported food, clothing, and household items. A recent study found that in a world of no trade, the poorest tenth of consumers would lose a staggering 63 percent of their purchasing power, more than double what the richest consumers would lose.[99] Tariffs or quotas on raw materials and basic goods would also hurt downstream industries, which employ many more American workers than do upstream industries. For example, imposing tariffs on Chinese steel might help the 147,000 Americans employed in the steel industry, but harm the 6.5 million Americans employed in steel-using industries.[100]

A better way to protect American workers would be to invest directly in them. As shown in chapter 5, the United States spends six times less than other rich nations as a percentage of GDP on job training, job-search assistance, and hiring and wage subsidies; and three times less on family benefits, such as childcare support and early education programs. Closing this investment gap would allow the United States to protect American workers without resorting to protectionism.

Third, the United States should maintain high levels of immigration, but prioritize high-skilled immigrants and refugees fleeing war, famine, and other disasters. Currently the United States is doing the opposite; it is reducing immigration, capping visas for high-skilled workers, and selecting immigrants primarily on family connections rather than merit or need. This system is the worst of all worlds. By reducing immigration, the United States betrays its values and cuts itself off from a vital source of human capital.[101] By selecting immigrants primarily based on family ties, the United States ends up rejecting many desperate refugees and talented workers and, instead, taking in a disproportionate number of low-skill workers, thereby reducing the wages and benefits of low-skill native-born workers—the most vulnerable group in the American workforce.[102]

The United States should reform this system by raising the annual cap on H-1B visas for high-skilled workers from 65,000 to at least 100,000 and shifting to a points-based immigration system similar to Canada's, which admits immigrants based on a range of factors in addition to family ties, including education, age, language ability, and refugee status. Americans already support such a system in overwhelming numbers.[103] Politicians need to rally this centrist majority behind a comprehensive immigration reform bill.

Finally, the United States should double funding for its international affairs programs, including foreign aid, peacekeeping, and diplomacy. Currently the United States spends 0.3 percent of its GDP on these programs—10 times less than it spends on the military—and the Trump administration wants to get this number down to 0.2 percent of GDP by slashing foreign aid, gutting the State Department, and reducing U.S. contributions to UN peacekeeping and World Bank development projects.

Instead of cutting the international affairs budget, the United States should double it, bringing total spending to 0.6 percent of GDP, which is what the United States spent during the 1980s under President Ronald Reagan. Aid, peacekeeping, and diplomacy are not frills or charity; they are vital tools of U.S. national security, because they prevent catastrophes (e.g. wars, terrorist attacks, refugee crises, pandemics) at a fraction of the cost of addressing them once full-blown. This rationale is backed by scientific research and was endorsed by 120 former three- and four-star generals and admirals in an open letter to Congress in 2017.[104]

Advocates of a "Fortress America" model, in which the United States limits its international engagement to military strikes, forget that many of America's greatest foreign policy victories were won through sustained diplomacy and aid.[105] The Louisiana Purchase doubled the size of the country. The Marshal Plan and the formation of NATO and the Bretton Woods institutions contained communism. The Nuclear Nonproliferation Treaty slowed the spread of nuclear weapons. Richard Nixon's opening to China swung the Cold War in America's favor.

By contrast, military power has often failed to secure U.S. interests. The United States sent millions of troops to Vietnam and still lost. Military victory in the 1991 Persian Gulf War did not produce a sustainable peace. The 2003 invasion of Iraq incited a brutal insurgency and enhanced Iranian influence. The U.S. military has occupied Afghanistan for nearly two decades, yet the Taliban controls more territory today than at any time since 9/11. American airstrikes helped topple the government of Libya in 2011, and now the country is a hotbed of Islamic radicalism.

These missions failed not because the U.S. military lacked valor or skill, but because the United States did not turn battlefield success into durable political settlements. Unrivaled military power counts for little if it is not buttressed by aid and diplomacy. The U.S. Foreign Service is an indispensable guardian of American interests and should be funded as such.

Interests aside, Americans might spare a thought for how history will remember them. When the sun finally sets on the American empire, the first paragraph of its obituary will surely be about America's unprecedented wealth and power. But the second paragraph, about America's purpose, remains up for grabs. The United States may have built the liberal order, but now it threatens to abandon it. It may have lifted the world onto a higher plane of peace and prosperity, championed democracy and human rights, and welcomed immigrants of all colors and creeds, but now it ranks 22nd in foreign aid, coddles dictators, and bans refugees based on their religion. Every great power leaves a legacy. What will America's be?

Compared to slaying the forces of fascism and communism, maintaining the liberal order may seem like an underwhelming call to greatness. It is not a mission that Americans are any more eager to undertake than the great geopolitical campaigns of the twentieth century. But it is just as virtuous and just as vital.

Notes

1. Why America?

1. Strauss 2016; World Economic Forum 2016.
2. United Nations 2015; U.S. Central Intelligence Agency 2015; Humphreys 2017.
3. World Bank 2016; Helliwell, Layard, and Sachs 2016.
4. United Nations Environment Programme (UNEP) and United Nations University International Human Dimensions Programme on Global Environmental Change (UNU-IHDP) 2014; National Science Board 2016; Stockholm International Peace Research Institute 2017a.
5. "The Global Forbes 2000," http://www.forbes.com/global2000/; Institute of Higher Education of Shanghai Jiao Tong University, "Academic Ranking of World Universities," http://www.shanghairanking.com.
6. U.S. Department of Defense 2015; Brooks and Wohlforth 2015–16.
7. Kennedy 2002, 12.
8. For works that challenge this conventional wisdom, see Brooks and Wohlforth 2015–16; Nye 2015; Christensen 2015; Zeihan 2015; Joffe 2014; Lieber 2012; Kagan 2012; Beckley 2011–12; Norrlof 2010; Chestnut and Johnston 2009. For Chinese sources on this point, see Song 2017; Chu 2016; Song 2010; Xu 2008.
9. Krauthammer 1990–91; Waltz 1993; Layne 1993; Huntington 1999. For Chinese sources on this point, see Cui 2016; Cui 2010; Chen 2009.
10. Zakaria 2012; Rachman 2017. See also Allison 2017.
11. National Intelligence Council 2017; 2012; 2008.
12. "Top News Stories of the 21st Century," Global Language Monitor, http://www.languagemonitor.com/top-news/bin-ladens-death-one-of-top-news-stories-of-21th-century/.
13. Pew Research Center 2016a.
14. For a few of many examples, see Allison 2017; Rachman 2017; National Intelligence Council 2012; Subramanian 2011.
15. For seminal works, see Gilpin 1981; Kennedy 1987; Layne 1993; Modelski 1978.
16. Allison 2017.
17. Wohlforth 1999.
18. Barma, Ratner, and Weber 2014; Zakaria 2012.
19. Walt 2005.
20. Monteiro 2014.

21. Morris 2010.
22. Layne 1993; Gilpin 1981.
23. Waltz 1979.
24. Gerschenkron 1962; Baumol 1986. For applications of the theory to world politics, see Subramanian 2011; Layne 1993; Modelski 1978; Kennedy 1987; Gilpin 1981.
25. Walt 1987; Wohlforth 1999; Levy and Thompson 2010; Mearsheimer 2014a.
26. Wohlforth 1999; Brooks and Wohlforth 2008; Walt 2005; Pape 2005; Lieber and Alexander 2005.
27. Pritchett 1997; Rodrik 2013; Sharma 2016a.
28. Mitton 2016; Zeihan 2015; McCord and Sachs 2013; Gallup, Sachs, and Mellinger 1999. On natural resources, see Brooks and Kurtz 2016; Wrigley 2010; Allen 2009a; Pomeranz 2000; Wright and Czelusta 2004. On transport infrastructure, see Emran and Hou 2013; Storeygard 2016; Zeihan 2015; Redding and Turner 2014; Limao and Venables 2001; Romer 1996; Rappaport and Sachs 2003. On buffers, see Walt 1987; Mearsheimer 2014a, 114–28; Levy and Thompson 2010.
29. Acemoglu and Johnson 2012; Acemoglu et al. 2015; Beaulieu, Cox, and Saiegh 2012; Schultz and Weingast 2003; Friedberg 2000; Haggard and Tiede 2010.
30. On population age, see Sharma 2016c; Bloom, Canning, and Sevilla 2003. On health, see United Nations Environment Programme (UNEP) and United Nations University International Human Dimensions Programme on Global Environmental Change (UNU-IHDP) 2014; Strittmatter and Stunde 2013; Lopez-Casasnovas, Rivera, and Currais 2005; Carstensen and Gundlach 2006. On education, see Becker, Hornung, and Woessman 2011; Goldin and Katz 2010, chap. 1.
31. Allison 2017.
32. Jervis 2002.
33. Monteiro 2014; Goldstein 2013; Christensen 2015, chap. 4.
34. Jervis 2003; Jervis 2006; Betts 2012; Snyder 2003; Kennedy 1987; Gilpin 1981.
35. Walt 2016; Desch 1996.
36. Christensen 2015, chap. 5.
37. Zeihan 2017.
38. Brooks and Wohlforth 2016; Lieber 2016; Brands 2015.

2. The Pillars of Power

1. Russell 1938, 10-12; Mearsheimer 2014, 12.
2. Nye 1990a, 177.
3. Nye 2011, 3.
4. Mearsheimer 2014a, 57–60; Nye 2011, chap. 1; Tellis et al. 2000, chap. 2.
5. Kennedy 1987; Gilpin 1981; Mearsheimer 2014a, chap. 3; Nye 2011, chap. 3; Modelski and Thompson 1996; Beckley 2010; Paarlberg 2004; Tellis et al. 2000, chap. 5.
6. Art 1980; Mearsheimer 2014a, chaps. 3–4; Nye 2011, chap. 2; Tellis et al. 2000, chap. 6.
7. Baldwin 1989.
8. For examples, see Dahl 1957; Nye 2004; Bachrach and Baratz 1962; Keohane and Nye 1989; Barnett and Duvall 2005; Guzzini 1993; Lukes 2005.
9. Beckley 2018.
10. Mack 1975; Arreguin-Toft 2001.
11. Davis 1954.
12. Knorr 1956, 231.
13. Karabell 2014, 158.
14. Karabell 2014, 50, 158.
15. Coyle 2014.
16. Kennedy 1987.
17. I am grateful to Jonathan Markowitz for introducing me to the inclusive wealth index. United Nations Environment Programme (UNEP) and United Nations University International Human Dimensions Programme on Global Environmental Change (UNU-IHDP) 2014.

18. Brooks and Wohlforth 2016, 31–32.
19. Tarrow 1995, 473.
20. For example, see "At the Double," *The Economist*, March 15, 2014.
21. Singer, Bremer, and Stuckey 1972.
22. Biddle 2004; Beckley 2010.
23. Biddle 2004, 1.
24. Biddle 1996.
25. Robertson and Sin 2017.
26. For example, see Subramanian 2011.
27. Casetti 2003, 663.
28. Knorr 1956.
29. Singer, Bremer, and Stuckey 1972.
30. Citations calculated from Google scholar.
31. Bairoch 1976, 282.
32. Beckley 2010.
33. On great powers, see *Correlates of War Project. 2017.* "State System Membership List, v2016." http://correlatesofwar.org. On rivalries, Bennett 2017; Klein, Goertz, and Diehl 2006.
34. Maddison 2003; Broadberry, Guna, and Li 2013; Ko, Koyama, and Sng 2017.
35. Lovell 2011; Spence 1991, chap. 7–8.
36. Moulder 1977, 100–102.
37. Morris 2010, 515.
38. Lovell 2011, 36–37.
39. Maddison 2003; Vries 2012, 19; Lovell 2011, 111–13.
40. Morris 2010, 502; Bairoch 1982, 281.
41. Kennedy 1987, 145.
42. Allen et al. 2011.
43. Ibid.
44. Sng 2014.
45. Ibid.
46. Vries 2012, 19; Feurenwerker 1969, 80–83.
47. The indemnity after the Boxer Rebellion, for example, was 1.8 times the Chinese government's total annual revenue. See Spence 1991, 235.
48. Lovell 2011, 111–13.
49. Platt 2014.
50. Lovell 2011, 113–14. On the number of British troops stationed in Britain, see Burroughs 1994, 162. For total numbers of British troops, see Singer, Bremer, and Stuckey 1972.
51. Lovell 2011, 113–14.
52. Desch 1989.
53. Lovell 2011, 110–14.
54. Crowley 1966, chap. 1; Duus 1976, chap. 8; Spence 1991, chap. 10.
55. Bairoch 1982, 281; Allen et al. 2011, 20; Singer, Bremer, and Stuckey 1972; Ma 2004, 369, 373.
56. Duus 1976, 137.
57. Feurenwerker 1969, 121; Flath 2014, 52.
58. Feurenwerker 1969, 168; Moulder 1977, 191; Spence 1991, 235.
59. Crawcour 1997, 52.
60. Moulder 1977, 184; Duus 1976, 142.
61. Chi 1992.
62. Williamsen 1992, 135.
63. Ibid., 170–71.
64. Chi 1992, 173.
65. Williamsen 1992, 148.
66. Chi 1992, 168–69.
67. Chi 1992, 171.
68. Chi 1992, 174–76.
69. On troop ratio, see Singer, Bremer, and Stuckey 1972.
70. Jelavich 1964, vii. See also Anderson 2003; Fuller 1998.

71. Fuller 1998, 292.
72. Snyder and Lieber 2008.
73. Nove 1990, 5.
74. Bairoch 1976.
75. Goldsmith 1961, 441.
76. Allen 2009b, 25.
77. Goldsmith 1961, 472–75.
78. Wohlforth 2001.
79. Hobson 1993, 478–79; Kennedy 1987, 174.
80. Adelman 1985, 88–92.
81. Mearsheimer 2014a, 72.
82. Kennedy 1987, 172.
83. Fuller 1998, 253.
84. Kennedy 1987, 236–37.
85. Singer, Bremer, and Stuckey 1972; Norris and Kristensen 2010; National Science Foundation 1989, 278, 313; National Science Foundation 1987, 228.
86. Cline 1977.
87. Brooks and Wohlforth 2000–2001.
88. Shifrinson 2018, chap. 3.
89. Brands 2016.
90. Easterly and Fischer 1995; International Monetary Fund 1991; Brooks and Wohlforth 2000–2001, 14–20; Allen 2009b, 190–200.
91. Krugman 1994.
92. Gaidar 2007, 75.
93. Oneal 1989.
94. National Science Foundation 1989, 278; National Science Foundation 1987, 228.
95. Ofer 1987.
96. Kontorovich 1990.
97. U.S. Bureau of the Census 1991, 4–9.
98. International Monetary Fund 1991, table II.2.3.
99. Gaidar 2007, 120; Alexeev and Gaddy 1993, 24.
100. Carter et al. 2006.
101. Zubok 2010, 95.
102. Firth and Noren 1998, 129–30.
103. Brooks and Wohlforth 2000–2001, 22.
104. Wolf et al. 1983.
105. Wolf et al. 1983; Carter et al. 2006.
106. Oneal 1989, 182.
107. Mearsheimer 1988, 183.
108. Betts 1995, 156–59.
109. Ibid.
110. Mearsheimer 1988; Posen 1984; Posen and Van Evera 1983.
111. Walt 1989.
112. Beckley 2018.

3. Economic Trends

1. A group of scholars are producing a new version of the Inclusive Wealth Report using modified methods. See Managi 2018. I received a draft manuscript of this new report, but have decided not to use the data, because the new methods have produced nonsensical results. For example, according to the 2018 report, India is eight times wealthier than China and 5.5 times wealthier than the United States; Congo is supposedly twice as wealthy as the United States on a per capita basis; and Niger has five times the per capita human capital of the United States! I contacted the editor of the report, Shunsuke Managi, inquiring about these bizarre results, and

his response led me to believe that the new methods massively overweight the economic value of population growth. Here is his response in full: "Basically, the reason for confusion comes from the Health Capital data. This health capital is the main contributor to the very high human capital of India and African countries. The longevity effect of health capital is measured in Stochastic Frontier Approach. So, the growing number of young population in India and Africa generating higher values, which show the discounted current value for health which is part of IW." Email correspondence with author on January 10, 2018.

2. Wallace 2016; Nakamura, Steinsson, and Liu 2015; Magnier 2016.

3. Balding 2016; Pettis 2017.

4. World Bank 2006, vii, xiv, 4, 20, 28; United Nations Environment Programme (UNEP) and United Nations University International Human Dimensions Programme on Global Environmental Change (UNU-IHDP) 2014, chap. 1.

5. UNU-IHDP 2014.

6. On workforce participation rates, see World Bank 2016. On American job losses, see Acemoglu et al. 2016; Autor, Dorn, and Hanson 2016.

7. Mossavar-Rahmani 2016, 53–54.

8. *The Economist* 2016k.

9. Ibid; Normile 2017.

10. Bradsher 2013.

11. OECD 2017; National Bureau of Statistics of China 2010.

12. World Bank, World Development Indicators, pupils per teacher in tertiary education; Phillips and Elkington 2016; Bland 2017b.

13. Ferrara 2015; Institute of Higher Education of Shanghai Jiao Tong University, "Academic Ranking of World Universities," http://www.shanghairanking.com.

14. Institute of Higher Education of Shanghai Jiao Tong University, "Academic Ranking of World Universities," http://www.shanghairanking.com.

15. Chen, Mourshed, and Grant 2013; Woetzel et al. 2016; Farrell and Grant 2005.

16. Laboissiere and Mourshed 2017.

17. Zakaria 2016; Cappelli 2015.

18. Woetzel 2016, 101.

19. Dan and Yao 2013.

20. Zweig and Wang 2013, 608.

21. *The Economist* 2013b.

22. Zweig and Wang 2013, 592; Chen 2017.

23. Huang 2011.

24. Yu 2015, 1148.

25. "Ticking Time Bombs: China's Health Care System Faces Issues of Access, Quality, and Cost," *Knowledge@Wharton*, June 26, 2013.

26. Huang 2011, 124; Beardson 2013, 149.

27. Rohde and Muller 2015; Albert and Xu 2016; Caiazzo et al. 2013.

28. Mossavar-Rahmani et al. 2016, 37.

29. Ministry of Environmental Protection of the People's Republic of China, "MEP Releases the 2014 Report on the State of Environment in China," June 4, 2015. See also, Stanway and Chen 2015; Tao and Xin 2014; Albert and Xu 2016; Economy 2014; *The Economist* 2013a.

30. Qiu 2011, 745.

31. Crane 2015; *The Economist* 2013a.

32. Chen et al. 2015; Volodzko 2016.

33. WHO Mortality Database 2017.

34. Pei 2016; Du and Mickiewicz 2015; Feng, Johansson, and Zhang 2015.

35. Du and Mickiewicz 2015, 23.

36. Litan and Hathaway 2017; Bessen 2016.

37. Transparency International 2016; Haley and Haley 2013; Anderlini 2013; Li and Hu 2013; Pei 2016.

38. U.S. Department of Agriculture, U.S. Agricultural Trade Data; Gale, Hansen, and Jewison 2015.

39. Woetzel et al. 2016, 22.
40. Rodrik 2013.
41. Woetzel et al. 2016, 21–22.
42. U.S. data from International Labor Office, ILO Laborstat Database. China data from National Bureau of Statistics of China. See also Ang 2012.
43. Lee 2014; OECD 2017.
44. Gopnik 2012.
45. *The Economist* 2017a.
46. Guo 2016.
47. Strauss 2017.
48. UNU-IHDP 2014; Enright 2016.
49. Enright 2016. See also, Xing 2014.
50. Hale and Hobijin 2011.
51. For example, each iPhone adds nearly $300 to the U.S. trade deficit with China, but manufacturers in China receive only $10 or less per phone. As one study of the iPhone's production chain concludes: "While these products, including most of their components, are manufactured in China, the primary benefits go to the U.S. economy as Apple continues to keep most of its product design, software development, product management, marketing and other high-wage functions in the U.S." See Kraemer, Linden, and Dedrick 2011, 2. See also, Xing 2014.
52. Conference Board 2017; Wu 2014; 2016.
53. Conference Board 2017; Jorgenson, Ho, and Samuels 2014.
54. Conference Board 2017.
55. To put China's investment rate in perspective, consider that Soviet investment was only 15 percent of GDP in 1950, under Stalin, and topped out in 1981 at 33 percent. Japan, South Korea, and Taiwan had investment rates around 35 percent during their high-growth years. Thailand, Malaysia, and Singapore experienced investment rates greater than 40 percent for a few years at a time, but these investment drives were short short-lived phenomena and stemmed mostly from an influx of foreign investment. By contrast, China has maintained an average investment rate above 40 percent since 1990, and most of this investment comes from domestic sources. On these points, see Naughton 2016, 108.
56. Brenda Goh, "Lovely Airport, Where Are the Planes? China's White Elephants Emerge," *Reuters*, April 10, 2015.
57. Ansar et al. 2016.
58. Chi et al. 2015; Shepard 2015.
59. American Society of Civil Engineers, *2017 Infrastructure Report Card.* https://www.infrastructurereportcard.org/americas-grades/.
60. World Economic Forum, *Global Competitiveness Rankings 2016–2017.* https://www.weforum.org/reports/the-global-competitiveness-report-2016-2017-1. On U.S. infrastructure improvements, see Harrison 2017.
61. European Chamber of Commerce in China 2016.
62. *The Economist* 2016a.
63. Ibid.
64. Perlez and Huang 2017.
65. Miller 2017.
66. *The Economist* 2017e.
67. Wildau 2017.
68. Wildau 2017.
69. *The Economist* 2016g.
70. Sharma 2012, 265.
71. Dobbs et al. 2015; Eichengreen 2012. On America's economic advantages more broadly, see Norrlof 2010. On the dollar's undisputed status as the world's reserve currency, see Sindreu and Bird 2017.
72. *The Economist* 2016h.
73. Ibid.; Bloomberg 2015.

74. Huo and Wu 2015; Amaro 2017.

75. Woetzel et al. 2016, 5.

76. Mossavar-Rahmani et al. 2016, 50; *The Economist* 2016g.

77. Tsai 2002.

78. Wei and Davis 2013; *The Economist* 2016h.

79. *The Economist* 2016i.

80. Tham 2017.

81. Conley 2013.

82. State Council of the People's Republic of China, "Guojia zhongchangji kexue fazhan guihua gangyao, 2006–2020" [National medium- and long-term science and technology development pro- gram outline, 2006–2020], February 9, 2006; McLaughlin 2016; U.S. Commission on the Theft of American Intellectual Property 2017.

83. Woetzel et al. 2016.

84. Ibid.

85. Ibid.

86. Wubbeke et al. 2016; Enright 2016; Xing 2014.

87. BCG 2014; Deloitte 2016.

88. Gilpin 1975, 70.

89. National Science Board 2018.

90. Ahmadpoor and Jones 2017.

91. Litan 2015.

92. *The Economist* 2016b; Bessen 2016.

93. *The Economist* 2017d.

94. For a review of these arguments, see Irwin 2016.

95. Gordon 2016.

96. The OECD defines these industries as "knowledge- and technology-intensive industries" that are capable of "altering lifestyles and the way business is conducted across a wide range of sectors."

97. U.S.-China Economic and Security Review Commission 2017b. chap. 4.

98. *The Economist* 2017b.

99. Ibid.

100. Ibid. See also, Lucas 2017.

101. Ibid.

102. National Science Board 2018, "Value-Added in Knowledge- and Technology-Intensive Industries," table 6-2.

103. State Council of the People's Republic of China, "Made in China 2025," May 19, 2015.

104. "Science Friction," Business Week, May 29, 2006. See also MacDonald 2016; Barbash 2015; Jacobs 2010; *Wall Street Journal* 2015.

105. *Business Week* 2006.

106. Wu 2011; *The Economist* 2013c; Yang and Zhang 2017.

107. *Zhongguo keji tongji nianjian 2064* [China statistical yearbook on science and technology 2016] (Beijing: China Bureau of Statistics, 2016), 94–95.

108. Gilboy 2004, 46.

109. Kennedy 2017, 21; *Zhongguo keji tongji nianjian 2016* [China statistical yearbook on science and technology 2016] (Beijing: China Bureau of Statistics, 2016), 96–97.

110. On Chinese firms, see ibid., 94–95. On Korean and Japanese firms, see Gilboy 2004, 43.

111. Wubbeke et al. 2016, 14.

112. World Bank and Development Research Center of the State Council of China 2013, 35. For an alternative but similar assessment, see Cao et al. 2013.

113. Wubbeke et al. 2016, 8.

114. Chin and Spegele 2014.

115. Vegetarianism is rare in China. The idea that an individual would deliberately abstain from eating meat seems counterintuitive, even offensive, in a culture where meat has been a sign of prosperity for millennia. Meat is now central to almost every middle-class meal, and pork is so important to Chinese society that the government maintains a strategic pork reserve

to stabilize prices during supply crunches. On the strategic pork reserve, see Taylor 2015. On the central place of meat in Chinese diets and why it guarantees a massive rise in Chinese meat and grain consumption, see Ma and Adams 2013, 56–61.

116. Li et al. 2014. See also Ghose 2014.

117. Marin 2014.

118. Shambaugh 2016, 83.

119. *The Economist* 2012b.

120. Ma and Adams 2013, 123.

121. World Bank 2016; Deloitte 2012.

122. *The Economist* 2016k.

123. *Xinhua* 2015.

124. World Bank 2016.

125. Canipe 2017.

126. Jourdan and Hirschier 2016; Deloitte 2015; Economist Intelligence Unit 2016.

127. Specifically, I include the combined budgets of the Departments of Defense, State, Veterans Affairs, Homeland Security, Justice, and the U.S. intelligence community; the Department of Energy's budget for the maintenance and modernization of the U.S. nuclear arsenal; state and local spending on law enforcement and prisons; and the Overseas Contingency Operations (OCO) fund, which funded the wars in Iraq and Afghanistan and continues to support a variety of defense programs and operations. The Department of Homeland Security funds U.S. Customs and Border Protection, Immigration, the Secret Service, the Air Marshals, the Coast Guard, and the Transportation Security Agency. The Department of Justice funds the Federal Bureau of Investigation; the Federal Bureau of Prisons; the Drug Enforcement Agency; the Bureau of Alcohol, Tobacco, and Firearms; and the U.S. Marshals Service. The U.S. Intelligence Community consists of sixteen agencies: the Central Intelligence Agency, the National Security Agency, the Defense Intelligence Agency, the Twenty-Fifth Air Force, the Intelligence and Security Command, Coast Guard Intelligence, the Office of Intelligence and Counterintelligence, the Office of Intelligence Analysis, the Bureau of Intelligence and Research, the Office of Terrorism and Financial Intelligence, the Office of National Security Intelligence, the Intelligence Branch of the FBI, the Marine Corps Intelligence Activity, the National Geospatial-Intelligence Agency, the National Reconnaissance Office, and the Office of Naval Intelligence. Most of these agencies are funded through the budgets of the U.S. Departments of Defense, Homeland Security, or Justice. Although the wars in Iraq and Afghanistan are officially over, the OCO budget remains, coming in at around $59 billion in 2016. Part of this funding supports ongoing operations in the Middle East and Afghanistan, but at least half of it is being used to pay for routine defense programs. For this reason, some analysts characterize OCO spending as a "slush fund" that enables the Department of Defense to get around budget caps. On this point, see Korb and Goepel 2016; Alexander 2010.

128. "What Does China Really Spend on Its Military?" *Center for Strategic and International Studies,* http://chinapower.csis.org/military-spending/; Chen 2013, 61; Fewsmith 2015, 61; Ma and Adams 2013, 246–48.

129. For examples, see "Political Stability and Absence of Terrorism/Violence," Worldwide Governance Indicators database (Washington, DC: World Bank, 2016); J. J. Messner et al., *The Fragile States Index 2016* (Washington, DC: Fund for Peace, 2016); Monty G. Marshall and Benjamin R. Cole, *Global Report 2014: Conflict, Governance, and State Fragility* (Vienna, VA: Center for Systemic Peace, 2014); Mark Gibney et al., "The Political Terror Scale, 1976–2015," *Political Terror Scale,* 2016, http://www.politicalterrorscale.org/; and *International Country Risk Guide* (East Syracuse, NY: PRS, 2016).

130. Orlik 2011.

131. Tanner 2014, 3.

132. Fravel 2008.

133. Smith 2015.

134. Kurlantzick 2015.

135. Mankoff 2015.

136. Page 2017.

137. "China," *Jane's World Armies*, December 24, 2016.
138. Rajagopalan 2017; *The Economist* 2014a; *The Economist* 2014b.
139. UNU-IHDP 2014.
140. *The Economist* 2013a; Albert and Xu 2016; Ma and Adams 2013, 41–47.
141. A large river is one with catchment areas of 100 square kilometers or more. On the drying up of China's rivers, see *The Economist* 2013d.
142. International Energy Agency 2016.
143. *Oil & Gas* 2015; Mufson 2013; Fensom 2014; Hefner 2014.
144. Collins 2015; Zeihan 2015, 132.
145. *The Economist* 2013e.
146. Mossavar-Rahmani et al. 2016, 37; Roberts 2014.
147. Cho 2011.
148. Hornby 2015.
149. *The Economist* 2013e.
150. Zhao et al. 2015.
151. British Petroleum 2016, 44; Stocking 2015, 2–3.
152. Woetzel et al. 2016, 21–22.
153. Zhou et al. 2012; Swartz and Oster 2010; Fischetti 2012.
154. *The Economist* 2013e.
155. On the costs of China's water shortages, see Economy 2014. On U.S. costs, see Raasch 2012.
156. International Energy Agency 2016, 2.
157. *The Economist* 2015a.
158. Gale, Hansen, and Jewison 2015, 3–5.
159. Patton 2014.

4. Military Trends

1. *The Economist* 2012a; International Institute for Strategic Studies (IISS) 2013, 42.
2. Office of Management and Budget 2016, table 6.1.
3. IISS 2017, chap. 3.
4. Wong 2014a.
5. U.S. data are for 2015 and comes from Office of Management and Budget 2016, table 3.2, section 052. Data for China are for 2010 and comes from Robertson and Sin 2017, table 1. For the United States, "welfare" includes personnel, housing, and construction costs. For China, "welfare" includes only personnel and housing costs. For the United States, "weapons" includes R&D and procurement costs. For China, "weapons" includes R&D and procurement costs plus construction costs and the costs of maintenance, transportation, and storage of equipment. For the United States, "operations" includes operation costs plus the costs of maintenance, transportation, and storage of equipment. China's "operations" category only includes the costs of current operations. See Blasko et al. 2006 and Liff and Erickson 2013 for a detailed comparison of what is included in each category for each country.
6. Blasko et al. 2006, 11.
7. Blasko 2012, 111–13; Erickson and Kennedy 2016.
8. Chase et al. 2015, 53. See also Blasko et al. 2006, 22; Robertson and Sin 2017.
9. Liff and Erickson 2013; Gilboy and Heginbotham 2012, chap. 4; Blasko et al 2006.
10. Scobell et al 2015; Chen 2013; Wang and Minzer 2015; Wong 2014b.
11. Fravel 2008.
12. As shown earlier, personnel costs account for 34 percent of China's military budget. Homeland security forces account for half of China's personnel, so the personnel costs of these forces are probably close to half of the personnel budget.
13. Nathan and Scobell 2012, 135.
14. Belasco 2014, 6–8.
15. Ibid.

16. Crawford 2014.
17. Cliff 2015, 104. See also Biddle 2004.
18. Cliff 2015, chap. 5; Allen and Clemens 2014.
19. Jourdan 2014; Martinson 2016.
20. Cliff 2015, 135.
21. U.S. Office of Naval Intelligence 2015, chap. 3; Cliff 2015, chap. 6.
22. Rielage 2016; Cliff 2015, chap. 6; Chase et al. 2015, chap. 4; McCauley 2015.
23. Ibid., 135.
24. Ibid.
25. Heginbotham et al. 2015, 80.
26. China's lack of carrier experience is no small matter: it took the U.S. Navy forty years, 12,000 crashed aircraft, and the lives of 8,500 personnel to reduce aircraft accident rates on carriers to the same level as land-based aircraft; and studies show that naval pilots with 4,500 hours of flight time are three times less likely to crash on a carrier, twice as accurate in bombing exercises, and five times less likely to be shot down in simulated air-to-air combat than pilots with only 500 hours of flying time. On these points, see Cliff 2015, 106.
27. Cliff 2015, 131.
28. Lin and Garafola 2016, 23–25.
29. Murray 2014, 18.
30. Johnson et al. 2009, 234.
31. Ibid., 55.
32. Beckley 2010, 57–59; Millet, Murray, and Watman 2010.
33. Millet, Murray, and Watman 2010.
34. McGann 2016, table 14; Huang and Economy 2015.
35. Garnaut 2012. See also Mulvenon and Ragland 2012.
36. Chase et al. 2015, 49.
37. The most commonly used measure of public sector corruption is Transparency International's Corruption Perceptions Index, which aggregates corruption measures form twelve sources, including the World Bank, the World Economic forum, and the Economist Intelligence Unit. According to the 2015 version of this index, the Chinese public sector is more than twice as corrupt as the U.S. government.
38. Lim and Blanchard 2014.
39. Easton 2014b.
40. Blasko 2015.
41. IISS 2017; Fravel 2007.
42. "China," *Jane's World Armies*, December 24, 2016.
43. U.S. personnel numbers come from U.S. Department of Defense 2014, iii.
44. Erickson 2016; Holmes 2016.
45. Erickson 2016.
46. "China: Sub Fleet Grows, Still in U.S. Wake," Stratfor. China's five tactical nuclear-powered submarines have 6 torpedo tubes. Most analysts believe that the PLA puts missiles in 4 of these tubes and torpedoes in the remaining 2 tubes. By contrast, U.S. Virginia- and Los-Angeles-class submarines have 4 torpedo tubes and 12 vertical-launch cells dedicated solely to missiles, and U.S. Ohio-class submarines have 4 torpedo tubes and 154 vertical-launch cells filled with missiles. China is currently developing a new tactical nuclear-powered submarine, the Type 093B, which appears to have a vertical-launch system with 12 to 16 missile cells. It is unknown when this submarine will be deployed, however.
47. Page 2015; Cote 2011.
48. On U.S. submarines, see Cote 2011, 202. On China's surveillance system, see Fisher 2016.
49. Beng 2015; Axe 2013.
50. U.S. Arleigh-Burke-class destroyers have 96 vertical-launch tubes, 2 Harpoon missile launchers, and 2 helicopters whereas China's most advanced destroyer, the Luyang III, has 64 vertical-launch tubes and one helicopter. U.S. Ticonderoga-class cruisers have 122 vertical-launch tubes, 8 Harpoon missile launchers, and 2 helicopters. See Clemens, Collins, and

Gunness 2015. China has launched one new cruiser, the Type 055, that has stealth capabilities and carries 112–28 missile cells, though it is unclear when the Type 055 will reach initial operating capability. See Lin and Singer 2015.

51. Gibbons-Neff 2016.

52. The Pentagon claims the YJ-18 has a range of 290 nautical miles (330 miles), but some defense experts believe the true range is less than half that. See Carlson 2015; Gormley, Erickson, and Yuan 2014, 102.

53. Majumdar 2015a; Majumdar 2015b.

54. Whittle 2015.

55. Economist Intelligence Unit 2011.

56. Vinik 2015; Heginbotham et al. 2015, 259; Lindsay 2015; Lindsay 2014/15, 35.

57. Montgomery 2014.

58. Posen 2003.

59. Kelly, Gompert, and Long 2016, 88–93.

60. Montgomery 2014.

61. Heath 2016.

62. Heginbotham et al. 2015, 48–55.

63. Finding, identifying, targeting, and striking a moving ship is a difficult task, so one should not assume that China's antiship ballistic missile is a one-shot, one-kill weapon. The seas near China encompass more than 5 million square miles, and thousands of ships pass through them every day. China's over-the-horizon skywave radar system has targeting errors ranging between ten to sixty-five miles, so it is not accurate enough to identify ships in the vast expanse of the East and South China Seas where U.S. ships would operate, let alone guide a ballistic missile to a U.S. aircraft carrier conducting evasive maneuvers and deploying all manner of radar jammers, decoys, countermeasures, and defensive systems. China has satellites that could provide targeting information for antiship missiles, but these satellites collectively provide images of a given point on earth only once every 2.6 hours, assuming perfect weather, and often only once every few days. For now, therefore, China's cruise missiles launched from ships and aircraft are much larger threats to U.S. aircraft carriers in Asia than China's shore-based antiship ballistic missile. For a discussion of the challenges facing China's antiship ballistic missile system, see Heginbotham et al. 2015, 154–71.

64. The United States has deployed 330 stealth fighters and 20 stealth bombers and plans to procure more than 2,500 stealth fighters and 100 "next generation" stealth bombers by the 2020s. At present, these aircraft can penetrate Chinese air space undetected. The United States also has converted four Ohio-class ballistic missile submarines into "underwater arsenal ships" that can loiter undetected in China's littorals and fire salvos of 154 Tomahawk missiles at China's missile batteries, radar installations, and bases. These submarines will be decommissioned between 2026 and 2028, but by then the United States will have deployed 22 new Virginia-class submarines each with expanded payloads of 40 Tomahawk missiles, supplementing the current fleet of 12 Virginia-class boats. The U.S. Air Force currently has 1,450 air-launched cruise missiles with ranges greater than 500 miles and is planning to purchase 3,000 more by the 2020s. The U.S. Navy currently has 700 air-launched cruise missiles with a range of 230 miles and has procured an initial batch of 30 new antiship air-launched cruise missile with a range of 570 miles. As noted earlier, U.S. ships and submarines already carry Tomahawk missiles with a range greater than 1,000 miles. On U.S. strike aircraft, see Majumdar 2015a; Heginbotham et al. 2015, 112. On U.S. submarines, see Beng 2015. On U.S. missiles, see Heginbotham et al. 2015, 106; Jane's Air-Launched Weapons, "AGM-158C Long Range Antiship Missile," February 6, 2016.

65. The U.S. Navy has aquired 114 EA-18G Growler aircraft, which are converted F/A-18Fs that accompany and cloak strike aircraft in a cloud of eletromagnetic noise. In 2021, the U.S. military will equip its fighter aircraft with the Next Generation Jammer, which can conduct both electromagnetic and cyber attacks against enemy radars, and active phased array radars that allow aircraft to broadcast powerful radar signals while remaining stealthy. See Clark and Gunzinger 2015.

66. Dyer 2014; De Luce 2015; Pietrucha 2015a.

67. Cliff 2014, 4.
68. Heginbotham et al. 2015, 92.
69. Ibid., chap. 6.
70. U.S. Department of Defense 2016, 26.
71. Dutton, Erickson, and Martinson 2014.
72. Clemens, Collins, and Gunness 2015.
73. U.S. Office of Naval Intelligence 2015, 20.
74. Erickson, Goldstein, and Murray 2009, 25–40.
75. Goldstein 2015a.
76. Melia 1991; Hartmann and Truver 1991.
77. Goldstein 2015a.
78. Heginbotham et al. 2015, 196.
79. The PLA only has 4 fixed-wing antisubmarine aircraft, which are similar to U.S. Cold War–era P-3C Orions, and 70 antisubmarine helicopters, which have limited combat radii (100–200 miles) and endurance (2–3 hours). These platforms have limited radar ranges (15–20 miles), so the PLA would have trouble finding U.S. submarines, let alone targeting them. China's diesel-powered submarines are poor antisubmarine platforms because they are slow and have limited endurance and would have extreme difficulty finding U.S. submarines. On the near invulnerability to U.S. submarines to Chinese antisubmarine warfare, see Cote 2011; Goldstein 2011; Mizokami 2017.
80. The United States has turned China's near seas into a "sensor-rich" environment by combining the existing U.S. underwater Sound Surveillance System (SOSUS) with hordes of new drones carrying thermal and optical sensors, active and passive sonar, magnetic anomaly detectors, and wake detection, light detection, and ranging systems. The navy has acquired roughly 160 aerial drones and 16 underwater drones, all of which can be deployed from submarines and perform reconnaissance over hundreds of miles. The U.S. military also has developed drone submarines (the Large Displacement Unmanned Underwater Vehicle) and unmanned surface ships (Anti-submarine Warfare Continuous Trail Unmanned Vessel) that can autonomously patrol for enemy submarines for 90 days and sweep areas of thousands of square miles. See Eckstein 2016; Gady 2016.
81. Heginbotham et al. 2015, 213.
82. Heginbotham et al. 2015, 222–24.
83. The United States is building two Virginia-class submarines per year from 2012 to 2025 and three submarines every two years thereafter until 2046. Submarines built after 2018 will have extra vertical-launch tubes, increasing their missile capacity from 12 to 40. The United States also will operate four Ohio-class cruise missile submarines, each with 154 Tomahawks, until at least 2025. The U.S. Navy will suffer a submarine "shortfall" in the mid-2020s, as Cold War–era Los Angeles-class submarines are retired. The total number of attack submarines will drop from 52 in 2017 to 41 in 2029 before rising back to 48 in 2037 and exceeding 50 in the 2040s. To put those numbers in perspective, the United States had 100 attack submarines at the height of the Cold War. To offset this temporary shortfall, the navy has accelerated production of Virginias, extended the service life of some Los Angeles-class submarines by one or two years each, lengthened submarine deployments from six to eight months, and procured 12 large undersea drones (the Large Displacement Unmanned Undersea Vehicle) to be deployed in 2025. These measures ensure that the United States will have at least 32 attack submarines ready for war at all times, and this updated fleet will be more capable than America's larger Cold War–era fleet, because Virginia-class boats are quieter and have more than three times the armaments of the Los Angeles-class boats they are replacing, and Virginias use fly-by-wire ship control systems that provide better shallow-water ship handling and carry more advanced sonar arrays. On these points, see O'Rourke 2016, 7–15; Cavas 2016a; Osborn 2016; Majumdar 2015b.
84. Benson 2014.
85. Seligman 2016.
86. Heginbotham et al. 2015, 188.
87. Tomkins 2016.

88. Pietrucha 2015b.
89. IISS 2017; U.S. Office of Naval Intelligence 2015, 21; Truver 2011, 60–61.
90. Gholz 2016.
91. For example, see Montgomery 2014.
92. U.S. Department of Defense 2016, ii, 40; Pillsbury 2015; Friedberg 2012; Mearsheimer 2014a, chap. 10.
93. The next section draws from Beckley 2017.
94. Crisher and Souva 2014.
95. Lafeber 2013.
96. Council on Hemispheric Affairs, "The U.S. Military's Presence in the Greater Caribbean Basin," http://www.Coha.Org/the-U-S-Militarys-Presence-in-the-Greater-Caribbean-Basin-More-a-Matter-of-Trade-Strategy-and-Ideology-Than-Drugs/.
97. Crowley 1966.
98. Erickson and Kennedy 2016.
99. Mollman 2016; Morris 2016.
100. Kane 2011.
101. Wachman 2007.
102. Peng and Yao 2005, 327.
103. O'Hanlon 2000.
104. Heginbotham et al. 2015, xxiii.
105. Lostumbo et al. 2016, 14; Shlapak et al. 2009, 51; Murray 2014, 6.
106. Easton 2014a.
107. Ibid., 31.
108. Easton 2014b.
109. Ibid.
110. Ibid.
111. Lostumbo et al. 2016, 4.
112. Easton 2014a, 35–45; Easton and Schriver 2014, 9.
113. Rosenau 2001, chap. 3.
114. Andrew 2009.
115. Shapiro 2013.
116. Cited in Easton 2014a, 13–14.
117. O'Hanlon 2000, 54–56.
118. Heginbotham et al. 2015, 203.
119. Ibid.
120. IISS 2017; Jane's Information Group 2016.
121. Shambaugh 2002, 324–27.
122. Ibid., 325–26; O'Hanlon 2000, 63.
123. Shlapak et al. 2009, 101.
124. Heginbotham et al. 2015, 205.
125. O'Hanlon 2000, 68.
126. Cliff 2015, 161.
127. O'Hanlon 2000, 71.
128. Shlapak et al. 2009, 115.
129. Ibid., 113.
130. Ibid., 98–99.
131. Bialik 2014.
132. Shlapak et al. 2009, 112.
133. Heginbotham et al. 2015, 211.
134. Grubb 2007.
135. Ibid.
136. Ibid., 89; O'Hanlon 2000, 76.
137. Glosny 2004.
138. Doughty 1982, 19; Navias and Hooton 1996, 86.

139. United Nations Conference on Trade and Development Statistics, http://unctad.org/en/Pages/statistics.aspxNCTAD 2016.

140. Mearsheimer 2014a, 90–96.

141. Glosny 2004, 145–46.

142. Election Study Center, National Chengchi University, "Taiwanese/Chinese Idenfication Trend Distribution," http://esc.nccu.edu.tw/course/news.php?Sn=166#.

143. Easton 2014a, 49.

144. On nonmilitary measures, see Gompert and Binnendijik 2016. On a U.S. blockade of China, see Hughes and Long 2014–15; Mirski 2013.

145. IISS 2017.

146. Cote Jr. 2011; Biddle and Oelrich 2016, 30–33.

147. Hughes and Long 2014–15, 174–78.

148. Ibid., 175. See also, Navias and Hooton 1996.

149. Seven cases took place during the world wars, but both wars were won on the ground. Italy bombed Ethiopia in 1936, but had to invade it to conquer the country. The Soviet Union bombed Afghanistan throughout the 1980s, but withdrew in defeat in 1989. The U.S. military bombed North Korea during the Korean War and conducted two bombing campaigns against North Vietnam during the Vietnam War, but failed to win either conflict. In the Gulf War, a U.S.-led coalition bombed Iraq, but had to invade Iraq to accomplish their aims. In the 1999 Kosovo War, NATO bombed Yugoslavia for seventy-eight days, but other factors ultimately impelled Yugoslavia's surrender, including the threat of a NATO ground invasion; pressure from Russia, Yugoslavia's vital ally; financial sanctions on Serbian political elites; and concessions by NATO that eventually made the terms of surrender more palatable. Moreover, the Kosovo case cannot be neatly applied to a China-Taiwan war, as NATO was not seeking to conquer Yugoslavia, and Yugoslavia was a weak nation led by an especially vulnerable regime.

150. Mearsheimer 2014a, 99–110.

151. Election Study Center, National Chengchi University, "Taiwan Independence vs. Unification with the Mainland Trend Distribution in Taiwan," http://esc.nccu.edu.tw/course/news.php?Sn=166#.

152. Dolven, Manyin, and Kan 2014.

153. Holmes 2017.

154. "East China Sea Tensions: Approaching a Slow Boil," Center for Strategic and International Studies, Asian Maritime Transparency Initiative, April 16, 2016, https://amti.csis.org/east-china-sea-tensions/.

155. Morris 2017.

156. IISS 2017; SIPRI 2017a.

157. Fannell and Cheney-Peters 2017.

158. "Playing Chicken in the East China Sea," Asia Maritime Transparency Initiative, CSIS, April 28, 2017, https://amti.csis.org/playing-chicken-east-china-sea/; Kelly and Kubo 2015.

159. Ball and Tanter 2015.

160. Yoshihara 2015.

161. IISS 2017.

162. Ibid.

163. Ibid.

164. Ibid.

165. "Japan," *Jane's World Air Forces*, December 23, 2016.

166. "Japan," *Jane's World Navies*, March 29, 2017; "Japan," *Jane's World Air Forces*, March 29, 2017.

167. Ibid.

168. Yoshihara and Holmes 2011.

169. Hayton 2014; Kaplan 2014.

170. Thayer 2014.

171. Fisher 2016.

172. Werrell 1988, 112.

173. "Vietnam Receives First Israeli-made SPYDER Air Defense Missile System," *Defence Blog*, July 18, 2016; "Vietnam Is Negotiating to Buy S-400 Triumph Anti-aircraft Missiles," *Defence Blog*, July 4, 2016.
174. IISS 2017.
175. "Vietnam," *Jane's World Air Forces*, May 18, 2016; Heginbotham et al. 2015, 90–95.
176. Goldstein 2015b.
177. Thayer 2017.
178. Roblin 2016a.
179. "Vietnam," *Jane's World Navies*, May 18, 2016.
180. Roblin 2016b.
181. Kaplan 2014, chap. 3.
182. Erickson 2016.
183. IISS 2017.
184. Gady 2016.
185. "Indonesia," *Jane's World Navies*, March 29, 2017.
186. "Indonesia," *Jane's World Navies*, April 20, 2016.
187. Ibid.; Rahmat 2016.
188. "Indonesia," *Jane's World Air Forces*, May 13, 2016.
189. Ibid.
190. "Malaysia," *Jane's World Navies*, March 29, 2017.
191. IISS 2017.
192. "Malaysia," *Jane's World Navies*, January 5, 2017.
193. IISS 2017.
194. Rapp-Hooper 2016, 76–82.
195. Torode 2016.
196. Heginbotham et al. 2015, 88.
197. Ibid.
198. "Airpower in the South China Sea" (Washington, DC: Asia Maritime Transparency Initiative, CSIS, 2015).
199. Heginbotham et al. 2015, 88.
200. Ibid., 48.
201. Ibid., 66.
202. Pettyjohn and Kavangh 2016, 138–39.
203. Gramer 2017a.
204. Heydarian 2017.
205. PettyJohn and Vick 2013, 26–27.
206. Heginbotham et al. 2015, 92.
207. Ibid., 91.
208. Gady 2017; Gibbons-Neff 2016; Heginbotham et al. 2015, 106; U.S. Department of Defense 2016, 27.
209. Cote 2011; Osborn 2016.
210. Heginbotham et al. 2015, 186–89.
211. Benson 2014; Eckstein 2016.
212. Heginbotham et al. 2015, 192–98, 222–24.

5. Future Prospects

1. For applications of both theories, see Layne 1993; Gilpin 1981.
2. Morgenthau 1973; Waltz 1979, chaps. 5–6; Waltz 1993; Layne 1993; Mearsheimer 2014a, chaps. 2–3; Monteiro 2014, chaps. 4–5; Walt 1987, chaps. 1–2.
3. Wohlforth 1999; Brooks and Wohlforth 2008.
4. Pape 2005; Brooks and Wohlforth 2008; Lieber and Alexander 2005; Walt 2005; Fiammenghi 2011; Monteiro 2014.
5. Brooks and Wohlforth 2008; Lieber and Alexander 2005.

6. Walt 1987; Mearsheimer 2014.
7. Wohlforth 1999, 31.
8. Walt 1987, 36.
9. Gowa and Ramsay 2017.
10. For example, see Daalder 2017.
11. SIPRI 2017a.
12. Jane's Information Group 2017b; Gorst 2011.
13. Jane's Information Group 2017b; Defense Intelligence Agency 2017, 20–21.
14. Oxenstierna 2016; Jane's Information Group 2017b.
15. Nelson 2017, 8.
16. Berman 2015; Berman 2017.
17. Daalder 2017; Peel and Bond 2017; Birnbaum and Gibbons-Neff 2017.
18. Rogin 2017; Schwartz 2017.
19. IISS 2013.
20. Shlapak and Johnson 2016a.
21. Kofman 2016.
22. Kofman 2015.
23. Lanoszka and Hunzeker 2016; Grygiel and Mitchell 2014.
24. Sagan 2011, C-1.
25. Ibid.
26. Hymans 2012.
27. Gavin 2015, 21; Yusuf 2009.
28. Gavin 2015; Miller 2017.
29. Beckley 2015.
30. Palmer et al. 2015.
31. Pape 2005; Layne 2004; Ikenberry 2004.
32. Baltrusaitis 2008, 10–18.
33. Brooks and Wohlforth 2008, chap. 2.
34. Selden 2013.
35. Walt 1987.
36. Chen 2001. For an engaging history of the U.S.-China relationship, see Pomfret 2016.
37. For example, see sources cited in Saradzhyan 2010.
38. Mankoff 2013. See also Mankoff 2015; Kaplan 2017; Menon 2009.
39. SIPRI 2017b; Blank 2014; Backes 2013.
40. Mankoff 2015; Muraviev 2014.
41. International Crisis Group 2017; Freeman 2017.
42. Freeman 2018.
43. Moravcsik 2010; Posen 2008; Kupchan 2007.
44. Eilstrup-Sangiovanni 2014; Toje 2010.
45. Norman and Barnes 2017.
46. Huffbauer et al. 2012. In 2014, Russia retaliated for U.S. sanctions on Russia by banning food imports from the United States and prohibiting several U.S. leaders, including President Obama, from traveling to Russia.
47. Rosenberg et al. 2016.
48. Gompert and Binnendijk 2016, 22–24; Hughes and Long 2014/15.
49. Bremmer 2015; Rosenberg et al. 2016, 38.
50. Goldman and Rosenberg 2015, 8; Gompert and Binnendijk 2016, 17. For an in-depth examination of how the U.S. Treasury Department manipulates global financial flows to impose sanctions on U.S. adversaries, see Zarate 2013.
51. Rosenberg et al. 2016.
52. Collins 2017, 3.
53. Ibid.
54. For excellent analyses of China's economic statecraft, see Feigenbaum 2017a; Feigenbaum 2017b; Norris 2016.
55. Chan 2016.

56. Villamor 2017.
57. Gramer 2017.
58. Gholz 2014; *Wall Street Journal* 2016.
59. Mogato 2017.
60. Perlez, Landler, and Sang-Hun 2017.
61. Council on Foreign Relations 2017.
62. For example, Romanosky 2016 estimates that the cost of cyber events worldwide is only $8.5 billion. For the U.S. government estimate, see U.S. Commission on the Theft of American Intellectual Property 2017, 1.
63. On China's efforts, see Osnos 2018.
64. Sindreu and Bird 2017.
65. Ikenberry and Lim 2017.
66. Kaushik 2018.
67. Miller 2017. See also, Larmer 2017.
68. Walker 2016.
69. Walker and Ludwig 2017.
70. Walker and Ludwig 2017. For an extensive list of China's global media influence, see U.S.-China Economic and Security Review Commission 2017b, section 5.
71. *Economist* 2017h.
72. Dorell 2017; Horwitz, Nakashim, and Gold 2017.
73. For example, see Boot 2017.
74. Downes and O'Rourke 2016.
75. Pew Research Center 2017.
76. Osnos 2017.
77. *Economist* 2017i.
78. Johnson 2017.
79. Qing and Shiffman 2015.
80. *Economist* 2017i.
81. Redden 2017.
82. Entous, Nakashima, and Jaffe 2017.
83. Quoted in Walker and Ludwig 2017.
84. Whereas 64 percent of foreign publics had confidence in Barack Obama to "do the right thing," only 22 percent have confidence in Donald Trump. Wike et al. 2017.
85. Ibid.
86. Brooks and Wohlforth 2012/13, 23.
87. Walt 2017a.
88. O'Rourke 2018.
89. Porter 2017; Barry 2011.
90. Nye 2004; Nye 2013.
91. Nye 2013.
92. Vice 2017; McClory 2017.
93. Kennedy 1987, xx.
94. Gerschenkron 1962; Baumol 1986. For applications of the theory, see Subramanian 2011; Layne 1993; Modelski 1978; Kennedy 1987; Gilpin 1981.
95. Gerschenkron 1962, chap. 1.
96. Kim 1997, 88–93, 193–94; Findlay 1978; Das 1987; Bitzinger 1994.
97. Citigroup 2011, 1.
98. Gilpin 1981, 179. See also Kennedy 1987; Layne 1993; Modelski 1978.
99. Rodrik 2013.
100. Pritchett 1997, 3.
101. Sharma 2016a; Sharma 2014; Sharma 2012; Rodrik 2013.
102. Beckley, Horiuchi, and Miller 2017.
103. Pritchett 1997, 4.
104. Kennedy 1987.
105. Rodrik 2013, 3.

106. These factor are reviewed in Beckley 2011–12.

107. Gordon 2004, 3.

108. Mitton 2016; Zeihan 2015; McCord and Sachs 2013; Gallup, Sachs, and Mellinger 1999. On natural resources, see Wrigley 2010; Allen 2009a; Pomeranz 2000; Griffin 2010, chaps. 7–8; Wright and Czelusta 2004. On transport infrastructure, see Emran and Hou 2013; Storeygard 2016; Zeihan 2015; Redding and Turner 2014; Limao and Venables 2001; Sokoloff 1988; Romer 1996; Wright 1990; Rappaport and Sachs 2003. On buffers, see Morgenthau 1973, 117–18; Walt 1987; Mearsheimer 2014a, 114–28; Levy and Thompson 2010.

109. Fernihough and O'Rourke 2014.

110. Wrigley 2010; Allen 2009; Pomeranz 2000; Griffin 2010, chaps. 7–8.

111. Morris 2010, 497.

112. Wright 1990; Irwin 2003.

113. BP 2016, 41; Alexeev and Conrad 2009; Allcott and Keniston 2015.

114. McCord and Sachs 2013.

115. Sachs and Warner 1995; Sala-i-Martin and Subramanian 2003; Ross 2003; Mazaheri 2016.

116. Kennedy and Tiede 2013; van der Ploeg 2011; Sachs and Warner 2001.

117. Brooks and Kurtz 2016.

118. Wright and Czelusta 2004; Mehlum, Moene, and Torvik 2006; Robinson, Torvik, and Verdier 2006.

119. Emran and Hou 2013; Storeygard 2016; Zeihan 2015, chap. 3.

120. Limao and Venables 2001.

121. Redding and Turner 2014.

122. Sokoloff 1988; Romer 1996.

123. Smith 1976, 25.

124. Gallup, Sachs, and Mellinger 1999.

125. Redding and Venables 2004.

126. See the studies cited in Bosker and Garretsen 2012.

127. On the Dutch Republic, see Vries and van der Woude 1997. On Britain, see Smith 1976. On the United States, see Wright 1990; Rappaport and Sachs 2003. On Germany, see Zeihan 2015.

128. Morgenthau 1973, 117–18.

129. Kennedy 1987; Gilpin 1981, chap. 4

130. Mearsheimer 2014a, 114–28; chap. 7.

131. Levy and Thompson 2010.

132. Acemoglu and Johnson 2005; Acemoglu et al 2016; Besley and Persson 2011; Beaulieu, Cox, and Saiegh 2012; Schultz and Weingast 2003; Friedberg 2000; Haggard and Tiede 2010.

133. For examples, see Johnson 1982; Amsden 1989; Wade 1990; Evans 1995.

134. Herbst 2000; Centeno 2002.

135. Besley and Persson 2011; Acemoglu, Garcia-Jimeno, and Robinson 2015.

136. Allen 2009b.

137. Acemoglu and Robinson 2012.

138. Besley and Ghatak 2010; Asoni 2008; Drezner 2001; Knack and Keefer 1995; Clague et al. 1999.

139. Marshall, Gurr, and Jaggers 2017; World Bank 2016.

140. Achen and Bartels 2016.

141. Acemoglu and Robinson 2012. Other scholars use different phrases, but the meaning is largely the same. For example, Douglas North, Barry Weingast, and their coauthors use the phrase "open access orders" and contrast them with "limited access orders." See North et al. 2011.

142. For examples, see Glaeser et al. 2004; Kurtz and Schrank 2007; Thomas 2010; Hoyland, Moene, and Willumsen 2012; Voigt 2013.

143. For a defense of the World Governance Indicators, see Kaufmann, Kraay, and Mastruzzi 2007; Kaufmann, Kraay, and Mastruzzi 2010.

144. Glaeser et al. 2004.

145. Acemoglu, Johnson, and Robinson 2001, 404–7; Acemoglu et al. 2018.

146. Acemoglu, Johnson, and Robinson 2001; Rodrik, Subramanian, and Trebbi 2004.

147. For examples, see Goldstein and Udry 2008; Frye 2004; Hornbeck 2010; Markus 2012.

148. Acemoglu et al. 2018.

149. On population age, see Sharma 2016c; Bloom, Canning, and Sevilla 2003. On health, see United Nations Environment Programme (UNEP) and United Nations University International Human Dimensions Programme on Global Environmental Change (UNU-IHDP) 2014; Strittmatter and Stunde 2013; Lopez-Casasnovas, Rivera, and Currais 2005; Carstensen and Gundlach 2006. On education, see Becker, Hornung, and Woessman 2011; Goldin and Katz 2010, chap. 1.

150. Kennedy 1987, chap. 4.

151. Bloom, Canning, and Sevilla 2002.

152. Sharma 2016c.

153. Ibid.

154. Ibid.

155. Ibid.

156. Cohen and Levinthal 1990; Bloom, Canning, and Sevilla 2002; Horowitz 2010.

157. Burgess 2016; Hanushek, Ruhose, and Woessmann 2015; Manuelli and Seshardi 2014.

158. On Germany, see Becker, Hornung, and Woessman 2011. On the United States, see Goldin and Katz 2010, chap. 1.

159. International Energy Agency 2016.

160. U.S. Energy Information Administration 2016; International Energy Agency 2016; BP 2016.

161. BP 2016.

162. Movchan 2017, 7; *The Economist* 2014c.

163. Aron 2013.

164. World Bank 2016.

165. Zeihan 2015, 124–28.

166. Cited in Odgaard and Delman 2014, 114.

167. Farchy 2014.

168. Hefner 2014.

169. Hill and Gaddy 2013, 344.

170. Ibid., 224.

171. Maugeri 2013, 2.

172. Ibid., 1.

173. Zeihan 2015, 126; Cook and Olson 2016.

174. Kurtzman 2014, chap. 4.

175. O'Sullivan 2017, 110. See also, Zeihan 2015, 129; Hosseinzadeh et al. 2014; Hefner 2014, 14; Verleger 2012, 9; Yergin 2013.

176. Aslund et al. 2012, 24.

177. Ibid.; Emerson and Winner 2014; Hughes 2014.

178. Aslund et al. 2012, 23.

179. Sun 2014; Odgaard and Delman 2014, 109.

180. Polak 2015.

181. Kauzlarich 2016; Johnson 2015; O'Sullivan 2017, chap. 8-9.

182. This subsection draws heavily on Zeihan 2015.

183. The Yangtze is China's sole navigable river and cuts through mountain chains and ridges on its path to the sea. Along many stretches, it lacks a floodplain even wide enough for a footpath. The elevation means that many of the basin's "nine thousand miles of navigability" are seasonal; if you eliminate any Yangtze River basin waterways that lack a channel of at least nine feet of depth for nine months of the year, that figure drops to seventeen hundred, and the number of navigable tributaries drops from over one hundred to just one. While it seems huge on a map, the area of usable territory it empowers is less than that of the Elbe. Aside from a short stretch of the Pearl River in the far south, none of the many southern Chinese rivers are navigable. On these points, see Zeihan 2015, 295–96.

184. Rappaport and Sachs 2003.

185. Zeihan 2015, 48.
186. World Bank 2016.
187. Zeihan 2015, 63–65.
188. Ibid.
189. Ibid., 67.
190. Ibid., 66–67.
191. U.S. Department of Defense 2015.
192. For a full description of the World Bank's methodology, including links to the source data and scholarly articles debating the merits of the indicators, see http://info.worldbank.org/governance/wgi/index.aspx#doc-sources.
193. These veto players include a president with equal democratic legitimacy to Congress; a powerful upper house of Congress whose approval is needed on virtually all legislation; an independent judiciary that can overturn legislative acts; and a federal system that allocates powers to state and local governments. Most parliamentary systems have far fewer veto players, and are therefore able to pass legislation more easily. In such systems, the executive branch is not a competing power center, but rather the administrative instrument of the legislative majority. On these points, see Fukuyama 2013.
194. Calculated as a three-year moving average. Data from OECD 2017.
195. Fukuyama 2012; Fukuyama 2015.
196. Zakaria 1998.
197. Friedberg 2000.
198. For a comparison of U.S., European, and Japanese welfare states, see Grusky, Mattingly, and Varner 2016. On poverty rates, see OECD 2017.
199. OECD 2017; Furman 2016, 134; *The Economist* 2016m.
200. Joint Committee on Taxation 2017.
201. Guzman and Stern 2016.
202. World Bank 2016. "Ease of Doing Business Indicators." Calculations based on data for all available years (2004 to 2017).
203. On starting, owning, and investing in new businesses, see Global Entrepreneurship Monitor 2017. Calculations based on data for all available years (2005 to 2015).
204. OECD 2015, figure 7.1.
205. On hiring and firing, see World Economic Forum 2016. On hours worked and productivity, see The Conference Board Total Economy Database™ (adjusted version), November 2016, http://www.conference-board.org/data/economydatabase/. On wages, see OECD 2017, average annual wages indicator.
206. Linz 1990.
207. Miller 2018; Hedberg 2016; Hill and Gaddy 2013; Ledeneva 2013.
208. Sakwa 2010, 32.
209. Kotkin 2015. For an example of Putin intervening forcefully to impose policy, see Brooke and Gans-Morse 2016.
210. Quoted in Hendley 2012.
211. On surveys of law compliance, see Hendley 2012. On police incomes and corruption, see Taylor 2011. On corruption, see Transparency International 2016. On crony capitalism, see "Comparing Crony Capitalism around the World," *The Economist*, May 5, 2016.
212. Lorentzen, Landry, and Yasuda 2014; Rithmire 2014; Landry 2008; Bergsten et al. 2008, chap. 4.
213. Lau, Qian, and Roland 2000. For a critique of this argument, see Cai and Treisman 2006.
214. Pettis 2013.
215. These reforms are described in U.S.-China Business Council 2016.
216. Bai, Hsieh, and Song 2016.
217. Pettis 2013, 40.
218. Han and Miller 2017; Wolf 2016; Wildau 2016.
219. Fisher 2015.
220. On India's tiny tax base, see Nageswaran and Najarajan 2016, 37–39. For data on tax revenues as a share of GDP, see IMF 2017.

221. Nageswaran and Natarajan 2016, 39.
222. Gupta et al. 2014, 6.
223. Ganguly and Thompson 2017, 185–86.
224. Gupta et al. 2014; Ganguly and Thompson 2017, 2033–34, 2133–34; World Bank 2016; *The Economist* 2015b.
225. *The Economist* 2016j.
226. Gupta et al. 2014, 132.
227. Fukuyama 2013.
228. Kessler 2013.
229. Blinder 2017; Yglesias 2017.
230. Stigler 1971.
231. Tocqueville 2000.
232. Dahl 1961.
233. Bartels 2008; Gilens 2014; Hacker and Pierson 2012; Gilens and Page 2014; Leighley and Nagler 2013.
234. For example, see Chayes 2017.
235. Transparency International 2017.
236. Zimmerman 2014.
237. *The Economist* 2017g. See also, Dawisha 2014; Judah 2013; Hill and Gaddy 2013.
238. *The Economist* 2017g; *The Economist* 2016n.
239. Ibid.
240. Taylor 2015.
241. Economy 2014. See also *The Economist* 2016c; Hernandez 2017a.
242. Nathan 2017.
243. Chen 2015; Hsieh and Song 2015; Milhaupt and Zheng 2015.
244. Abrami, Kirby, and McFarlan 2014; Wong and Dou 2017.
245. King, Pan, and Roberts 2013.
246. Ibid.; King, Pan, and Roberts 2017; Bland 2017a; Bland 2017b; Garnaut 2017.
247. Freedom House 2017.
248. Chin and Wong 2016.
249. Browne 2017; Fan, Khan, and Lin 2017.
250. Osnos 2018, 43.
251. Ibid.
252. U.S. Congressional-Executive Commission on China 2017.
253. Lee 2012. On financial repression, see Pettis 2013.
254. On party officials as managers of state-owned enterprises, see Pei 2016. On bank lending to state-owned enterprises, see Lee 2012; Magnier 2016.
255. Li and Hu 2013.
256. Pei 2016.
257. Forsythe 2015.
258. Ibid.
259. Hernandez 2017b.
260. Vaishnav 2017. See also *The Economist* 2016l; Chandra 2016.
261. Ganguly and Thompson 2017, tables 9.1 and 9.2.
262. Jeffrey 2015.
263. UN Population Database.
264. Zeihan 2017, chap. 8.
265. Berman 2013.
266. Eberstadt 2011; Neufield and Rehm 2013.
267. On Russian public health initiatives, see Brooke and Gans-Morse 2016. For data on death rates by country, see CIA 2017.
268. Gupta et al. 2014, 48.
269. World Bank 2016.
270. den Boer and Hudson 2014.
271. Barro and Lee 2013.

272. OECD 2017. India does not participate in PISA, but India almost certainly would score much lower than the other major powers. Almost 70 percent of India's working-age population has not attended high school and nearly 50 percent of prime working-age adults (ages to 54) has no education at all. Only 12 percent of Indian eighth graders can read at a first-grade level and only 20 percent could recognize numbers above ten. On India's educational failings, see Gupta et al. 2014, 22, 70.

273. "Massachusetts Students Score among World Leaders on PISA Reading, Science, and Math Tests," Massachusetts Department of Education, December 6, 2016.

274. Gneezy et al. 2017.

275. Mehta 2013; Ripley 2013.

276. Master, Sun, and Loeb 2017; Auguste, Kihn, and Miller 2010; Mehta 2013.

277. Chetty, Friedman, and Rockoff 2014.

278. Mehta 2013, 8.

279. Fraumeni 2015.

280. These points are developed in Hanushek and Woessman 2015, 443–46.

281. Hanson and Slaughter 2015.

282. National Science Foundation 2016, table 2-13 and table 3-17.

6. The Unipolar Era

1. Rosseau 2010, Kindle Location 1184. This quote also appears in Huntington 1988, 96.

2. Barma, Ratner, and Weber 2014; Zakaria 2012; Rachman 2017; Glaser 2011; Legro 2011.

3. Allison 2017.

4. Roser 2016.

5. Goldstein 2011; Anderson 2017.

6. Maddison 2003; World Bank 2016.

7. Pinker 2011.

8. Violence of all kinds has declined over the course of human history. Changing social norms, the rise of the nation-state, and the spread of commerce help explain this long-term trend. On these points, see Pinker 2011. However, I do not think they fully explain the sudden drop in warfare after 1991.

9. Between 1989 and 1999, the number of democracies in the world and the level of globalization (measured in international flows of trade, finance, people, and data) both increased by roughly 60 percent and the number of peacekeeping operations doubled. On democracy, see Roser 2017. On globalization, see KOF Index of Globalization 2017. On peacekeeping operations, see UN 2017. On the argument that the spread of democracy has reduced the likelihood of war, see Dafoe, Oneal, and Russet 2013. On the argument that globalization has reduced the likelihood of war, see Gartzke 2007. On the argument that peacekeeping has reduced the likelihood of war, see Goldstein 2011.

10. Wohlforth 1999.

11. Jervis 2002.

12. Morgan 2008; Goldstein 2013; Gompert and Kelly 2013.

13. Christensen 2006.

14. Rovner 2017.

15. Denmark 2018; Posen 2017; Barno and Bensahel 2017.

16. Here I am paraphrasing Krauthammer 1984.

17. Demick 2017; Panda and Narang 2017.

18. Trump 2017a.

19. Karako, Williams, and Rumbaugh 2017.

20. Lieber and Press 2017.

21. Manzo and Warden 2017.

22. Friedman 2017.

23. Mastro 2018.

24. On the military requirements of securing North Korea after a collapse, see Bennett and Lind 2011.

25. Ibid., 63.
26. Goldstein 2015c; Steinberg and O'Hanlon 2014.
27. Gholz, Press, and Sapolsky 1997; Layne 2006, chap. 8; Carpenter 2008.
28. On past successful cases of retrenchment, see Parent and MacDonald 2011.
29. On the costs of retrenchment, see Brooks and Wohlforth 2016; Lieber 2016; Brands 2015.
30. Christensen 2012.
31. Heginbotham et al. 2015, chap. 14; Kelly, Gompert, and Long 2016.
32. Chollet et al. 2017.
33. Murray 2008.
34. Lanoszka and Hunzeker 2016; Grygiel and Mitchell 2014.
35. Gompert and Binnendijik 2016.
36. Ibid. On the coercive power of U.S. financial sanctions, see Zarate 2013. On the United States' ability to control international shipping, see Hughes and Long 2014–15. On U.S. cyber capabilities, see Vinik 2015.
37. Ibid., 9.
38. Rovner 2017a.
39. Bradley 2015; Christensen 2012.
40. Kennedy 1987; Gilpin 1981, chap. 4.
41. Layne 2006, 152–53.
42. Jervis 2006, 13–14.
43. For an insightful look at great power conquest in the periphery, see MacDonald 2014.
44. Gilpin 1981, 148.
45. Layne 2011, 149. See also Betts 2012; Carpenter 2008; Posen 2014; Snyder 2003; Jervis 2006; Jervis 2003; Layne 2006.
46. Posen 2014.
47. Zakaria 2015.
48. Betts 2014.
49. For an application of this doctrine to the civil war in Syria, see Walt 2013.
50. Edelstein 2008.
51. The next few paragraphs draw heavily from Weissman 2017.
52. Bader and Pollack 2017.
53. Flores-Macias and Kreps 2016.
54. For an excellent analysis showing that the American public calculates costs and benefits when deciding whether to support a war, see Gelpi, Feaver, and Reifler 2009.
55. Rovner and Talmadge 2014; Mearsheimer and Walt 2016; Glaser and Kelanic 2017; Simon and Stevenson 2015.
56. Rovner 2016; Rovner and Talmadge 2014; Glaser and Kelanic 2017.
57. Gholz 2009; Talmadge 2008.
58. "More than 1 Million Saudis on Unemployment Benefit," *Reuters*, March 28, 2012.
59. Talmadge 2008; Rovner and Talmadge 2014. Alternatively, Iran could fire missiles at Saudi oil infrastructure, but such an attack would not seriously disrupt Saudi production, because Iran's missiles are inaccurate, and Saudi Arabia could compensate for destroyed facilities by activating its ample extra production and export capacity. On this point, see Shifrinson and Priebe 2011.
60. Mueller and Stewart 2016, chaps. 1–2.
61. Ibid.
62. Priest and Arkin 2011, 12, 25–26, 86; Mueller and Stewart 2011, introduction.
63. Lake 2016.
64. Edelstein 2008.
65. This literature is summarized in Desch 1996 and Walt 2016.
66. Ibid.
67. For statistical evidence that increases in relative power increase domestic polarization, see Bafumi and Parent 2012.
68. Ibid.
69. Ibid.

70. Friedberg 2000.
71. Poole and Rosenthal 2016; Shor and McCarty 2015; Bateman, Clinton, and Lapinski 2016; Pew 2016b.
72. Drutman 2017.
73. Office of Management and Budget 2018.
74. Klein 2011.
75. The following recommendations come from Gehl and Porter 2017.
76. Kalla and Broockman 2016.
77. O'Donnell 2016.
78. See Kalla and Broockman 2016 and the sources cited therein.
79. For a good summary of this research, see LaRaja and Schaffner 2014.
80. Ikenberry 2001; Ikenberry 2011; Brooks and Wohlforth 2016; Lieber 2016; Brands 2015.
81. Kagan 2013.
82. Drezner 2014.
83. Zeihan 2017.
84. For two excellent analyses from leading scholars on the threat the Trump administration poses to the liberal order and what other actors can do about it, see Ikenberry 2017; Nye 2017.
85. Ikenberry 2011, 58.
86. On the argument that China will play this role, see Feng 2017.
87. Fukuyama 1992.
88. Keohane 2005.
89. Kagan 2009; Mearsheimer 2014; Kennedy 1987.
90. Gilpin 1981.
91. Brendon 2010.
92. For two thoughtful analyses on the fate of the liberal order, see Emmott 2017 and Luce 2017.
93. Haas 2018. See also, Kagan 2013; Brooks and Wohlforth 2016.
94. Stein 1984.
95. Mastanduno 2009.
96. Brands 2018.
97. Wright 2017.
98. Johannesson and Mavroidis 2016.
99. Fajgelbaum and Khandelwal 2016.
100. Irwin 2017, 50.
101. For additional evidence that immigration is a net positive for the U.S. economy, see Blau and Mackie 2017.
102. Blau and Mackie 2017, parts II and III.
103. Hainmueller and Hopkins 2015.
104. Lamothe 2017.
105. The next three paragraphs draw heavily from Walt 2017b.

Works Cited

Abrami, Regina M., William C. Kirby, and F. Warren McFarlan. 2014. "Why China Can't Innovate." *Harvard Business Review* (March): 107–11.

Abramowitz, Alan I. 2013. *The Polarized Public: Why American Government Is So Dysfunctional*. New York: Pearson.

Acemoglu, Daron, David H. Autor, David Dorn, Gordon H. Hanson, and Brendan Price. 2016. "Import Competition and the Great U.S. Employment Sag of the 2000s." *Journal of Labor Economics* 34, no. 1 (January): 141–98.

Acemoglu, Daron, Camilo Garcia-Jimeno, and James Robinson. 2015. "State Capacity and Economic Development: A Network Approach." *American Economic Review* 105, no. 8 (August): 2364–409.

Acemoglu, Daron, and Simon Johnson. 2005. "Unbundling Institutions." *Journal of Political Economy* 113, no. 5 (October): 949–95.

Acemoglu, Daron, Simon Johnson, and James A. Robinson. 2001. "The Colonial Origins of Comparative Development: An Empirical Investigation." *American Economic Review* 91, no. 5 (December): 1369–401.

Acemoglu, Daron, Suresh Naidu, Pascual Restrepo, and James A. Robinson. 2018. "Democracy Does Cause Growth." *Journal of Political Economy*. Forthcoming.

Acemoglu, Daron, and James Robinson. 2012. *Why Nations Fail: The Origins of Power, Prosperity, and Poverty*. New York: Crown Business.

Achen, Christopher H., and Larry M. Bartels. 2016. *Democracy for Realists: Why Elections Do Not Produce Responsive Government*. Princeton: Princeton University Press.

Adelman, Jonatha R. 1985. *Revolution, Armies, ad War: A Political History*. Boulder: Lynne Reinner.

Ahmadpoor, Mohammad, and Benjamin F. Jones. 2017. "The Dual Frontier: Patented Innovations and Prior Scientific Advance." *Science* 357, no. 6351 (August 11): 583–87.

Albert, Eleanor, and Beina Xu. 2016. "China's Environmental Crisis." Council on Foreign Relations Backgrounder. January 18.

Albouy, David. 2012. "The Colonial Origins of Comparative Development: An Empirical Investigation: Comment." *American Economic Review* 102, no. 6 (October): 3059–76.

Alexander, Michelle. 2010. *The New Jim Crow: Mass Incarceration in the Age of Colorblindness.* New York: The New Press.

Alexeev, Michael, and Robert Conrad. 2009. "The Elusive Curse of Oil." *Review of Economics and Statistics* 91, no. 3: 586–98.

Alexeev, Michael V., and Clifford G. Gaddy. 1993. "Income Distribution in the USSR in the 1980s." *Review of Income and Wealth* 39, no. 1 (March): 23–36.

Allcott, Hunt, and Daniel Keniston. 2017. "Dutch Disease or Agglomeration? The Local Economic Effects of Natural Resource Booms in Modern America." NBER Working Paper No. 20508. National Bureau of Economic Research. June.

Allen, Kenneth, and Morgan Clemens. 2014. *The Recruitment, Education, and Training of PLA Navy Personnel.* Newport: U.S. Naval War College.

Allen, Robert C. 2009a. *The British Industrial Revolution in Global Perspective.* Cambridge: Cambridge University Press.

———. 2009b. *Farm to Factory: A Reinterpretation of the Soviet Industrial Revolution.* Princeton: Princeton University Press.

Allen, Robert C., Jean-Pascal Bassino, Debin Ma, Christine Moll-Murata, and Jan Luiten Van Zanden. 2011. "Wages, Prices, and Living Standards in China, 1738–1925: In Comparison with Europe, Japan, and India." *Economic History Review* 64, no. S1 (February): 8–38.

Allison, Graham. 2017. *Destined for War: Can America and China Escape Thucydides's Trap?* New York: Houghton Mifflin Harcourt.

Amaro, Silvia. 2017. "China's Debt Surpasses 300 Percent of GDP, IIF Says, Raising Doubts over Yellen's Crisis Remarks." *CNBC.* June 28.

Amsden, Alice H. 1989. *Asia's Next Giant: South Korea and Late Industrialization.* New York: Oxford University Press.

Anderlini, Jamil. 2013. "Chinese Industry: Ambitions in Excess." *Financial Times.* June 16.

Anderson, M. S. 2003. *The Ascendancy of Europe: 1815–1914.* 3rd ed. Harlow: Pearson Education.

Anderson, Noel. 2017. "Competitive Intervention and Its Consequences for Civil Wars." University of Toronto, Department of Political Science.

Andrew, Martin. 2009. "Revisiting the Lessons of Operation Allied Force." *Air Power Australia Analyses* 6, no. 4 (June).

Ang, Yuen Yuen. 2012. "Counting Cadres: A Comparative View of the Size of China's Public Employment." *China Quarterly* 211 (September): 676–96.

Ansar, Atif, Bent Flyvberg, Alexander Budzier, and Daniel Lunn. 2016. "Does Infrastructure Investment Lead to Economic Growth or Economic Fragility? Evidence from China." *Oxford Review of Economic Policy* 32, no. 3 (October): 360–90.

Aron, Leon. 2013. "The Political Economy of Russian Oil and Gas." American Enterprise Institute. May 29.

Arreguin-Toft, Ivan. 2001. "How the Weak Win Wars: A Theory of Asymmetric Conflict." *International Security* 26, no. 1 (summer): 93–128.

Art, Robert J. 1980. "To What Ends Military Power?" *International Security* 4, no. 4 (spring): 3–35.

Aslund, Anders, Ariel Cohen, Gary Kleiman, John Lee, Dan Mahaffee, Joseph S. Nye Jr., Daniel Pipes, Raymond Tanter, and Charles Wolf. 2012. "The Geopolitics of U.S. Energy Independence." *International Economy* 26, no. 3 (summer): 22–28.

Asoni, Andrea. 2008. "Protection of Property Rights and Growth as Political Equilibria." *Journal of Economic Surveys* 22, no. 5 (December): 953–87.

Auguste, Byron, Paul Kihn, and Matt Miller. 2010. *Closing the Talent Gap: Attracting and Retaining Top Third Graduates to a Career in Teaching*. New York: McKinsey.

Autor, David H., David Dorn, and Gordon H. Hanson. 2016. "The China Shock: Learning from Labor-Market Adjustment to Large Changes in Trade." *Annual Review of Economics* 8: 205–40.

Axe, David. 2013. "China's Overhyped Sub Threat." *War Is Boring*. June 13.

Babones, Salvatore. 2016. "How Weak Is China? The Real Story Behind the Economic Indicators." *Foreign Affairs*. January 31.

Bachrach, Peter, and Morton S. Baratz. 1962. "Two Faces of Power." *American Political Science Review* 56, no. 4 (December): 947–52.

Backes, Oliver. 2013. "The Traditional Friend: Russia-India Military-Technical Cooperation and Defense Procurement Ties Post-Dpp-2013." Center for Strategic and International Studies. October 28.

Bader, Jeffrey and Jonathan D. Pollack. 2017. "Time to Restrict the President's Power to Wage Nuclear War." *New York Times*. September 12.

Bafumi, Joseph, and Joseph M. Parent. 2012. "International Polarity and America's Polarization." *International Politics* 49, no. 1 (January): 1–35.

Bai, Chong-En, Chang-Tai Hsieh, and Zheng Michael Song. 2016. "The Long Shadow of a Fiscal Expansion." NBER Working Paper No. 22801. National Bureau of Economic Research. November.

Bairoch, Paul. 1976. "Europe's Gross National Product: 1800–1975." *Journal of European Economic History* 5, no. 2 (fall): 273–340.

———. 1982. "International Industrialization Levels from 1750 to 1980." *Journal of European Economic History* 11, no. 2 (fall): 269–333.

Balding, Christopher. 2016. "Further Questions About Chinese GDP Data." *Financial Times*. August 2.

Baldwin, David A. 1989. *Paradoxes of Power*. New York: Basil Blackwell.

———. 2016. *Power and International Relations*. Princeton: Princeton University Press.

Ball, Desmond, and Richard Tanter. 2015. *The Tools of Owatatsuni: Japan's Ocean Surveillance and Coastal Defence Capabilities*. Canberra: Australia National University Press.

Baltrusaitis, Daniel F. 2008. "Friends Indeed? Coalition Burden Sharing and the War in Iraq." Unpublished manuscript. Georgetown University.

Bank for International Settlements. 2017. "Total Credit to Non-Financial Sector, Adjusted for Breaks, for United States, Retrieved from Fred, Federal Reserve Bank of St. Louis." Basel, Switzerland.

Barbash, Fred. 2015. "Major Publisher Retracts 43 Scientific Papers Amid Wider Fake Peer-Review Scandal." *Washington Post*. March 27.

Barma, Naazneen, Ely Ratner, and Steven Weber. 2014. "Welcome to the World without the West." *National Interest*. November 12.

Barnhart, Michael. 1987. *Japan Prepares for Total War: The Search for Economic Security*. Ithaca: Cornell University Press.

Barnett, Michael, and Raymond Duvall. 2005. "Power in International Politics." *International Organization* 59, no. 1 (January): 39–75.

Barno, David, and Nora Bensahel. 2017. "The Growing Danger of a U.S. Nuclear First Strike on North Korea." *War on the Rocks*. October 10.

Barro, Robert, and Jong-Wha Lee. 2013. "A New Data Set of Educational Attainment in the World, 1950–2010." *Journal of Development Economics*. 104 (September): 184–98.

Barry, John. 2011. "America's Secret Libya War: U.S. Spent $1 Billion on Covert Ops Helping NATO." *Daily Beast*. August 30.

Bartels, Larry M. 2008. *Unequal Democracy: The Political Economy of the New Gilded Age*. Princeton: Princeton University Press.

Bateman, David A., Joshua D. Clinton, and John S. Lapinski. 2017. "A House Divided? Roll Calls, Polarization, and Policy Differences in the U.S. House, 1877–2011." *American Journal of Political Science*. 61, no. 3 (July): 698–714.

Baumol, William J. 1986. "Productivity Growth, Convergence, and Welfare: What the Long-Run Data Show." *American Economic Review* 76 (December): 1072–85.

Beardson, Timothy. 2013. *Stumbling Giant: The Threats to China's Future*. New Haven: Yale University Press.

Beaulieu, Emily, Gary W. Cox, and Sebastian Saiegh. 2012. "Sovereign Debt and Regime Type: Reconsidering the Democratic Advantage." *International Organization* 66, no. 4 (October): 709–38.

Becker, Sascha O., Erik Hornung, and Ludger Woessmann. 2011. "Education and Catch-up in the Industrial Revolution." *American Economic Journal: Macroeconomics* 3 (July): 92–126.

Beckley, Michael. 2010. "Economic Development and Military Effectiveness." *Journal of Strategic Studies* 33, no. 1 (February): 43–79.

———. 2011–12. "China's Century? Why America's Edge Will Endure." *International Security* 36, no. 3 (winter): 41–78.

———. 2015. "The Myth of Entangling Alliances: Reassessing the Security Risks of U.S. Defense Pacts." *International Security*. 39, no. 4 (spring): 7–48.

———. 2017. "The Emerging Military Balance in East Asia: How China's Neighbors Can Check Chinese Naval Expansion." *International Security*. 42, no. 2 (fall): 78–119.

———. 2018. "The Power of Nations: Measuring What Matters." *International Security*, forthcoming.

Beckley, Michael, Yusaku Horiuchi, and Jennifer M. Miller. 2017. "America's Role in the Making of Japan's Economic Miracle." *Journal of East Asian Studies* 17, no. 3 (November).

Belasco, Amy. 2014. "The Cost of Iraq, Afghanistan, and Other Global War on Terror Operations since 9/11." Congressional Research Service. December 8.

Beng, Ben Ho Wan. 2015. "The Chinese Submarine Threat." *Diplomat*. December 10.

Bennet, Bruce W., and Jennifer Lind. 2011. "The Collapse of North Korea: Military Missions and Requirements." *International Security* 36, no. 2 (fall): 84–119.

Bennett, Scott. 2017. "Coding Notes for Interstate/Enduring Data." Unpublished Manuscript, updated version. May 1.

Benson, Lt. Cmdr. Jeff W. 2014. "A New Era in Anti-Submarine Warfare." *USNI News*. August 27.

Bergen, Peter, Albert Ford, Alyssa Sims, and David Sterman. 2017. "Terrorism in America after 9/11." New America, International Security Program, accessed on August 8, 2017. https://www.newamerica.org/in-depth/terrorism-in-america/.

Bergsten, C. Fred, Charles Freeman, Nicholas R. Lardy, and Derek J. Mitchell. 2008. *China's Rise: Challenges and Opportunities*. Washington, DC: Peterson Institute for International Economics.

Berman, Ilan. 2013. *Implosion: The End of Russia and What It Means for America.* Washington, DC: Regnery.

———. 2015. "Paradise Lost in Crimea. How Russia Is Paying for the Annexation." *Foreign Affairs.* September 8.

———. 2017. "How Russian Rule Has Changed Crimea." *Foreign Affairs.* July 13.

Besley, Timothy, and Maitreesh Ghatak. 2010. "Property Rights and Economic Development." In *Handbook of Development Economics*, edited by Dani Rodrik and Mark Rosenzweig, chapter 68. New York: Elsevier.

Besley, Timothy, and Torsten Persson. 2011. *Pillars of Prosperity: The Political Economics of Development Clusters.* Princeton: Princeton University Press.

Bessen, James. 2016. "Lobbyists Are Behind the Rise in Corporate Profits." *Harvard Business Review.* May 26.

Betts, Richard K. 1995. *Military Readiness: Concepts, Choices, Consequences.* Washington, DC: Brookings Institution Press.

———. 2012. *American Force: Dangers, Delusions, and Dilemmas in National Security.* New York: Columbia University Press.

———. 2014. "Pick Your Battles: Ending America's Era of Permanent War." *Foreign Affairs* 93, no. 6 (November/December): 15–24.

Bialik, Carl. 2014. "The Challenge of Counting D-Day's Dead." *FiveThirtyEight.* June 6.

Biddle, Stephen. 1996. "Victory Misunderstood: What the Gulf War Tells Us About the Future of Conflict." *International Security* 21, no. 2 (fall): 139–79.

———. 2004. *Military Power: Explaining Victory and Defeat in Modern Battle.* Princeton: Princeton University Press.

Biddle, Stephen, and Ivan Oelrich. 2016. "Future Warfare in the Western Pacific: Chinese Antiaccess/Area Denial, U.S. Airsea Battle, and Command of the Commons in East Asia." *International Security* 41, no. 1 (summer): 7–48.

Birnbaum, Michael, and Thomas Gibbons-Neff. 2017. "NATO Allies Boost Defense Spending in the Wake of Trump Criticism." *Washington Post.* June 28.

Bitzinger, Richard A. 1994. "The Globalization of the Arms Industry: The Next Proliferation Challenge." *International Security* 19, no. 2 (autumn): 170–98.

Blank, Stephen. 2014. "Russia and Vietnam Team up to Balance China." *National Interest.* April 7.

Bland, Ben. 2017a. "China Rewrites History with New Censorship Drive." *Financial Times.* September 4.

———. 2017b. "Outcry as Latest Global Publisher Bows to Chinese Censors." *Financial Times.* November 1.

Blasko, Dennis J. 2012. *The Chinese Army Today: Tradition and Transformation for the 21st Century.* New ed. New York: Routledge.

———. 2015. "Ten Reasons Why China Will Have Trouble Fighting a Modern War." *War on the Rocks.* February 18.

Blasko, Dennis J., Chas W. Freeman, Stanley A. Horowitz, Evan S. Medeiros, and James C. Mulvenon. 2006. "Defense-Related Spending in China: A Preliminary

Analysis and Comparison with American Equivalents." United States–China Policy Foundation.

Blau, Max. 2017. "Stat Forecast: Opioids Could Kill Nearly 500,000 Americans in the Next Decade." *STAT.* June 27.

Blau, Francine D. and Christopher Mackie, eds. 2017. *The Economic and Fiscal Consequences of Immigration.* Washington, DC: National Academies Press.

Blinder, Alan S. 2017. "Almost Everything Is Wrong With the New Tax Law." *Wall Street Journal.* December 27.

Bloom, David E., David Canning, and Jaypee Sevilla. 2002. "Technological Diffusion, Conditional Convergence, and Economic Growth." NBER Working Paper No. 8713. National Bureau of Economic Research. January.

———. 2003. *The Demographic Dividend: A New Perspective on the Economic Consequences of Population Change.* Santa Monica, CA: RAND.

Bloomberg. 2015. "China Has a $1.2 Trillion Ponzi Finance Problem." November 19.

Boot, Max. 2017. "Donald Trump: A Modern Manchurian Candidate?" *New York Times.* January 11.

Bosker, Maarten, and Harry Garretsen. 2012. "Economic Geography and Economic Development in Sub-Saharan Africa." *World Bank Economic Review* 26, no. 1 (February): 1–43.

BCG. 2014. "The BCG Global Manufacturing Cost-Competitiveness Index." *BCG Perspectives.* August 19.

BP. 2017. *BP Statistical Review of World Energy 2017.* London: BP.

Bradley, Jennifer. 2015. "Increasing Uncertainty: The Dangers of Relying on Conventional Forces for Nuclear Deterrence." *Air and Space Power Journal* 29, no. 4 (July/August): 72–83.

Bradsher, Keith. 2013. "Next Made-in-China Boom: College Graduates." *New York Times.* January 16.

Brands, Hal. 2015. *The Limits of Offshore Balancing.* Carlisle, PA: U.S. Army War College.

———. 2016. *Making the Unipolar Moment: U.S. Foreign Policy and the Rise of the Post-Cold War Order.* Ithaca: Cornell University Press.

———. 2018. *American Grand Strategy in the Age of Trump.* Washington, DC: Brookings Institution Press.

Brendon, Piers. 2010. *The Decline and Fall of the British Empire, 1781-1997.* New York: Vintage.

British Petroleum (BP). 2016. "BP Energy Outlook 2016 Edition: Outlook to 2035."

Broadberry, Stephen, Hanhui Guan, and David Daokui Li. 2014. "China, Europe, and the Great Divergence: A Study in Historical National Accounting, 980–1850." Unpublished manuscript. London School of Economics.

Brooke, Henry St. George, and Jordan Gans-Morse. 2016. "Putin's Crackdown on Mortality." *Problems of Post-Communism* 63, no. 1: 1–15.

Brooks, Sarah M., and Marcus J. Kurtz. 2016. "Oil and Democracy: Endogenous Natural Resources and the Political "Resource Curse.'" *International Organization* 70, no. 2 (spring): 279–311.

Brooks, Stephen G., and William C. Wohlforth. 2000–2001. "Power, Globalization, and the End of the Cold War: Reevaluating a Landmark Case for Ideas." *International Security* 25, no. 3 (winter): 5–53.

———. 2008. *World Out of Balance: International Relations and the Challenge of American Primacy*. Princeton: Princeton University Press.

———. 2012/13. "Don't Come Home, America: The Case against Retrenchment." *International Security* 37, no. 3 (Winter): 7–51.

———. 2015–16. "The Rise and Fall of the Great Powers in the Twenty-First Century: China's Rise and the Fate of America's Global Position." *International Security* 40, no. 3 (winter): 7–53.

———. 2016. *America Abroad: The United States' Global Role in the 21st Century*. New York: Oxford University Press.

Browne, Andrew 2017. "China Uses "Digital Leninism" to Manage Economy and Monitor Citizens." *Wall Street Journal*. October 17.

Brunnschweiler, Christa N. 2007. "Cursing the Blessings? Natural Resource Abundance, Institutions, and Economic Growth." *World Development* 36, no. 3: 399–419.

Burgess, Simon. 2016. "Human Capital and Education: The State of the Art in the Economics of Education." IZA Discussion Paper 9885, April.

Burroughs, Peter. 1994. "An Unreformed Army? 1815–1868." In *The Oxford History of the British Army*, edited by David Chandler and Ian Beckett, chapter 8. Oxford: Oxford University Press.

Business Week. 2006. "Science Friction." May 29.

Cai, Hongbin, and Daniel Treisman. 2006. "Did Government Decentralization Cause China's Economic Miracle?" *World Politics* 58, no. 4 (July): 505–35.

Caiazzo, Fabio, Akshay Ashok, Ian A. Waitz, Steve H. L. Yim, and Steven R. H. Barrett. 2013. "Air Pollution and Early Deaths in the United States, Part I: Quantifying the Impact of Major Sectors in 2005." *Atmospheric Environment* 79 (November): 198–208.

Canipe, Chris. 2017. "The High Cost of Health Care in America." *Wall Street Journal*. March 15.

Cappelli, Peter H. 2015. "Skill Gaps, Skill Shortages, and Skill Mismatches: Evidence and Arguments for the United States." *ILR Review* 68, no. 2: 251–90.

Carlson, Capt. Christopher P. (ret.) 2015. "Inside the Design of China's Yuan-Class Submarine." *USNI News*, August 31.

Carpenter, Ted Galen. 2008. *Smart Power: Toward a Prudent Foreign Policy for America*. Washington, DC: CATO.

Carstensen, Kai, and Erich Gundlach. 2006. "The Primacy of Institutions Reconsidered: Direct Income Effects of Malaria Prevalence." *World Bank Economic Review* 20, no. 3: 309–39.

Carter, Susan B., Richard Sutch, Scott Sigmund Gartner, Michael R. Haines, Alan L. Olmstead, and Gavin Wright, eds. 2006. *Historical Statistics of the United States*. Vol. E. Cambridge: Cambridge University Press.

Case, Anne, and Angus Deaton. 2015. "Rising Morbidity and Mortality among White Non-Hispanic Americans in the 21st Century." *Proceedings of the National Academy of Sciences of the United States of America*. 112, no. 49: 15078–83.

Casetti, Emilio. 2003. "Power Shifts and Economic Development: When Will China Overtake the USA?" *Journal of Peace Research* 40, no. 6 (November): 661–75.

Centeno, Miguel A. 2002. *Blood and Debt: War and Nation-State in Latin America*. Princeton: Princeton University Press.

Chan, Sewell. 2016. "Norway and China Restore Ties 6 Years after Nobel Prize Dispute." *New York Times*. December 19.

Chandra, Kanchan. 2016. "Authoritarian India: The State of the World's Largest Democracy." *Foreign Affairs*. June 16.

Chase, Michael S., Jeffrey Engstrom, Tai Ming Cheung, Kristen A. Gunness, Scott Warren Harold, Susan Puska, and Samuel P. Berkowitz. 2015. *China's Incomplete Military Transformation: Assessing the Weaknesses of the People's Liberation Army (PLA)*. Santa Monica, CA: RAND.

Chayes, Sarah. 2017. "Kleptocracy in America: Corruption is Reshaping Governments Everywhere." *Foreign Affairs* 96, no. 5 (September/October): 142-150.

Chen, Jian. 1994. *China's Road to the Korean War*. New York: Columbia University Press.

———. 2001. *Mao's China and the Cold War*. Chapel Hill: University of North Carolina Press.

Chen, Li-Kai, Mona Mourshed, and Andrew Grant. 2013. "The $250 Billion Question: Can China Close the Skills Gap?" *McKinsey Global Institute*. May.

Chen, Stephen. 2017. "Top Chinese Researcher's Move to U.S. Sparks Soul-Searching in China." *South China Morning Post*. May 9.

Chen, Xi. 2013. "The Rising Cost of Stability." *Journal of Democracy* 24, no. 1 (January): 57–64.

Chen, Yugang. 2009. "Jinrong weiji, Meiguo shuailuo yu guoji guanxi geju bianpinghua." *Shijie Jingji yu Zhengzhi* 5: 28–34.

Chen, Zhiwu. 2015. "China's Dangerous Debt: Why the Economy Could Be Headed for Trouble." *Foreign Affairs* 94, no. 3 (May/June): 13–18.

Chen, Zhengming, Richard Peto, Maigeng Zhou, Andri Iona, Margaret Smith, Ling Yang, Yu Guo et al. 2015. "Contrasting Male and Female Trends in Tobacco-Attributed Mortality in China: Evidence from Successive Nationwide Prospective Cohort Studies." *Lancet* 386, no. 10002 (October): 1447–56.

Chestnut, Sheena, and Alastair Iain Johnston. 2009. "Is China Rising?" In *Global Giant: Is China Changing the Rules of the Game?* edited by Eva Paus, Penelope B. Prime, and Jon Western, chapter 9. New York: Palgrave.

Chetty, Raj, John N. Friedman, and Jonah E. Rockoff. 2014. "Measuring the Impacts of Teachers II: Teacher Value-Added and Student Outcomes in Adulthood." *American Economic Review* 104, no. 9 (September): 2633–79.

Chetty, Raj, David B. Grusky, Maximilian Hell, Nathaniel Hendren, Robert Manduca, and Jimmy Narang. 2017. "The Fading American Dream: Trends in Absolute Income Mobility since 1940." *Science* 356 (April 28): 398–406.

Chetty, Raj, Nathaniel Hendren, Patrick Kline, Emmanuel Saez, and Nicholas Turner. 2014. "Is the United States Still a Land of Opportunity? Recent Trends in Intergenerational Mobility." *American Economic Review: Papers and Proceedings* 104, no. 5 (May): 141–47.

Chi, Guanghua, Yu Liu, Zhengwei Wu, and Haishan Wu. 2015. "'Ghost Cities' Analysis Based on Positioning Data in China." Big Data Lab, Baidu Research.

Chi, Hsi-sheng. 1992. "The Military Dimension, 1942–1945." In *China's Bitter Victory: War with Japan, 1937–45*, edited by James C. Hsiung and Steven I. Levine, chapter 7. New York: Routledge.

Chin, Josh, and Brian Spegele. 2014. "China Details Vast Extent of Soil Pollution." *Wall Street Journal*. April 17.

Chin, Josh, and Gillian Wong. 2016. "China's New Tool for Social Control: A Credit Rating for Everything." *Wall Street Journal*. November 28.

China Bureau of Statistics. 2016. *Zhongguo Keji Tongji Nianjian*. Beijing.

China, People's Republic of, Ministry of Environmental Protection. 2015. "MEP Releases the 2014 Report on the State of Environment in China." June 4.

China, State Council of the People's Republic of. 2015. "Made in China 2025." Beijing.

Cho, Renee. 2011. "How China Is Dealing with Its Water Crisis." Earth Institute, Columbia University. May 5.

Chollet, Derek, Eric S. Edelman, Michele Flournoy, Stephen J. Hadley, Martin S. Indyk, Bruce Jones, Robert Kagan, Kristen Silverberg, Jake Sullivan, and Thomas Wright. 2017. *Building Situations of Strength: A National Security Strategy for the United States*. Washington, DC: Brookings Institution.

Christensen, Thomas J. 1996. *Useful Adversaries: Grand Strategy, Domestic Mobilization, and Sino-American Conflict, 1947–1958*. Princeton: Princeton University Press.

———. 2006. "Windows and War: Changes in the International System and China's Decision to Use Force." In *New Approaches to China's Foreign Relations: Essays in Honor of Allen S. Witting*, edited by Alastair Iain Johnston and Robert Ross, chapter 3. Stanford: Stanford University Press.

———. 2012. "The Meaning of the Nuclear Evolution: China's Strategic Modernization and U.S.-China Security Relations." *Journal of Strategic Studies* 35, no. 4 (August): 447–87.

———. 2015. *The China Challenge: Shaping the Choices of a Rising Power*. New York: Norton.

Chu, Shulong. 2016. "Dui guanyu meiguo de ji ge zhongda wenti de renshi yu panduan." *Xiandai Guoji Guanxi* 7: 7–12.

Citigroup Global Markets. 2011. "Global Growth Generators: Moving Beyond 'Emerging Markets' and 'BRIC.'" Global Economics View. London. February 21.

Clague, Christopher, Philip Keefer, Stephen Knack, and Mancur Olson. 1999. "Contract-Intensive Money: Contract Enforcement, Property Rights, and Economic Performance." *Journal of Economic Growth* 4, no. 2 (June): 185–211.

Clark, Bryan, and Mark Gunzinger. 2015. *Winning the Air Waves: Regaining America's Dominance in the Electromagnetic Spectrum*. Washington, DC: Center for Strategic and Budgetary Assessments.

Clemens, Morgan, Gabriel Collins, and Kristen Gunness. 2015. "The Type 054/054a Frigate Series: China's Most Produced and Deployed Large Modern Surface Combatant." *China Signpost*. August 2.

Cliff, Roger. 2015. *China's Military Power: Assessing Current and Future Capabilities*. Cambridge: Cambridge University Press.

Cline, Ray S. 1977. *World Power Assessment: A Calculus of Strategic Drift*. Boulder: Westview Press.

Cohen, Eliot A. 2016. *The Big Stick: The Limits of Soft Power and the Necessity of Military Force*. New York: Basic Books.

Cohen, Wesley M., and Daniel A. Levinthal. 1990. "Absorptive Capacity: A New Perspective on Learning and Innovation." *Administrative Science Quarterly* 35, no. 1 (March): 128–52.

Colby, Elbridge, and Jonathan Solomon. 2015–16. "Facing Russia: Conventional Defence and Deterrence in Europe." *Survival* 57, no. 6 (December/January): 21–50.

Collins, Gabriel. 2015. "China Peak Oil: 2015 Is the Year." *Diplomat*. July 7.

———. 2017. *Russia's Use of the "Energy Weapon" in Europe*. Issue Brief. Baker Institute for Public Policy. July 18.

Conference Board. 2017. "Total Economy Database."

Conley, Tom. 2013. "China's Foreign Exchange Reserves and Debt." *Big P Political Economy*. October 15.

Cook, Lynn, and Bradley Olson. 2016. "Two Years into Oil Slump, U.S. Shale Firms Are Ready to Pump More." *Wall Street Journal*. September 27.

Cote, Owen R., Jr. 2011. "Assessing the Undersea Balance between the United States and China." In *Competitive Strategies for the 21st Century*, edited by Thomas G. Mahnken, chapter 11. Stanford: Stanford University Press.

Council on Foreign Relations. 2017. "Cyber Operations Tracker." Accessed on December 24, 2017 at https://www.cfr.org/interactive/cyber-operations.

Coyle, Diane. 2014. *GDP: A Brief but Affectionate History*. Princeton: Princeton University Press.

Crane, Keith. 2015. "Smog Solutions: A Fix to China's Pollution Problem Is Expensive but Worth It." *U.S. News and World Report*. January 17.

Crawcour, E. Sydney. 1997. "Industrialization and Technological Change, 1885–1920." In *The Economic Emergence of Modern Japan*, edited by Kozo Yamamura, chapter 2. Cambridge: Cambridge University Press.

Crawford, Neta C. 2014. "U.S. Costs of Wars through 2014: $4.4 Trillion and Counting." Cost of Wars Project. June 25.

Credit Suisse. 2017. *Global Wealth Report 2017*. Zurich: Credit Suisse.

Crisher, Brian Benjamin, and Mark Souva. 2014. "Power at Sea: A Naval Power Dataset, 1865–2011." *International Interactions* 40, no. 4: 602–29.

Crowley, James B. 1966. *Japan's Quest for Autonomy: National Security and Foreign Policy, 1930–1938*. Princeton: Princeton University Press.

———. 1996. *Japan's Quest for Autonomy; National Security and Foreign Policy, 1930–1938*. Princeton: Princeton University Press.

Cui, Liru. 2010. "Quanqiu shidai yu duoji shijie." *Xiandai Guoji Guanxi*. 1: 1–4.

———. 2016. "Guoji geju yanbian yu duo ji shidai de zhixu jaingou (shang)." *Shijie Jingji yu Zhengzhi*. 1: 1–18.

Cui, Carolyn, and Lingling Wei. 2016. "Beneath a Quieter Yuan, Fears over China Are Rising." *Wall Street Journal*. August 29.

Daalder, Ivo. 2017. "Responding to Russia's Resurgence: Not Quiet on the Eastern Front." *Foreign Affairs*. 96, no. 6 (November/December): 30–38.

Dahl, Robert A. 1957. "The Concept of Power." *Behavioral Science* 2 (July): 201–15.

———. 1961. *Who Governs? Democracy and Power in an American City*. New Haven: Yale University Press.

Dan, He, and Yang Yao. 2013. "Brain Drain May Be World's Worst." *China Daily*. July 7.

Das, Sanghamitra. 1987. "Externalities and Technology Transfer through Multinational Corporations." *Journal of International Economics* 22, no. 1–2 (February): 171–82.

Davis, Kingsley. 1954. "The Demographic Foundations of National Power." In *Freedom and Control in Modern Societies*, edited by Monroe Berger, Theodore Abel, and Charles H. Page, 206–42. New York: Van Nostrand.

Dawisha, Karen. 2014. *Putin's Kleptocracy: Who Owns Russia?* New York: Simon and Schuster.

Defense Intelligence Agency. 2017. *Russia Military Power: Building a Military to Support Great Power Aspirations.* Washington, DC: Defense Intelligence Agency.

Deloitte. 2012. "Reflections on the Development of the Private Education Industry in China." New York.

———. 2015. "2015 Healthcare Outlook: China." New York.

———. 2016. "2016 Global Manufacturing Competitiveness Index."

Demick, Barbara. 2017. "Escalating Tension Has Experts Simulating a New Korean War, and the Scenarios Are Sobering." *Los Angeles Times.* September 25.

Denyer, Simonn. 2017. "Chinese Universities Scramble to Open Centers to Study Xi Jinping Thought." *Washington Post.* November 1.

De Luce, Dan. 2015. "The U.S. Navy Wants to Show China Who's Boss." *Foreign Policy.* December 14.

Den Boer, Andrea, and Valerie M. Hudson. 2014. "The Security Risks of China's Abnormal Demographics." *Washington Post.* April 30.

Denmark, Abraham M. 2018. "The Myth of the Limited Strike on North Korea." *Foreign Affairs.* January 9.

Desch, Michael C. 1989. "The Keys That Lock up the World: Identifying American Interests in the Periphery." *International Security* 14, no. 1 (summer): 86–121.

———. 1996. "War and Strong States, Peace and Weak States?" *International Organization* 50, no. 2 (spring): 237–68.

Dettrey, Bryan J., and James E. Campbell. 2013. "Has Growing Income Inequality Polarized the American Electorate? Class, Party, and Ideological Polarization." *Social Science* 94, no. 4 (December): 1062–83.

DeVries, Jan, and Frederick Van der Ploeg. 1997. *The First Modern Economy: Success, Failure, and Perseverance of the Dutch Economy, 1500–1815.* Cambridge: Cambridge University Press.

Dobbs, Richard, Susan Lund, Jonathan Woetzel, and Mina Mutafchieva. 2015. "Debt and (Not Much) Deleveraging." McKinsey Global Institute. February.

Dolven, Ben, Mark E. Manyin, and Shirley A. Kan. 2014. *Maritime Territorial Disputes in East Asia: Issues for Congress.* Washington, DC: Congressional Research Service.

Dorell, Oren. 2017. "Alleged Russian Political Meddling Documented in 27 Countries Since 2004." *USA Today.* September 7.

Doughty, Martin. 1982. *Merchant Shipping and War: A Study in Defence Planning in Twentieth-Century Britain.* London: Royal Historical Society.

Downes, Alexander B., and Lindsey A. O'Rourke. 2016. "You Can't Always Get What You Want: Why Foreign-Imposed Regime Change Seldom Improves Interstate Relations." *International Security* 41, no. 2 (Fall): 43–89.

Drezner, Daniel. 2001. "State Structure, Technological Leadership and the Maintenance of Hegemony." *Review of International Studies.* 27, no. 1 (January): 3–25.

———. 2014. *The System Worked: How the World Stopped Another Great Depression.* Oxford: Oxford University Press.

Drutman, Lee. 2017. "Political Divisions in 2016 and Beyond." Democracy Fund Voter Study Group.

Du, Jun, and Tomasz Mickiewicz. 2015. "Subsidies, Rent Seeking, and Performance: Being Young, Small, or Private in China." *Journal of Business Venturing* 31, no. 1 (January): 22–38.

Dutton, Peter, Andrew S. Erickson, and Ryan Martinson, eds. 2014. *China's near Seas Combat Capabilities.* Newport, RI: U.S. Naval War College.

Duus, Peter. 1976. *The Rise of Modern Japan*. Boston: Houghton Mifflin.

Dyer, Geoff. 2014. "U.S. Spreads Military Presence across Asia." *Financial Times*. April 28.

Easterly, William, and Stanley Fischer. 1995. "The Soviet Economic Decline." *World Bank Economic Review* 9, no. 3 (September): 347–71.

Easton, Ian. 2014a. *Able Archers: Taiwan Defense Strategy in an Age of Precision Strike*. Arlington: Project 2049 Institute.

———. 2014b. "China's Deceptively Weak (and Dangerous) Military." *Diplomat*. January 31.

Easton, Ian, and Randall Schriver. 2014. *Standing Watch: Taiwan and Maritime Domain Awareness in the Western Pacific*. Arlington: Project 2049 Institute.

Eberstadt, Nicholas. 2011. "The Dying Bear: Russia's Demographic Disaster." *Foreign Affairs* 90, no. 6 (November/December): 95–108.

Eckstein, Megan. 2016. "Navy: Future Undersea Warfare Will Have Longer Reach, Operate with Network of Unmanned Vehicles." *USNI News*. March 24.

The Economist. 2012a. "The Dragon's New Teeth." April 7.

———. 2012b. "Social Security with Chinese Characteristics." April 11.

———. 2013a. "A Bay of Pigs Moment." March 12.

———. 2013b. "Age Shall Weary Them." May 11.

———. 2013c. "Looks Good on Paper." September 28.

———. 2013d. "Desperate Measures." October 12.

———. 2013e. "All Dried Up." October 12.

———. 2014a. "Spreading the Net." August 9.

———. 2014b. "A Chechnya in the Making." August 9.

———. 2014c. "What's Gone Wrong with Russia's Economy." December 16.

———. 2015a. ""China's Inefficient Agricultural System." May 21.

———. 2015b. "A Better Lifeline." May 23.

———. 2016a. "The March of the Zombies." February 27.

———. 2016b. "Too Much of a Good Thing." March 26.

———. 2016c. "Beware the Cult of Xi." April 2.

———. 2016f. "Crony Capitalism around the World." May 5.

———. 2016g. "Big but Brittle." May 7.

———. 2016h. "The Coming Debt Bust." May 7.

———. 2016i. "Breaking Bad." May 7.

———. 2016j. "Dropping the Scales." May 21.

———. 2016k. "The Class Ceiling." June 4.

———. 2016l. "Two Stumbles Forward, One Back." June 25.

———. 2016m. "Coming and Going." October 1.

———. 2016n. "Milk without the Cow." October 22.

———. 2017a. "Jail Break." *Economist*, May 27.

———. 2017b. "The Algorithm Kingdom." July 15.

———. 2017d. "Whack-a-Passenger." April 22.

———. 2017e. "The Belt-and-Road Express." May 4.

———. 2017f. "Boozing." August 17.

———. 2017g. "A Tsar Is Born." October 26.

———. 2017h. "At the Sharp End." December 14.

———. 2017i. "The Subtleties of Soft Power." May 23.

Economist Intelligence Unit. 2016. "Navigating through China's Evolving Health-care Market: Healthcare 2020." London.

Economy, Elizabeth C. 2014. "China's Imperial President: Xi Jinping Tightens His Grip." *Foreign Affairs* 93, no. 6 (November/December): 80–91.

Edelstein, David M. 2008. *Occupational Hazards: Success and Failure in Military Occupation*. Ithaca: Cornell University Press.

Eichengreen, Barry. 2012. *Exorbitant Privilege: The Rise and Fall of the Dollar and the Future of the International Monetary System*. Reprint ed. Oxford: Oxford University Press.

Eilstrup-Sangiovanni, Mette. 2014. "Europe's Defence Dilemma." *The International Spectator* 49, no. 2 (June): 83–116.

Election Study Center. 2017. "Taiwanese/Chinese Identification Trend Distribution." National Chengchi University.

Emerson, Sarah A., and Andrew C. Winner. 2014. "The Myth of Petroleum Independence and Foreign Policy Isolation." *Washington Quarterly* 37, no. 1 (spring): 21–34.

Emmott, Bill. 2017. *The Fate of the West: The Battle to Save the World's Most Successful Political Ideas*. London: Economist Books.

Emran, M. Shahe, and Zhaoyang Hou. 2013. "Access to Markets and Rural Poverty: Evidence from Household Consumption in China." *Review of Economics and Statistics* 95, no. 2 (May): 682–97.

Enright, Michael J. 2016. *Developing China: The Remarkable Impact of Foreign Direct Investment*. New York: Routledge.

Entous, Adam, Ellen Nakashima, and Greg Jaffe. 2017. "Kremlin Trolls Burned Across Internet as Washington Debated Options." *Washington Post*. December 25.

Erickson, Andrew S. 2016. "How Does China's First Aircraft Carrier Stack Up?" China Power Project, Center for Strategic and International Studies.

Erickson, Andrew S., Lyle J. Goldstein, and William S. Murray. 2009. *Chinese Mine Warfare: A PLA Navy "Assassin's Mace" Capability*. Newport, RI: U.S. Naval War College.

Erickson, Andrew S., and Conor M. Kennedy. 2016. "China's Maritime Militia: What It Is and How to Deal with It." *Foreign Affairs*. June 23.

European Chamber of Commerce in China. 2016. *Overcapacity in China: An Impediment to the Party's Reform Agenda*. Beijing.

Evans, Peter. 1995. *Embedded Autonomy: States and Industrial Transformation*. Princeton: Princeton University Press.

Fajgelbaum, Pablo D., and Amit K. Khandelwal. 2016. "Measuring the Unequal Gains from Trade." *Quarterly Journal of Economics* 131, no. 3 (August): 1113–80.

Fan, Wenxin, Natasha Khan, and Liza Lin. 2017. "China Snares Innocent and Guilty Alike to Build World's Biggest DNA Database." *Wall Street Journal*. December 26.

Fannell, James A., and Scott Cheney-Peters. 2017. "Defending against a Chinese Navy of 500 Ships." *Wall Street Journal*. January 19.

Farchy, Jack. 2014. "Russia Oil: Between a Rock and a Hard Place." *Financial Times*. October 29.

Farrell, Diana, and Andrew Grant. 2005. "Addressing China's Looming Talent Shortage." McKinsey Global Institute, October.

Feigenbaum, Evan. 2017a. "Is Coercion the New Normal in China's Economic Statecraft?" *Marco Polo.* July 25.

———. 2017b. "China and the World: Dealing with a Reluctant Power." *Foreign Affairs* 96, 1 (January–February): 33–40.

Feng, Yujun. 2017. "Guoji xingshi xin bianhua yu Zhongguo de zhanlüe xuanze." *Xiandai Guoji Guanxi.* 3: 9–15.

Feng, Xunan, Anders C. Johansson, and Tianyu Zhang. 2015. "Mixing Business with Politics: Political Participation by Entrepreneurs in China." *Journal of Banking and Finance* 59: 220–35.

Fensom, Anthony. 2014. "China: The Next Shale-Gas Superpower?" *National Interest.* October 9.

Fernihough, Alan, and Kevin Hjortshøj O'Rourke. 2014. "Coal and the European Industrial Revolution." NBER Working Paper No. 19802. National Bureau of Economic Research. January.

Ferrara, Mark S. 2015. *Palace of Ashes: China and the Decline of American Higher Education.* Baltimore: Johns Hopkins University Press.

Feurenwerker, Albert. 1969. *The Chinese Economy, 1870–1949.* Ann Arbor: University of Michigan Press.

Fewsmith, Joseph. 2015. "Domestic Drivers of China's Future Military Modernization." In *The Chinese People's Liberation Army in 2025,* edited by Roy Kamphausen and David Lai, chapter 3. Carlisle, PA: Strategic Studies Institute.

Fiammenghi, Davide. 2011. "The Security Curve and the Structure of International Politics: A Neorealist Synthesis." *International Security* 35, no. 4 (Spring): 126–54.

Findlay, Ronald. 1978. "Relative Backwardness, Direct Foreign Investment, and the Transfer of Technology: A Simple Dynamic Model." *Quarterly Journal of Economics* 92, no. 1 (February): 1–16.

Fiorina, Morris P., and Samuel J. Abrams. 2012. *Disconnect: The Breakdown of Representation in American Politics.* Kindle ed. Norman: University of Oklahoma Press.

Firth, Noel E., and James H. Noren. 1998. *Soviet Defense Spending: A History of CIA Estimates, 1950–1990.* Houston: Texas A&M University Press.

Fischetti, Mark. 2012. "Which Nations Consume the Most Water?" *Scientific American.* June 1.

Fisher, Max. 2015. "China's Authoritarianism Is Dooming Its Economy." *Vox.* July 9.

Fisher, Richard D. 2016. "Vietnamese Military Trains Deployment of Bastion-P Coastal Defence System." *Jane's Defence Weekly.* August 16.

Flath, David. 2014. *The Japanese Economy.* Oxford: Oxford University Press.

Flintoff, Corey. 2012. "Where Does America Get Its Oil? You May Be Surprised." *NPR.* April 12.

Forsythe, Michael. 2015. "Billionaire Lawmakers Ensure the Rich Are Represented in China's Legislature." *New York Times.* March 2.

Frank, Thomas. 2017. "Civil Engineers Say Fixing Infrastructure Will Take $4.6 Trillion." *CNN.* March 9.

Fraumeni, Barbara M. 2015. "Choosing a Human Capital Measure: Educational Attainment Gaps and Rankings." NBER Working Paper No. 21283. National Bureau of Economic Research.

Fravel, M. Taylor. 2007. "Securing Borders: China's Doctrine and Force Structure for Frontier Defense." *Journal of Strategic Studies* 30, no. 4 (August): 705–37.

———. 2008. *Strong Borders, Secure Nation: Cooperation and Conflict in China's Territorial Disputes.* Princeton: Princeton University Press.

Freedom House 2017. "Freedom of the Press, 2017." www.freedomhouse.org.

Freeman, Carla P. 2018. "New Strategies for an Old Rivalry? China-Russia Relations in Central Asia after the Energy Boom." *Pacific Review* 31, no. 2 (March): 1–20.

Friedberg, Aaron L. 2000. *In the Shadow of the Garrison State: America's Anti-Statism and Its Cold War Grand Strategy.* Princeton: Princeton University Press.

———. 2012. *A Contest for Supremacy: China, America, and the Struggle for Mastery in Asia.* New York: Norton.

Friedman, Uri. 2017. "Can Trump Make a Deal with North Korea?" *Atlantic.* August 17.

Fruhling, Stephan, and Guillaume Lasconjarias. 2016. "NATO, A2/Ad, and the Kaliningrad Challenge." *Survival* 58, no. 2 (April/May): 95–116.

Frye, Timothy. 2004. "Credible Commitment and Property Rights: Evidence from Russia." *American Political Science Review* 98, no. 3 (August): 453–66.

Fukuyama, Francis. 1992. *The End of History and the Last Man.* New York: Macmillan.

———. 2012. *The Origins of Political Order: From Prehuman Times to the French Revolution.* New York: Farrar, Straus and Giroux.

———. 2013. "The Decay of American Political Institutions." *The American Interest* 9, no. 3 (January/February): 6–19.

———. 2015. *Political Order and Political Decay: From the Industrial Revolution to the Globalization of Democracy.* New York: Farrar, Straus and Giroux.

Fuller, William C. 1998. *Strategy and Power in Russia, 1600–1914.* New York: Free Press.

Furman, Jason. 2016. "The Truth about American Unemployment." *Foreign Affairs* 95, no. 4 (July/August): 127–38.

Gady, Franz-Stefan. 2016. "South Korea Launches First Indonesian Stealth Submarine." *Diplomat.* March 29.

———. 2017. "U.S. Navy Tests New Long-Range Anti-Ship Missile." *Diplomat.* April 6.

Gaidar, Yegor. 2007. *Collapse of an Empire: Lessons for Modern Russia.* Washington, DC: Brookings Institution Press.

Gale, Fred, James Hansen, and Michael Jewison. 2015. "China's Growing Demand for Agricultural Imports." U.S. Department of Agriculture, Economic Information Bulletin No. 136. February.

Gallup, John Luke, Jeffery D. Sachs, and Andrew D. Mellinger. 1999. "Geography and Economic Development." *International Regional Science Review* 22, no. 2 (August): 179–232.

Ganguly, Sumit, and William R. Thompson. 2017. *Ascending India and Its State Capacity: Extraction, Violence, and Legitimacy.* Kindle ed. New Haven: Yale University Press.

Garnaut, John. 2012. "Rotting from Within: Investigating the Massive Corruption of the Chinese Military." *Foreign Policy.* April 16.

Gavin, Francis. 2010. "Same as It Ever Was: Nuclear Alarmism, Proliferation, and the Cold War." *International Security* 34, no. 3 (winter): 7–37.

————. 2015. "Strategies of Inhibition: U.S. Grand Strategy, the Nuclear Revolution, and Nonproliferation." *International Security* 40, no. 1 (summer): 9–46.

Gartzke, Erik. 2007. "The Capitalist Peace." *American Journal of Political Science* 51, no. 1 (January): 166–91.

Gehl, Katherine M., and Michael E. Porter. 2017. *Why Competition in the Politics Industry Is Failing America: A Strategy for Reinvigorating Our Democracy.* Cambridge: Harvard Business School.

Gelpi, Christopher, Peter D. Feaver, and Jason Reifler. 2009. *Paying the Human Costs of War: American Public Opinion and Casualties in Military Conflicts.* Princeton: Princeton University Press.

Gerschenkron, Alexander. 1962. *Economic Backwardness in Historical Perspective.* Cambridge: Harvard University Press.

Gholz, Eugene. 2009. "Threats to Oil Flows through the Strait of Hormuz." LBJ School of Public Affairs Hormuz Working Group. Austin. December.

————. 2014. *Rare Earth Elements and National Security.* Energy Report. Council on Foreign Relations. October.

————. 2016. "No Man's Sea: Implications for Strategy and Theory." Paper presented at the annual meeting of the International Studies Association. Atlanta. March 16–19.

Gholz, Eugene, Daryl G. Press, and Harvey M. Sapolsky. 1997. "Come Home, America: The Strategy of Restraint in the Face of Temptation." *International Security* 21, no. 4 (spring): 5–48.

Ghose, Bishwajit. 2014. "Food Security and Food Self-Sufficiency in China: From Past to 2050." *Food and Energy Security* 3, no. 2 (December): 86–95.

Gibbons-Neff, Thomas. 2016. "Navy Ships and Submarines to Carry New Anti-Ship Tomahawk Missile, Report Says." *Washington Post.* February 18.

Gilboy, George J. 2004. "The Myth behind China's Miracle." *Foreign Affairs* 83, no. 4: 33–48.

Gilboy, George J., and Eric Heginbotham. 2012. *Chinese and Indian Strategic Behavior: Growing Power and Alarm.* Cambridge: Cambridge University Press.

Gilens, Martin. 2014. *Affluence and Influence: Economic Inequality and Political Power in America.* Princeton: Princeton University Press.

Gilens, Martin, and Benjamin I. Page. 2014. "Testing Theories of American Politics: Elites, Interest Groups, and Average Citizens." *Perspectives on Politics* 12, no. 3 (September): 564–81.

Gilli, Andrea, and Mauro Gilli. 2018. "Military-Technological Superiority, Systems Integration and the Challenges of Imitation, Reverse Engineering, and Cyber-Espionage." *International Security.* Forthcoming.

Gilpin, Robert. 1975. *U.S. Power and the Multinational Corporation: The Political Economy of Foreign Direct Investment.* New York: Basic Books.

————. 1981. *War and Change in World Politics.* Cambridge: Cambridge University Press.

Glaeser, Edward L., Rafael La Porta, Florencio Lopez de Silanes, and Andrei Shleifer. 2004. "Do Institutions Cause Growth?" *Journal of Economic Growth* 9, no. 3: 271–303.

Glaser, Charles L. 2011. "Why Unipolarity Doesn't Matter (Much)." *Cambridge Review of International Affairs* 24, no. 2 (June): 135–47.

Glaser, Charles L., and Rosemary A. Kelanic. 2017. "Getting Out of the Gulf." *Foreign Affairs* 96, no. 1 (January/February): 122–31.

Global Entrepreneurship Monitor. 2017. Boston, MA.

Glosny, Michael A. 2004. "Strangulation from the Sea? A PRC Submarine Blockade of Taiwan." *International Security* 28, no. 4 (spring): 125–60.

Goh, Brenda. 2015. "Lovely Airport, Where Are the Planes? China's White Elephants Emerge." *Reuters.* April 10.

Goldin, Claudia, and Lawrence F. Katz. 2010. *The Race between Education and Technology.* Cambridge: Harvard University Press.

Goldsmith, Raymond W. 1961. "The Economic Growth of Tsarist Russia, 1860–1913." *Economic Development and Cultural Change* 9, no. 3 (April): 441–75.

Goldstein, Avery. 2013. "First Things First: The Pressing Danger of Crisis Instability in U.S.-China Relations." *International Security* 37, no. 4 (spring): 49–89.

Goldstein, Joshua S. 2011. *Winning the War on War: The Decline of Armed Conflict Worldwide.* New York: Penguin.

Goldstein, Lyle J. 2015a. "Old-School Killers: Fear China's Sea Mines." *National Interest.* October 14.

——. 2015b. "China's Nightmare: Vietnam's New Killer Submarines." *National Interest.* March 29.

——. 2015c. *Meeting China Halfway: How to Defuse the Emerging U.S.-China Rivalry.* Washington, DC: Georgetown University Press.

Goldstein, Markus, and Christopher Udry. 2008. "The Profits of Power: Land Rights and Agricultural Investment in Ghana." *Journal of Political Economy* 116, no. 6 (December): 981–1022.

Goldman, Zachary K., and Elizabeth Rosenberg. 2015. *American Economic Power and the New Face of Financial Warfare.* Washington, DC: Center for a New American Security.

Gompert, David C., and Hans Binnendijk. 2016. *The Power to Coerce: Countering Adversaries without Going to War.* Santa Monica, CA: RAND.

Gompert, David C., and Terrence K. Kelly. 2013. "Escalation Cause: How the Pentagon's New Strategy Could Trigger War with China." *Foreign Policy.* August 3.

Gopnik, Adam. 2012. "The Caging of America." *New Yorker.* January 30.

Gordon, John Steele. 2004. *An Empire of Wealth: The Epic History of American Economic Power.* New York: Harper Collins.

Gordon, Robert J. 2016. *The Rise and Fall of American Growth: The U.S. Standard of Living since the Civil War* Princeton: Princeton University Press.

Gorst, Isabel. 2011. "Russian Military Budget Sapped by Corruption." *Financial Times.* May 24.

Gormley, Dennis M., Andrew S. Erickson, and Jingdong Yuan. 2014. "A Potent Vector: Assessing Chinese Cruise Missile Developments." *Joint Forces Quarterly* 75 (October): 98–105.

Gneezy, Uri, John A. List, Jeffrey A. Livingston, Sally Sadoff, Xiangdong Qin, and Yan Xu. 2017. "Measuring Success in Education: The Role of Effort on the Test Itself." National Bureau of Economic Research, Working Paper 24004, November.

Gramer, Robbie. 2017a. "Philippines to Deploy Troops to Disputed Islands in the South China Sea." *Foreign Policy*. April 6.

———. 2017b. "First U.S. Natural Gas Shipped to Poland." *Foreign Policy*. June 8.

Griffin, Emma. 2010. *A Short History of the British Industrial Revolution*. New York: Palgrave.

Grubb, Lieutenant Michael C. 2007. "Merchant Shipping in a Chinese Blockade of Taiwan." *Naval War College Review* 60, no. 1 (winter): 81–102.

Grusky, David B., Marybeth J. Mattingly, and Charles E. Varner. 2016. "The Poverty and Inequality Report." *Pathways* Special Issue.

Grygiel, Jakub, and A. Wess Mitchell. 2014. "A Preclusive Strategy to Defend the NATO Frontier." *American Interest*. August 17.

Guo, Jeff. 2016. "America Has Locked up So Many Black People It Has Warped Our Sense of Reality." *Washington Post*. February 26.

Gupta, Rajat, Shirish Sankhe, Richard Dobbs, Jonathan Woetzel, Anu Madgavkar, and Ashwin Hasyagar. 2014. "From Poverty to Empowerment: India's Imperative for Jobs, Growth, and Effective Basic Services." McKinsey Global Institute.

Guzman, Jorge, and Scott Stern. 2016. "The State of American Entrepreneurship: New Estimates of the Quantity and Quality of Entrepreneurship for 15 U.S. States, 1988–2014." NBER Working Paper No. 22095. National Bureau of Economic Research. March.

Guzzini, Stefano. 1993. "Structural Power and the Limits of Neorealist Power Analysis." *International Organization* 47, no. 3 (summer): 443–78.

Haas, Richard. 2018. *A World in Disarray: American Foreign Policy and the Crisis of the Old Order*. New York: Penguin Press.

Hacker, Jacob S., and Paul Pierson. 2012. *Winner-Take-All Politics: How Washington Made the Rich Richer—and Turned Its Back on the Middle Class*. New York: Pearson.

Haggard, Stephan, and Lydia Tiede. 2010. "The Rule of Law and Economic Growth: Where Are We?" *World Development* 39, no. 5: 673–85.

Hainmueller, Jens, and Daniel J. Hopkins. 2015. "The Hidden American Immigration Consensus: A Conjoint Analysis of Attitudes toward Immigrants." *American Journal of Political Science* 59, no. 3 (July): 529–48.

Hale, Galina, and Bart Hobijn. 2011. "The U.S. Content of 'Made in China.'" FRBSF Economic Letter. Federal Reserve Bank of San Francisco.

Haley, Usha, and George Haley. 2013. *Subsidies to Chinese Industry: State Capitalism, Business Strategy, and Trade Policy*. New York: Oxford University Press.

Han, Alice, and Chris Miller. 2017. "China's Awkward Debt Problem." *Wall Street Journal*. July 7.

Hanson, Gordon H., and Matthew J. Slaughter. 2015. "High-Skilled Immigration and the Rise of Stem Occupations in U.S. Employment." NBER Working Paper National Bureau of Economic Research. September.

Hanushek, Eric A., Jens Ruhose, and Ludger Woessmann. 2015. "Human Capital Quality and Aggregate Income Differences: Development Accounting for U.S. States." NBER Working Paper No. 21295. National Bureau of Economic Research. June.

Hanushek, Eric A., and Ludger Woessmann. 2015. "Skills, Mobility, and Growth." Paper prepared for the Ninth Biennial Federal Reserve System Community Development Research Conference, Washington, DC. April 2–3.

Harrison, David. 2017. "Much-Maligned U.S. Infrastructure Shows Signs of Improvement." *Wall Street Journal*. May 21.

Hartmann, Gregory K., and Scott C. Truver. 1991. *Weapons that Wait: Mine Warfare in the U.S. Navy*. Annapolis: Naval Institute Press.

Hayton, Bill. 2014. *The South China Sea: The Struggle for Power in Asia*. New Haven: Yale University Press.

Heath, Timothy. 2016. "How China's New Russian Air Defense System Could Change Asia." *War on the Rocks*. January 21.

Hedberg, Masha. 2016. "Top-Down Self-Organization: State Logics, Substitutional Delegation, and Private Governance in Russia." *Governance* 29, no. 1 (January): 67–83.

Hefner, Robert A., III. 2014. "The United States of Gas: Why the Shale Revolution Could Have Happened Only in America." *Foreign Affairs* 93, no. 3 (May/June): 9–14.

Heginbotham, Eric, Michael Nixon, Forrest E. Morgan, Jacob L. Heim, Jeff Hagen, Sheng Li, and Jeffrey Engstrom. 2015. *The U.S.-China Military Scorecard: Forces, Geography, and the Evolving Balance of Power, 1996–2017*. Santa Monica, CA: RAND.

Helliwell, John, Richard Layard, and Jeffrey Sachs, eds. 2016. *World Happiness Report 2016*. New York: United Nations.

Hendley, Kathryn. 2012. "Who Are the Legal Nihilists in Russia?" *Post-Soviet Affairs* 28, no. 2: 149–86.

Herbst, Jeffrey. 2000. *States and Power in Africa: Comparative Lessons in Authority and Control*. Princeton: Princeton University Press.

Hernandez, Javier C. 2017a. "China's "Chairman of Everything": Behind Xi Jinping's Many Titles." *New York Times*, October 25.

———. 2017b. "Xi Jinping Vows No Poverty in China by 2020. That Could Be Hard." *New York Times*. October 31.

Heydarian, Richard Javad. 2017. "Duterte Is under Pressure to End the Philippines-China Honeymoon." *National Interest*. April 13.

Hill, Fiona, and Clifford G. Gaddy. 2013. *Mr. Putin: Operative in the Kremlin*. Washington, DC: Brookings Institution Press.

Hobson, John M. 1993. "The Military Extraction Gap and the Wary Titan: The Fiscal Sociology of British Defense Policy, 1870–1913." *Journal of European Economic History* 22, no. 3: 461–506.

Holmes, James. 2014. "Strategic Features of the South China Sea: A Tough Neighborhood for Hegemons." *Naval War College Review* 67, no. 2 (spring): 30–51.

———. 2016. "Will China Become an Aircraft Carrier Superpower?" *Foreign Policy*. January 21.

———. 2017. "China's East China Sea ADIZ Represents a Thinly Veiled Grab for Sovereignty." *National Interest*. April 21.

Hornbeck, Richard. 2010. "Barbed Wire: Property Rights and Agricultural Development." *Quarterly Journal of Economics* 125, no. 2 (May): 767–810.

Hornby, Lucy. "Chinese Environment: Ground Operation." *Financial Times*. September 1.

Horowitz, Michael C. 2010. *The Diffusion of Military Power: Causes and Consequences for International Politics*. Princeton: Princeton University Press.

Horwitz, Sari, Ellen Nakashim, and Matea Gold. 2017. "DHS Tells States About Russian Hacking during 2016 Election." *Washington Post*. September 22.

Hosseinzadeh, Shaia, Norma MacDonald, Juan Hartsfield, Scott Roberts, Paul Curbo, Darin Turner, Joseph Tang, and Dean Newman. 2014. "Examining the Feasibility and Implications of U.S. Energy Independence." Invesco Global Investment Views. January 28.

Hoyland, Bjorn, Karl Moene, and Fredrik Willumsen. 2012. "The Tyranny of International Index Rankings." *Journal of Development Economics* 97, no. 1 (January): 1–14.

Hsieh, Chang-Tai, and Zheng Song. 2015. "Grasp the Large, Let Go of the Small: The Transformation of the State Sector in China." *Brookings Papers on Economic Activity* (spring): 295–366.

Huang, Yanzhong. 2011. "China's Health Costs Outstrip GDP Growth." *New York Times*. November 1

Huang, Yanzhong, and Elizabeth Economy. 2015. "Where China Can't Compete: Beijing's Think Tank Trouble." *Foreign Affairs*. September 21.

Huffbauer, Gary Clyde, Jeffrey J. Schott, Kimberly Ann Elliott, and Julia Muir. 2012. "Case Studies in Economic Sanctions and Terrorism." Peterson Institute for International Economics. Access at: https://piie.com/commentary/speeches-papers/case-studies-economic-sanctions-and-terrorism.

Hughes, Llewelyn. 2014. "The Limits of Energy Independence: Assessing the Implications of Oil Abundance for U.S. Foreign Policy." *Energy Research and Social Science* 3 (September): 55–64.

Hughes, Llewelyn, and Austin Long. 2014–15. "Is There an Oil Weapon? Security Implications of Changes in the Structure of the International Oil Market." *International Security* 39, no. 3 (winter): 152–89.

Humphreys, Keith. 2017. "Americans Use Far More Opioids Than Anyone Else in the World." *Washington Post*. March 15.

Huntington, Samuel P. 1999. "The Lonely Superpower." *Foreign Affairs* 78, no. 2 (March/April): 35–49.

———. 2004. *Who Are We? The Challenges to America's National Identity.*

Huo, Kan, and Hongyuran Wu. 2015. "Banks Raise Dams, Fend Off Toxic Debt Crisis." *Caixin*. December 1.

Hymans, Jacques E. C. 2012. *Achieving Nuclear Ambitions: Scientists, Politicians, and Proliferation.* Cambridge: Cambridge University Press.

Ikenberry, G. John. *After Victory: Strategic Restraint, and the Rebuilding of Order after Major Wars.* Princeton: Princeton University Press.

———. 2004. "The End of the Neoconservative Moment." *Survival* 46, no. 1 (spring): 7–22.

———. 2011. *Liberal Leviathan: The Origins, Crisis, and Transformation of the American World.* Princeton: Princeton University Press.

———. 2017. "The Plot against American Foreign Policy: Can the Liberal Order Survive?" *Foreign Affairs* 96, no. 3 (May/June): 2–9.

Ikenberry, G. John, and Darren J. Lim. 2017. *China's Emerging Institutional Statecraft: The Asian Infrastructure Investment bank and the Prospects for Counter-Hegemony.* Washington, DC: Brookings Institution.

International Crisis Group. 2017. *Central Asia's Silk Road Rivalries.* Brussels: International Crisis Group.

International Energy Agency. 2016. *World Energy Outlook 2016.* Paris.

International Institute for Strategic Studies (IISS). 2013. *The Military Balance.* London: IISS.

2017. *The Military Balance*. London: IISS.

International Monetary Fund (IMF). 1991. *A Study of the Soviet Economy*. Washington, DC.

———. 2017. *World Economic Outlook*. Washington, DC.

Irwin, Douglas A. 2003. "Explaining America's Surge in Manufactured Exports, 1880–1913." *Review of Economics and Statistics* 85, no. 2 (May): 364–76.

———. 2017. "The False Promise of Protectionism: Why Trump's Trade Policy Could Backfire." *Foreign Affairs* 96, no. 3 (May/June): 45–56.

Irwin, Neil. 2016. "Why Is Productivity So Weak? Three Theories." *New York Times*. April 28.

Jacobs, Andrew. 2010. "Rampant Fraud Threat to China's Brisk Ascent." *New York Times*. October 6.

Jane's Information Group. 2017a. *Jane's Defence Weekly*. London: Jane's Information Group.

———. 2017b. *Jane's Defence Procurement Budgets*. London: Jane's Information Group.

———. 2016. *Jane's World Armies*. London: Jane's Information Group.

Jeffrey, Craig. 2015. "Despite Its Anti-Corruption Creativity, India Is Still a One Man, One Bribe Democracy." *The Guardian*. April 6.

Jelavich, Barbara. 1964. *A Century of Russian Foreign Policy, 1814–1914*. Philadelphia: Lippincott.

Jervis, Robert. 2002. "Theories of War in an Era of Leading-Power Peace." *American Political Science Review* 96, no. 1 (March): 1–14.

———. 2003. "The Compulsive Empire." *Foreign Policy*, no. 137 (July/August): 82–87.

———. 2006. "The Remaking of a Unipolar World." *Washington Quarterly* 29, no. 3 (summer): 5–19.

Joffe, Josef. 2014. *The Myth of America's Decline: Politics, Economics, and a Half-Century of False Prophecies*. New York: Liveright.

Johannesson, Louise, and Petros C. Mavroidis. 2016. "The WTO Dispute Settlement System 1995–2016: a Dataset and Its Descriptive Statistics." EUI Working Papers. RSCAS 2016/72. European University Institute.

Johnson, Chalmers A. 1982. *MITI and the Japanese Miracle: The Growth of Industrial Policy, 1925–1975*. Stanford: Stanford University Press.

Johnson, David E., Jennifer D.P. Moroney, Roger Cliff, M. Wade Markel, Laurence Smallman, and Michael Spirtas. 2009. *Preparing and Training for the Full Spectrum of Military Challenges: Insights from the Experiences of China, France, the United Kingdom, India, and Israel*. Santa Monica, CA: RAND.

Johnson, Keith. 2015. "Putin's Energy Diplomacy Is Getting the Cold Shoulder." *Foreign Policy*. August 5.

Johnson, Ian. 2017. "Cambridge University Press Removes Academic Articles on Chinese Site." *New York Times*. August 18.

Johnston, Alastair Iain, and Mingming Shen. 2015. *Perception and Misperception in American and Chinese Views of the Other*. Washington, DC: Carnegie Endowment for International Peace.

Joint Committee on Taxation. 2017. *Macroeconomic Analysis of the "Tax Cut and Jobs Act" as Ordered Reported by the Senate Committee on Finance on November 16, 2017* (JCX-61-17). Washington, DC: U.S. Congress. November 30.

Jorgenson, Dale W., Mun S. Ho, and Jon D. Samuels. 2014. "Long-term Estimates of U.S. Productivity and Growth." Paper presented at the Third World KLEMS Conference. Tokyo. May 19.

Jourdan, Adam. 2014. "China Military Training Inadequate for Winning a War: Army Paper." *Reuters*. October 12.

Jourdan, Adam, and Ben Hirschier. 2016. "China Healthcare Costs Forcing Patients into Crippling Debt." *Reuters*. July 10.

Judah, Ben. 2013. *Fragile Empire: How Russia Fell In and Out of Love with Vladimir Putin*. New Haven: Yale University Press.

Kagan, Robert. 2009. *The Return of History and the End of Dreams*. NY: Vintage.

———. 2012. "Not Fade Away: The Myth of American Decline." *New Republic*. January 11.

———. 2013. *The World America Made*. New York: Vintage.

Kalla, Joshua L., and David E. Broockman. 2016. "Campaign Contributions Facilitate Access to Congressional Officials: A Randomized Field Experiment." *American Journal of Political Science* 60, no. 3 (July): 545–58.

Kane, Paul V. 2011. "To Save Our Economy, Ditch Taiwan." *New York Times*. November 10.

Kaplan, Robert D. 2014. *Asia's Cauldron: The South China Sea and the End of a Stable Pacific*. New York: Random House.

———. 2017. "The Quiet Rivalry Between China and Russia." *New York Times*. November 3.

Karabell, Zachary. 2014. *The Leading Indicators: A Short History of the Numbers That Rule Our World*. New York: Simon and Schuster.

Karako, Thomas, Ian Williams, and Wes Rumbaugh. 2017. *Missile Defense 2020: Next Steps for Defending the Homeland*. Washington, DC: Center for Strategic and International Studies.

Katz, Josh. 2017. "Drug Deaths in America Are Rising Faster Than Ever." *New York Times*. June 5.

Kaufmann, Daniel, Aart Kraay, and Massimo Mastruzzi. 2007. "Worldwide Governance Indicators Project: Answering the Critics." World Bank Policy Research Working Paper No. 4149. Washington, DC.

———. 2010. "The Worldwide Governance Indicators: Methodology and Analytical Issues." World Bank Policy Research Working Paper No. 5430. Washington, DC.

Kaushik, Narendra. 2018. "Indian Resistance Could Spell Trouble for RCEP." *Bangkok Post*. January 8.

Kauzlarich, Richard D. 2016. "Energizing U.S. Foreign Policy." *The American Interest*. May 10.

Kearns, Ian. 2015. "Avoiding War in Europe: The Risks from NATO-Russian Close Military Encounters." *Arms Control Today* 45, no. 9 (November): 8–13.

Keehan, Sean P., John A. Poisal, Gigi A. Cuckler, Andrea M. Sisko, Sheila D. Smith, Andrew J. Madison, Devin A. Stone, Christian J. Wolfe, and Joseph M. Lizonitz. 2016. "National Health Expenditure Projections, 2015–25: Economy, Prices, and Aging Expected to Shape Spending and Enrollment." *Health Affairs* 35, no. 8 (August): 1522–31.

Kelly, Terrence K., Anthony Atler, Todd Nichols, and Lloyd Thrall. 2013. *Employing Land-Based Anti-Ship Missiles in the Western Pacific*. Santa Monica, CA: RAND Corporation.

Kelly, Terrence K., David C. Gompert, and Duncan Long. 2016. *Smart Power, Stronger Partners*. Vol. 1. *Exploiting U.S. Advantages to Prevent Aggression*. Santa Monica, CA: RAND.

Kelly, Tim, and Nobuhiro Kubo. 2015. "Japan's Far-Flung Island Defense Plan Seeks to Turn Tables on China." *Reuters*. December 18.

Kennedy, Paul. 1987. *The Rise and Fall of the Great Powers: Economic Change and Military Conflict from 1500 to 2000*. New York: Random House.

———. 2002. "The Greatest Superpower Ever." *New Perspectives Quarterly* 19, no. 2 (spring): 8–18.

Kennedy, Ryan, and Lydia Tiede. 2013. "Economic Development Assumptions and the Elusive Curse of Oil." *International Studies Quarterly* 57: 760–71.

Kennedy, Scott. 2017. *The Fat Tech Dragon: Benchmarking China's Innovation Drive*. Washington, DC: Center for Strategic and International Studies.

Keohane, Robert O. 2005. *After Hegemony: Cooperation and Discord in the World Political Economy*. Princeton: Princeton University Press.

Keohane, Robert O., and Joseph S. Nye, Jr. 1989. *Power and Interdependence*. New York: Harper Collins.

Kessler, Glenn. 2013. "How Many Pages of Regulations for 'Obamacare?'" *Washington Post*. May 15.

Kim, Linsu. 1997. *Imitation to Innovation: The Dynamics of Korea's Technological Learning*. Boston: Harvard Business School Press.

Kindleberger, Charles P. 2013. *The World in Depression, 1929–1939*. 40th Anniversary ed. Berkeley: University of California Press.

King, Gary, Jennifer Pan, and Margaret E. Roberts. 2013. "How Censorship in China Allows Government Criticism but Silences Collective Expression." *American Political Science Review* 107, no. 2 (May): 1–18.

———. 2017. "How the Chinese Government Fabricates Social Media Posts for Strategic Distraction, Not Engaged Argument." *American Political Science Review* 111, no. 3 (August): 484–501.

Klare, Michael T. 2016. "The United States and NATO Are Preparing for a Major War with Russia." *The Nation*. July 7.

Klein, Ezra. 2011. "The U.S. Government: An Insurance Conglomerate Protected by a Large, Standing Army." *Washington Post*. February 14.

Klein, James P., Gary Goertz, and Paul F. Diehl. 2006. "The New Rivalry Dataset: Procedures and Patterns." *Journal of Peace Research* 43, no. 3 (May): 331–48.

Knack, Stephen, and Philip Keefer. 1995. "Institutions and Economic Performance: Cross-Country Tests Using Alternative Institutional Measures." *Economics and Politics* 7, no. 3 (November): 207–27.

Knorr, Klaus. 1956. *The War Potential of Nations*. Princeton: Princeton University Press.

Ko, Chiu Yu, Mark Koyama, and Tuan-Hwee Sng. 2017. "Unified China and Divided Europe." *International Economic Review*.

Kofman, Michael. 2016. "Fixing Deterrence in the East, or How I Learned to Stop Worrying and Love NATO's Crushing Defeat by Russia." *War on the Rocks*. May 12.

Kontorovich, Vladimir. 1990. "The Long-Run Decline in Soviet R&D Productivity." In *The Impoverished Superpower: Perestroika and the Soviet Military Burden*, edited by Henry S. Rowen and Charles Wolf, chapter 11. San Francisco: ICS Press.

Korb, Lawrence J., and Eric M. Goepel. 2016. "Does America Really Need to Spend More on Defense?" *National Interest*. August 4.

Kotkin, Stephen. 2015. "The Resistible Rise of Vladimir Putin: Russia's Nightmare Dressed Like a Daydream." *Foreign Affairs* 94, no. 2 (March/April): 140–53.

Kraemer, Kenneth L., Greg Linden, and Jason Dedrick. 2011. "Capturing Value in Global Networks: Apple's iPad and iPhone." Unpublished manuscript. July.

Krauthammer, Charles. 1984. "The Illusion of Star Wars." *New Republic.* 190, no. 20 (April): 13–17.

———. 1990–91. "The Unipolar Moment." *Foreign Affairs* 70, no. 1 (January/February): 23–33.

Krepenevich, Andrew F., Jr. 2015. "How to Deter China: The Case for Archipelagic Defense." *Foreign Affairs* 94, no. 2 (March/April): 78–86.

Kroenig, Matthew. 2015. "Facing Reality: Getting NATO Ready for a New Cold War." *Survival* 57, no. 1 (February/March): 49–70.

Krugman, Paul. 1994. "The Myth of Asia's Miracle." *Foreign Affairs* 73, no. 6 (November/December): 62–78.

Kupchan, Charles. 2007. *The End of the American Era: U.S. Foreign Policy and the Geopolitics of the Twenty-First Century.* New York: Vintage.

Kurlantzick, Joshua. 2015. "A China-Vietnam Military Clash." Council on Foreign Relations, Contingency Planning Memorandum No. 2. September.

———. 2016. *State Capitalism: How the Return of State Is Transforming the World.* New York: Oxford University Press.

Kurtz, Marcus J., and Andrew Schrank. 2007. "Growth and Governance: Models, Measures, and Mechanisms." *Journal of Politics* 69, no. 2 (May): 538–54.

Kurtzman, Joel. 2014. *Unleashing the Second American Century.* New York: Public Affairs.

Laboissiere, Martha, and Mona Mourshed. 2017. "Closing the Skills Gap: Creating Workforce-Development Programs That Work for Everyone." *McKinsey Insights.* February.

Lafeber, Walter. 2013. *The New Cambridge History of American Foreign Relations: The American Search for Opportunity, 1865–1913.* Vol. 2. Cambridge: Cambridge University Press.

Lake, David. 1993. "Leadership, Hegemony, and the International Economy: Naked Emperor or Tattered Monarch with Potential?" *International Studies Quarterly* 37, no. 4 (December): 459–89.

———. 2016. *The Statebuilding Dilemma; On the Limits of Foreign Intervention.* Ithaca: Cornell University Press.

Lamothe, Dan. 2017. "Retired Generals Cite Comments from Mattis While Opposing Trump's Proposed Foreign Aid Cuts." *Washington Post.* February 27.

Landry, Pierre F. 2008. *Decentralized Authoritarianism in China: The Communist Party's Control of Local Elites in the Post-Mao Era.* Cambridge: Cambridge University Press.

Lange, Glenn-Marie, and Kevin Carey, eds. 2018. *The Changing Wealth of Nations 2018.* Washington, DC: World Bank.

Lanoszka, Alexander, and Michael A. Hunzeker. 2016. "Confronting the Anti-Access/Area Denial and Precision Strike Challenge in the Baltic Region." *RUSI Journal* 161, no. 5 (December): 12–18.

LaRaja, Ray, and Brian Schaffner. 2014. "Want to Reduce Polarization? Give Parties More Money." *Washington Post.* July 21.

Larmer, Brook. "What the World's Emptiest International Airport Says about China's Influence." *New York Times Magazine.* September 13.

Lau, Lawrence, Yingyi Qian, and Gerard Roland. 2000. "Reform without Losers: An Interpretation of China's Dual-Track Approach to Transition." *Journal of Political Economy* 108, no. 1: 120–43.

Layne, Christopher. 1993. "The Unipolar Illusion: Why New Great Powers Will Rise." *International Security* 17, no. 4 (spring): 5–51.

———. 2004. "The War on Terrorism and the Balance of Power: The Paradoxes of American Hegemony." In *Balance of Power: Theory and Practice in the 21st Century,* edited by T. V. Paul, James J. Wirtz, and Michel Fortmann, chapter 4. Stanford: Stanford University Press.

———. 2006. *The Peace of Illusions: American Grand Strategy from 1940 to the Present.* Ithaca: Cornell University Press.

———. 2011. "The Unipolar Exit: Beyond Pax Americana." *Cambridge Review of International Affairs* 24, no. 2 (June): 149–64.

Ledeneva, Alena. 2013. *Can Russia Modernise? Sistema, Power Networks, and Informal Governance.* Cambridge: Cambridge University Press.

Lee, John. 2012. "China's Corporate Leninism." *American Interest* 7, no. 5 (April 10): 36–45.

———. 2014. "The Real Picture on China's State-Owned Enterprises." *Business Spectator.* December 12.

Legro, Jeffrey W. 2011. "Sell Unipolarity? The Future of an Overvalued Concept." In *International Relations Theory and the Consequences of Unipolarity,* edited by G. John Ikenberry, Michael Mastaunduno, and William C. Wohlforth, chapter 11. Cambridge: Cambridge University Press.

Leighley, Jan E., and Jonathan Nagler. 2013. *Who Votes Now? Demographics, Issues, Inequality, and Turnout in the United States.* Princeton: Princeton University Press.

Levendusky, Matthew. 2013. *How Partisan Media Polarize America.* Chicago: University of Chicago Press.

Levendusky, Matthew, and Neil Malhorta. 2016. "Does Media Coverage of Partisan Polarization Affect Political Attitudes?" *Political Communication* 33, no. 2: 283–301.

Levy, Jack S., and William R. Thompson. 2010. "Balancing on Land and at Sea: Do States Ally against the Leading Global Power?" *International Security* 35, no. 1 (summer): 7–43.

Li, Jianjun, and Fengyun Hu. 2013. "Zhongguo Zhongxiao Qiye Jinrong Jeigou Rongzi Chengben Yu Xinzi Xindai Shichang Fazhan" [Financing Structure and Cost of China's Small and Medium-Sized Enterprises and Development of Shadow Credit Market]. *hongguan jingji yanjiu* 5: 7–11.

Li, Zhiyuan, Zongwei Ma, Tsering Jan van der Kuijp, Zengwei Yuan, and Lei Huang. 2014. "A Review of Soil Heavy Metal Pollution from Mines in China: Pollution and Health Risk Assessment." *Science of the Total Environment* 468–69 (January): 843–53.

Lieber, Keir A., and Gerard Alexander. 2005. "Waiting for Balancing: Why the World Is Not Pushing Back." *International Security* 30, no. 1 (summer): 109–39.

Lieber, Keir A., and Daryl G. Press. 2017. "The New Era of Counterforce: Technological Change and the Future of Nuclear Deterrence." *International Security* 41, no. 4 (spring): 9–49.

Lieber, Robert J. 2012. *Power and Willpower in the American Future: Why the United States Is Not Destined to Decline.* Cambridge: Cambridge University Press.

———. 2016. *Retreat and Its Consequences: American Foreign Policy and the Problem of World Order.* Cambridge: Cambridge University Press.

Liff, Adam P., and Andrew S. Erickson. 2013. "Demystifying China's Defence Spending: Less Mysterious in the Aggregate." *China Quarterly* 216 (December): 805–30.

Lim, Benjamin Kang, and Ben Blanchard. 2014. "Disgraced China Military Officer Sold Hundreds of Posts." *Reuters.* April 1.

Limao, Nuno, and Anthony J. Venables. 2001. "Infrastructure, Geographical Disadvantage, and Transport Costs." *World Bank Economic Review* 15, no. 3 (October): 451–79.

Lin, Bonny, and Cristina L. Garafola. 2016. *Training the People's Liberation Army Air Force Surface-to-Air Missile (Sam) Forces.* Santa Monica, CA: RAND.

Lin, Jeffery, and P. W. Singer. 2015. "China's Getting Ready to Turn on Asia's Biggest Warship." *Popular Science.* June 4.

Linz, Juan J. 1990. "The Perils of Presidentialism." *Journal of Democracy* 1, no. 1 (winter): 51–69.

Lippman, Thomas W. 2016. "Saudi Arabian Oil and U.S. Interests." In *Crude Strategy: Rethinking the U.S. Military Commitment to Defend Persian Gulf Oil,* edited by Charles L. Glaser and Rosemary A. Kelanic, chapter 4. Washington, DC: Georgetown University Press.

Litan, Robert E. 2015. "Start-up Slowdown: How the United States Can Regain Its Entrepreneurial Edge." *Foreign Affairs* 94, no. 1 (January/February): 47–53.

Litan, Robert E., and Ian Hathaway. 2017. "Is America Encouraging the Wrong Kind of Entrepreneurs?" *Harvard Business Review.* June 13.

Lopez, German. 2017a. "In 2016, Drug Overdoses Likely Killed More Americans than the Entire Wars in Vietnam and Iraq." *Vox.* July 7.

———. 2017b. "America Leads the World in Drug Overdose Deaths—By a Lot." *Vox.* June 28.

Lopez-Casasnovas, Guillem, Berta Rivera, and Luis Currais. 2005. *Health and Economic Growth: Findings and Policy Implications.* Cambridge: MIT Press.

Lorentzen, Peter, Pierre Landry, and John Yasuda. 2014. "Undermining Authoritarian Innovation: The Power of China's Industrial Giants." *American Journal of Political Science* 76, no. 1 (January): 182–94.

Lostumbo, Michael J., David R. Frelinger, James Williams, and Barry Wilson. 2016. *Air Defense Options for Taiwan: An Assessment of Relative Costs and Operational Benefits.* Santa Monica, CA: RAND Corporation.

Lovell, Julia. 2011. *The Opium War: Drugs, Dreams, and the Making of Modern China.* London: Picador.

Lucas, Louise. 2017. "China Seeks Dominance of Global AI Industry." *Financial Times.* October 15.

Luce, Edward. 2017. *The Retreat of Western Liberalism.* New York: Atlantic Monthly Press.

Lukes, Steven. 2005. *Power: A Radical View.* New York: Palgrave Macmillan.

Ma, Debin. 2004. "Why Japan, Not China, Was the First to Develop in East Asia: Lessons from Sericulture, 1850–1937." *Economic Development and Cultural Change* 52, no. 2 (January): 369–94.

Ma, Damian, and William Adams. 2013. *In Line behind a Billion People: How Scarcity Will Define China's Ascent in the Next Decade*. New York: Pearson.

MacDonald, Fiona. 2016. "80 Percent of Data in Chinese Clinical Trials Have Been Fabricated." *Science Alert*. October 1.

MacDonald, Paul. 2014. *Networks of Domination: The Social Foundations of Peripheral Conquest in International Politics*. New York: Oxford University Press.

MacGregor, Richard. 2010. *The Party: The Secret World of China's Communist Rulers*. New York: Harper Collins.

Mack, Andrew J. R. 1975. "Why Big Nations Lose Small Wars: The Politics of Asymmetric Conflict." *World Politics* 27, no. 2 (January): 175–200.

Maddison, Angus. 2003. "Historical Statistics of the World Economy: 1–2008 AD." Unpublished manuscript.

Magnier, Mark. 2016. "As Growth Slows, China's Era of Easy Choices Is Over." *Wall Street Journal*. January 8.

Majumdar, Dave. 2015a. "America's F-35 Stealth Fighter vs. China's New J-31: Who Wins?" *National Interest*. September 25.

———. 2015b. "America's F-22 Rapter Vs. China's Stealth J-20: Who Wins?" *National Interest*. September 10.

Managi, Shunsuke, ed. 2018. *Inclusive Wealth Report 2018: Measuring Progress toward Sustainability*. New York: Routledge.

Mankoff, Jeffrey. 2013. "The Wary Chinese-Russian Partnership." *New York Times*. July 11.

———. 2015. "Russia's Asia Pivot: Confrontation or Cooperation?" *Asia Policy* 19 (January): 65–87.

Manuelli, Rodolfo E., and Ananth Seshardi. 2014. "Human Capital and the Wealth of Nations." *American Economic Review* 104, no. 9 (September): 2736–62.

Manzo, Vince A., and John K. Warden. 2017. "Want to Avoid Nuclear War? Reject Mutual Vulnerability with North Korea." *War on the Rocks*. August 29.

Marin, Richard A. 2014. "Surviving the Global Pension Crisis: Unfunded Liabilities and How We Can Fill the Gap." *CFA Institute Conference Proceedings Quarterly* 31, no. 4 (fourth quarter): 47–55.

Markus, Stanislav. 2012. "Secure Property as a Bottom-up Process: Firms, Stakeholders, and Predators in Weak States." *World Politics* 64, no. 2 (April): 242–77.

Marshall, Monty G., Ted Robert Gurr, and Keith Jaggers. 2017. "Polity Iv Project: Political Regime Characteristics and Transitions, 1800–2016." Center for Systemic Peace.

Martinson, Ryan D. 2016. "The Courage to Fight and Win: The PLA Cultivates Xuexing for the Wars of the Future." *China Brief* 16, no. 9: 11–14.

Massey, Douglas S. "The New Immigration and Ethnicity in the United States." *Population and Development Review* 21, No. 3 (September): 631–52.

Mastanduno, Michael. 2009. "System Maker, Privilege Taker: U.S. Power and the International Political Economy." *World Politics* 61, no. 1 (January): 121–54.

Master, Benjamin, Min Sun, and Susanna Loeb. 2017. "Teacher Workforce Developments: Recent Changes in Academic Competitiveness and Job Satisfaction of New Teachers." *Education Finance and Policy*.

Mastro, Oriana Skylar. 2018. "Why China Won't Rescue North Korea: What to Expect of Things Fall Apart." *Foreign Affairs* 97, no. 1 (January/February): 58–66.

Maugeri, Leonardo. 2013. "The Shale Oil Boom: A U.S. Phenomenon." Belfer Center for Science and International Affairs, Harvard Kennedy School. Discussion Paper 2013–05. June.

Mazaheri, Nimah. 2016. *Oil Booms and Business Busts: Why Resource Wealth Hurts Entrepreneurs in the Developing World*. Oxford: Oxford University Press.

McCarty, Nolan, Keith T. Poole, and Howard Rosenthal. 2006. *Polarized America: The Dance of Ideology and Unequal Riches*. Cambridge: MIT Press.

McCauley, Kevin N. 2015. "Incomplete Transformation: PLA Joint Training and Warfighting Capabilities." *China Brief* 15, no. 5 (March 6): 13–18.

McClory, Jonathan. 2017. *The Soft Power 30: A Global Ranking of Softpower, 2017*. CA: Portland Communications.

McCord, Gordon C., and Jeffrey D. Sachs. 2013. "Development, Structure, and Transformation: Some Evidence on Comparative Economic Growth." NBER Working Paper No. 19512. National Bureau of Economic Research. October.

McLaughlin, Kathleen. 2016. "Science Is a Major Plank in China's New Spending Plan." *Science*. March 7.

Mead, Walter Russell. 2015. "The Seven Great Powers." *American Interest*. January 4.

Mearsheimer, John J. 1988. "Numbers, Strategy, and the European Balance." *International Security* 12, no. 4 (spring): 174–85.

———. 2014a. *The Tragedy of Great Power Politics*. Updated ed. New York: Norton.

———. 2014b. "Why the Ukraine Crisis Is the West's Fault." *Foreign Affairs* 93, no. 5 (September/October): 1–12.

Mearsheimer, John J., and Stephen M. Walt. 2016. "The Case for Offshore Balancing: A Superior U.S. Grand Strategy." *Foreign Affairs* 95, no. 4 (July/August): 70–83.

Mehlum, Halvor, Karl Moene, and Ragnar Torvik. 2006. "Institutions and the Resource Curse." *Economic Journal* 116: 1–20.

Mehta, Jal. 2013. *The Allure of Order: High Hopes, Dashed Expectations, and the Troubled Quest to Remake American Schooling*. Oxford: Oxford University Press.

Melia, Tamara Moser. 1991. *"Damn the Torpedoes"*: *A Short History of U.S. Naval Mine Countermeasures, 1777–1991*. Washington, DC: Naval Historical Center.

Menon, Anand. 2009. "The Limits of the Chinese-Russian Partnership." *Survival* 51, no. 3 (July): 99–130.

Miguelez, Ernest, and Carsten Fink. 2013. "Measuring the International Mobility of Inventors: A New Database." World Intellectual Property Organization (WIPO). Working Paper No. 8. May.

Milhaupt, Curtis J., and Wentong Zheng. 2015. "Beyond Ownership: State Capitalism and the Chinese Firm." *Georgetown Law Journal* 103, no. 3 (March): 665–722.

Miller, Christopher. 2017. "One Belt, One Road, One Bluff." *American Interest*. May 23.

———. 2018. *Putinomics: Power and Money in Resurgent Russia*. Chapel Hill: University of North Carolina Press.

Miller, Nicholas. 2017. "Why Nuclear Energy Programs Rarely Lead to Proliferation." *International Security* 42, no. 2 (fall): 40–77.

Millett, Allan R., Williamson Murray, and Kenneth H. Watman. 2010. "The Effectiveness of Military Organizations." In *Military Effectiveness*, edited by Allan R. Millet and Williamson Murray, chapter 1. Cambridge: Cambridge University Press.

Mirski, Sean. 2013. "Stranglehold: The Context, Conduct and Consequences of an American Naval Blockade of China." *Journal of Strategic Studies* 36, no. 3 (February): 385–421.

Mitton, Todd. 2016. "The Wealth of Subnations: Geography, Institutions, and within-Country Development." *Journal of Development Economics* 118 (January): 88–111.

Mizokami, Kyle. 2017. "The U.S. Nuclear Submarine Russia and China Can't Beat in Battle." *National Interest*. September 21.

Modelski, George. 1978. "The Long Cycle of Global Politics and the Nation-State." *Comparative Studies in Society and History* 20 (April): 214–35.

Modelski, George, and William R. Thompson. 1996. *Leading Sectors and World Powers*. Columbia: University of South Carolina Press.

Mogato, Manuel. 2017. "Philippines Says U.S. Military to Use Bases, Defense Deal Intact." *Reuters*. January 26.

Mollman, Steve. 2016. "In a Threat to China, Malaysia Vows to Sink Illegal Fishing Boats in the South China Sea." *Quartz*. August 2.

Monteiro, Nuno P. 2014. *Theory of Unipolar Politics*. Cambridge: Cambridge University Press.

Montgomery, Evan Braden. 2014. "Contested Primacy in the Western Pacific: China's Rise and the Future of U.S. Power Projection." *International Security* 38, no. 4 (spring): 115–49.

Moravcsik, Andrew. 2010. "Europe: Quietly Rising Superpower in a Bipolar World." In *Rising States, Rising Institutions*, edited by Alan Alexandroff and Andrew Cooper, chapter 7. Washington, DC: Brookings Institution Press.

Morgan, Forrest E., Karl P. Mueller, Evan S. Medeiros, Kevin L. Pollpeter, and Roger Cliff. 2008. *Dangerous Thresholds*. Santa Monica, CA: RAND.

Morgenthau, Hans J. 1973. *Politics among Nations: The Struggle for Power and Peace*. New York: Knopf.

Morris, Ian. 2010. *Why the West Rules—for Now: The Patterns of History, and What They Reveal About the Future*. New York: Farrar, Straus and Giroux.

Morris, Lyle. 2016. "Indonesia-China Tensions in the Natuna Sea: Evidence of Naval Efficacy over Coast Guards?" *Diplomat*. June 28.

———. 2017. "The New "Normal" in the East China Sea." *Diplomat*. February 27.

Mossavar-Rahmani, Sharmin, Jiming Ha, Maziar Minovi, and Matheus Dibo. 2016. *Walled In: China's Great Dilemma*. New York: Goldman Sachs.

Moulder, Frances V. 1977. *Japan, China, and the Modern World Economy: Toward a Reinterpretation of East Asian Development, 1600–1918*. Cambridge: Cambridge University Press.

Movchan, Andrey. 2017. *Decline, Not Collapse: The Bleak Prospects for Russia's Economy*. Washington, DC: Carnegie Endowment for International Peace.

Mueller, John, and Mark G. Stewart. 2011. *Terror, Security, and Money: Balancing the Risks, Benefits, and Costs of Homeland Security*. New York: Oxford University Press.

———. 2016. *Chasing Ghosts: The Policing of Terrorism*. New York: Oxford University Press.

Mufson, Steven. 2013. "China Struggles to Tap Its Shale Gas." *Washington Post*. April 30.

Mullen, Adm. Mike (RET.), and Gen. James Jones (RET.). 2017. "Why Foreign Aid Is Critical to U.S. National Security." *Politico.* June 12.

Mulvenon, James, and Leigh Ann Ragland. 2012. "The Only Honest Man? General Liu Yuan Calls Out PLA Corruption." *China Leadership Monitor* 37 (spring): 1–15.

Muraviev, Alexey D. 2014. "Comrades in Arms: The Military-Strategic Aspects of China-Russia Relations." *Journal of Asian Security* 1, no. 2 (August): 163–85.

Murray, William S. 2008. "Revisiting Taiwan's Defense Strategy." *Naval War College Review* 61, no. 3 (summer): 13–38.

———. 2014. "Underwater Tels and China's Antisubmarine Warfare: Evolving Strength and a Calculated Weakness." In *China's Near Sea Combat Capabilities,* edited by Peter Dutton, Andrew S. Erickson, and Ryan Martinson, chapter 2. Newport: U.S. Naval War College.

Nageswaran, V. Anantha, and Gulzar Natarajan. 2016. *Can India Grow? Challenges, Opportunities, and the Way Forward.* Washington, DC: Carnegie Endowment for International Peace.

Nakamura, Emi, Jon Steinsson, and Miao Liu. 2015. "Are Chinese Growth and Inflation Too Smooth? Evidence from Engel Curves." NBER Working Paper No. 19893. National Bureau of Economic Research. February.

Nathan, Andrew J. 2000. "What's Wrong with American Taiwan Policy?" *Washington Quarterly* 23, no. 2 (spring): 93–106.

———. 2017. "What Is Xi Jinping Afraid Of? China's Regime Is Less Secure than It Looks." *Foreign Affairs.* December 8.

Nathan, Andrew J., and Andrew Scobell. 2012. "China's Overstretched Military." *Washington Quarterly* 35, no. 4 (fall): 135–48.

National Bureau of Statistics of China. 2010. *2010 Population Census.* Beijing.

National Equity Atlas. 2017. http://nationalequityatlas.org.

National Intelligence Council. 2008. *Global Trends 2025: A Transformed World.* Washington DC: Government Printing Office.

———. 2012. *Global Trends 2030: Alternative Worlds.* Washington DC: U.S. Government Printing Office.

———. 2017. *Global Trends: Paradox of Progress.* Washington, DC: U.S. Government Printing Office.

National Science Board. 2016. *Science and Engineering Indicators 2016.* Arlington: National Science Foundation.

———. 2018. *Science and Engineering Indicators 2018.* Arlington: National Science Foundation.

National Science Foundation (NSF). 1987. *Science and Engineering Indicators, 1987.* Washington, DC.

———. 1989. *Science and Engineering Indicators, 1989.* Washington, DC.

Naughton, Barry. 2016. "Rebalancing, Restructuring, and Reform: China 2016." Paper presented to the Reserve Bank of Australia Annual Conference 2016. Sydney. March 17–18.

Navias, Martin S., and E. R. Hooton. 1996. *Tanker Wars: The Assault on Merchant Shipping During the Iran-Iraq Crisis, 1980–1988.* New York: I. B. Tauris.

Nelson, Rebecca M. 2017. "U.S. Sanctions and Russia's Economy." Congressional Research Service. February 17.

Neufield, Maria, and Jurgen Rehm. 2013. "Alchohol Consumption and Mortality in Russia since 2000." *Alcohol and Alcoholism* 48, no. 2: 222–30.

Norman, Laurence, and Julian E. Barnes. "Brexit Leads EU to Circle Defense Weapons." *Wall Street Journal*. December 22.

Normile, Dennis. 2017. "One in Three Chinese Children Faces an Education Apocalypse." *Science*. September 21.

Norris, William J. 2016. *Chinese Economic Statecraft: Commercial Actors, Grand Strategy, and State Control*. Ithaca: Cornell University Press.

Norris, Robert S., and Hans M. Kristensen. 2010. "Global Nuclear Weapons Inventories, 1945–2010." *Bulletin of Atomic Scientists* 66, no. 4 (July): 77–83.

Norrlof, Carla. 2010. *America's Global Advantage: U.S. Hegemony and International Cooperation*. Cambridge: Cambridge University Press.

North, Douglas C., John Joseph Wallis, Steven B. Webb, and Barry R. Weingast. 2011. "Limited Access Orders: Rethinking the Problems of Development and Violence." Stanford University, January 25.

Nove, Alec. 1990. *An Economic History of the USSR*. New York: Penguin Books.

Nye, Joseph S., Jr. 1990. "The Changing Nature of World Power." *Political Science Quarterly* 105, no. 2 (summer): 177–92.

———. 2004. *Soft Power: The Means to Success in World Politics*. New York: Public Affairs.

———. 2011. *The Future of Power*. New York: Public Affairs.

———. 2013. "What China and Russia Don't Get about Soft Power." *Foreign Policy*. April 29.

———. 2015. *Is the American Century Over?* New York: Polity Press.

———. 2017. "Will the Liberal Order Survive? The History of the Liberal Order." *Foreign Affairs* 96, no. 1 (January/February): 10–16.

Odgaard, Ole, and Jorgen Delman. 2014. "China's Energy Security and Its Challenges Towards 2035." *Energy Policy* 71 (August): 107–17.

O'Donnell, Norah. 2016. "Are Members of Congress Becoming Telemarketers?" *60 Minutes*. April 24.

Ofer, Gur. 1987. "Soviet Economic Growth: 1928–1985." *Journal of Economic Literature* 25, no. 4 (December): 1767–833.

Office of Management and Budget. 2016. *Historical Tables*. Washington, DC.

———. 2018. *Historical Tables*. Washington, DC.

O'Hanlon, Michael E. 2000. "Why China Cannot Conquer Taiwan." *International Security* 25, no. 2 (fall): 51–86.

Oil & Gas. 2015. "Why China Will Never See a Shale Boom." November 2.

Oneal, John R. 1989. "Measuring the Material Base of the Contemporary East-West Balance of Power." *International Interactions* 15, no. 2: 177–96.

Organisation for Economic Co-operation and Development (OECD). 2015. *Entrepreneurship at a Glance*. Paris.

———. 2016. *Survey of Adult Skills: Readers Companion*. 2nd ed. Paris.

———. 2017. "Oecd.Stat." Paris.

Orlik, Tom. 2011. "Unrest on Rise as Economy Booms." *Wall Street Journal*. September 26.

O'Rourke, Lindsey A. 2018. *Regime Change: America's Covert Cold War*. Ithaca: Cornell University Press.

Osborn, Kris. 2016. "'Acoustic Superiority': U.S. Navy's Secret Submarine Plan to Dominate the Seas." *National Interest*. June 20.

Osnos, Evan. 2017. "Why the 2018 Midterms Are So Vulnerable to Hackers." *New Yorker*. December 28.

———. 2018. "Making China Great Again." *New Yorker.* January 8.

Oxenstierna, Susanne. 2016. "Russia's Defense Spending and the Economic Decline." *Journal of Eurasian Studies* 7, no. 1 (January): 60–70.

Paarlberg, Robert L. 2004. "Knowledge as Power: Science, Military Dominance, and U.S. Security." *International Security* 29, no. 1 (summer): 122–55.

Page, Jeremy. 2015. "Underwater Drones Join Microphones to Listen for Chinese Nuclear Submarines." *Wall Street Journal.* October 24.

———. 2017. "China Prepares for a Crisis Along North Korea Border." *Wall Street Journal.* July 24.

Palmer, Glenn, Vito D'Orazio, Michael Kenwick, and Matthew Lane. 2015. "The Mid4 Data Set, 2002–2010: Procedures, Coding Rules, and Description." *Conflict Management and Peace Science* 32, no. 2: 222–42.

Panda, Ankit, and Vipin Narang. 2017. "Deadly Overconfidence: Trump Thinks Missile Defenses Work against North Korea, and That Should Scare You." *War on the Rocks.* October 16.

Pape, Robert A. 2005. "Soft Balancing against the United States." *International Security* 30, no. 1 (summer): 7–45.

Parent, Joseph M., and Paul K. MacDonald. 2011. "Graceful Decline? The Surprising Success of Great Power Retrenchment." *International Security* 35, no. 4 (spring): 7–44.

Patton, Dominique. 2014. "More Than 40 Percent of China's Arable Land Degraded: Xinhua." *Reuters.* November 4.

Peel, Michael, and David Bond. "NATO Plans to Sharpen European Capabilities." *Financial Times.* November 7.

Pei, Minxin. 2016. *China's Crony Capitalism: The Dynamics of Regime Decay.* Cambridge: Harvard University Press.

Peng, Guangqian, and Youzhi Yao, eds. 2005. *The Science of Military Strategy.* Beijing: Military Science Publishing House.

Perlez, Jane, and Yufan Huang. 2017. "Behind China's $1 Trillion Plan to Shake up the Economic Order." *New York Times.* May 13.

Perlze, Jane, Mark Landler, and Choe Sang-Hun. 2017. "China Blinks on South Korea, Making Nice After a Year of Hostilities." *New York Times.* November 1.

Pettis, Michael. 2013. *Avoiding the Fall: China's Economic Restructuring.* Washington, DC: Carnegie Endowment for International Peace.

———. 2017. "Is China's Economy Growing as Fast as China's GDP?" Carnegie Endowment for International Peace. September 5.

Pettyjohn, Stacie L., and Jennifer Kavanagh. 2016. *Access Granted: Political Challenges to the U.S. Overseas Military Presence, 1945–2014.* Santa Monica, CA: RAND.

Pettyjohn, Stacie L., and Alan J. Vick. 2013. *The Posture Triangle: A New Framework for U.S. Air Force Global Presence.* Washington, DC: RAND Corporation.

Pew Research Center. 2016a. "Global Indicators Database: World's Leading Economic Power." Washington, DC.

———. 2016b. "A Wider Ideological Gap between More and Less Educated Adults." Washington, DC.

———. 2017. "Public Trust in Government: 1958–2017." Washington, DC.

Phillips, Tom, and Ed Elkington. 2016. "No Country for Academics: Chinese Crackdown Forces Intellectuals Abroad." *The Guardian.* May 24.

Pietrucha, Col. Michael W. 2015a. "Making Places, Not Bases a Reality." *Proceedings Magazine* 141, no. 10 (October).

———. 2015b. "Twenty-First-Century Aerial Mining." *Air and Space Power Journal* 29, no. 2 (March–April): 129–50.

Pillsbury, Michael. 2015. *The Hundred-Year Marathon: China's Secret Strategy to Replace America as the Global Superpower.* New York: Henry Holt.

Pinker, Stephen. 2011. *The Better Angels of Our Nature: Why Violence Has Declined.* New York: Penguin.

Platt, Stephen R. 2014. "Book Review: 'The Opium War' by Julia Lovell." *Wall Street Journal.* August 29.

Polak, Petr. 2015. "Europe's Low Energy: The Promise and Perils of the Energy Union." *Foreign Affairs.* September 9.

Pomeranz, Kenneth. 2000. *The Great Divergence: China, Europe, and the Making of the Modern World Economy.* Princeton: Princeton University Press.

Pomfret, John. 2016. *The Beautiful Country and the Middle Kingdom: America and China, 1776 to the Present.* New York: Henry Holt and Co.

Poole, Keith T., and Howard Rosenthal. 2016. "The Polarization of the Congressional Parties." Voteview. January 30.

Porter, Eduardo. 2013. "In Public Education, Edge Still Goes to Rich." *New York Times.* November 5.

Porter, Gareth. 2017. "How America Armed Terrorists in Syria." *American Conservative.* June 22.

Posen, Barry R. 1984. "Measuring the European Conventional Balance: Coping with Complexity in Threat Assessment." *International Security* 9, no. 3 (winter): 47–88.

———. 2003. "Command of the Commons: The Military Foundation of U.S. Hegemony." *International Security* 28, no. 1 (summer): 5–46.

———. 2008. "ESDP and the Structure of World Power." *The International Spectator* 39, no. 1: 5–17.

———. 2014. *Restraint: A New Foundation for U.S. Grand Strategy.* Ithaca: Cornell University Press.

———. 2017. "The Price of War with North Korea." *New York Times.* December 6.

Posen, Barry R., and Stephen Van Evera. 1983. "Defense Policy and the Reagan Administration: Departure from Containment." *International Security* 8, no. 1 (summer): 3–45.

Priest, Dana, and William Arkin. 2011. *Top Secret America: The Rise of the New American Security State.* New York: Little, Brown.

Pritchett, Lant. 1997. "Divergence, Big Time." *Journal of Economic Perspectives* 11, no. 3 (summer): 3–17.

Qian, Zhenchao, and Daniel T. Lichter. 2007. "Social Boundaries and Marital Assimilation: Interpreting Trends in Racial and Ethnic Intermarriage." *American Sociological Review* 72 (February): 68–94.

Qiu, Jane. 2011. "China to Spend Billions Cleaning up Groundwater." *Science* 334, no. 6057 (November): 745.

Qing, Koh Gui, and John Shiffman 2015. "Beijing's Covert Radio Network Airs China-friendly News across Washington and the World." *Reuters.* November 2.

Raasch, Chuck. 2012. "How the Drought Is Changing Business." *USA Today.* July 30.

Rachman, Gideon. 2017. *Easternisation: War and Peace in the Asian Century*. London: Bodley Head.

Rahmat, Ridzwan. 2016. "Indonesia Navy Plans for Submarine Base in South China Sea." *Jane's Defence Weekly*. March 31.

Rajagopalan, Megha. 2017. "This Is What a 21st-Century Police State Really Looks Like." *BuzzFeed*. October 17.

Rapp-Hooper, Mira. 2016. "Parting the South China Sea: How to Uphold the Rule of Law." *Foreign Affairs* 95, no. 5 (September/October): 76–82.

Rappaport, Jordan, and Jeffery D. Sachs. 2003. "The United States as a Coastal Nation." *Journal of Economic Growth* 8, no. 1 (March): 5–46.

Redden, Elizabeth. 2017. "New Scrutiny for Confucius Institutes." *Inside Higher Ed*. April 26.

Redding, Stephen J., and Matthew A. Turner. 2014. "Transportation Costs and the Spatial Organization of Economic Activity." NBER Working Paper No. 20235. National Bureau of Economic Research. June.

Redding, Stephen J., and Matthew A. Turner. 2014. "Transportation Costs and the Spatial Organization of Economic Activity." NBER Working Paper No. 20235. National Bureau of Economic Research. June.

Redding, Stephen, and Anthony J. Venables. 2004. "Economic Geography and International Inequality." *Journal of International Economics* 62, no. 1 (January): 53–82.

Rielage, Dale C. 2016. "Chinese Navy Trains and Takes Risks." *Proceedings Magazine* 142, no. 5 (May): 36–41.

Ripley, Amanda. 2013. *The Smartest Kids in the World: And How They Got That Way*. New York: Simon and Schuster.

Rithmire, Meg E. 2014. "China's "New Regionalism": Subnational Analysis in Chinese Political Economy." *World Politics* 66, no. 1 (January): 165–94.

Roberts, Dexter. 2014. "Think Air Pollution Is Bad? China Faces a Water Contamination Crisis." *Bloomberg Businessweek*. November 19.

Robertson, Peter E., and Adrian Sin. 2017. "Measuring Hard Power: China's Economic Growth and Military Capacity." *Defence and Peace Economics* 28, no. 1: 91–111.

Robinson, James, Ragnar Torvik, and Thierry Verdier. 2006. "Political Foundations of the Resource Curse." *Journal of Development Economics* 79: 447–68.

Roblin, Sebastien. 2016a. "Brahmos: India's Supersonic Mega Missile That China Should Fear." *National Interest*. August 27.

———. 2016b. "How the Falklands War (Thanks to a Stealthy Submarine) Could Have Gone Very Differently." *National Interest*. November 27.

Rodrik, Dani. 2013. "The Past, Present, and Future of Economic Growth." Global Citizens Foundation Working Paper 1. June.

Rodrik, Dani, Arvind Subramanian, and Francesco Trebbi. 2004. "Institutions Rule: The Primacy of Institutions over Geography and Integration in Economic Development." *Journal of Economic Growth* 9, no. 2 (June): 131–65.

Rogin, Josh. 2017. "Trump Administration Approves Lethal Arms Sales to Ukraine." *Washington Post*. December 20.

Rohde, Robert A., and Richard A. Muller. 2015. "Air Pollution in China: Mapping of Concentrations and Spaces." *PlosS ONE* 10, no. 8 (August 20): 1–14.

Romanosky, Sasha. 2016. "Examining the Costs and Causes of Cyber Incidents." *Journal of Cybersecurity*.

Romer, Paul M. 1996. "Why, Indeed, in America? Theory, History, and the Origins of Modern Economic Growth." *American Economic Review* 86, no. 2 (May): 202–6.

Rosenau, William. 2001. *Special Operations Forces and Elusive Enemy Ground Targets: Lessons from Vietnam and the Persian Gulf War*. Santa Monica, CA: RAND Corporation.

Roser, Max. 2016. "War and Peace." Published online at Our WorldInData.org. https://ourworldindata.org/war-and-peace/.

Ross, Michael. 2003. "The Natural Resource Curse: How Wealth Can Make You Poor." In *Options and Actions*, edited by Ian Bannon and Paul Collier, chapter 2. Washington, DC: World Bank.

Rosseau, Jean Jacques. 2010 (1762). *The Social Contract or Principles of Political Right*. Translated by G.D.H. Cole. Venice, CA: SWB Books.

Rovner, Joshua. 2015. "Dealing with Putin's Strategic Incompetence." *War on the Rocks*. August 12.

———. 2016. "After America: The Flow of Persian Gulf Oil in the Absence of U.S. Military Force." In *Crude Strategy: Rethinking the U.S. Military Commitment to Defend Persian Gulf Oil*, edited by Charles L. Glaser and Rosemary A. Kelanic, chapter 5. Washington, DC: Georgetown University Press.

———. 2017a. "Two Kinds of Catastrophe: Nuclear Escalation and Protracted war in Asia." *Journal of Strategic Studies* 40, no. 5 (February): 696–730.

———. 2017b. "The ABCs of Deterring North Korea." *War on the Rocks*. September 13.

Rovner, Joshua, and Caitlin Talmadge. 2014. "Less Is More: The Future of the U.S. Military in the Persian Gulf." *Washington Quarterly* 37, no. 3 (fall): 47–60.

Rubel, Capt. Robert C. (ret.). 2017. "Think Outside the Hull." *Proceedings Magazine* 143, no. 6 (June): 372.

Rumer, Eugene. 2016. "Russia and the Security of Europe." Washington, DC: Carnegie Endowment for International Peace.

Russell, Bertrand. 1938. *Power: A New Social Analysis*. London: George, Allen and Unwin.

Sachs, Jeffery D., and Andrew Warner. 2001. "Natural Resource Abundance and Economic Growth." *European Economic Review* 45, no. 4–6 (May): 827–38.

Sagan, Sott D. 1988. "The Origins of the Pacific War." *Journal of Interdisciplinary History* 28, no. 4 (spring): 893–922.

———. 2011. "The Causes of Nuclear Weapons Proliferation." *Annual Review of Political Science* 14: 225–44.

Sakwa, Richard. 2010. *The Crisis of Russian Democracy: The Dual State, Factionalism, and the Medvedev Succession*. Cambridge: Cambridge University Press.

Sala-i-Martin, Xavier, and Arvind Subramanian. 2003. "Addressing the Natural Resource Curse: An Illustration from Nigeria." NBER Working Paper No. 9804. National Bureau of Economic Research.

Saradzhyan, Simon. 2010. "The Role of China in Russia's Military Thinking." International Relations and Security Network, May 4.

Schultz, Kenneth A., and Barry R. Weingast. 2003. "The Democratic Advantage: Institutional Foundations of Financial Power in International Competition." *International Organization* 57, no. 1 (December): 3–42.

Scobell, Andrew, Arthur S. Ding, Philip C. Saunders, and Scott W. Harold, eds. 2015. *The People's Liberation Army and Contingency Planning in China*. Washington, DC: National Defense University Press.

Selden, Zachary. 2013. "Balancing against or Balancing with? The Spectrum of Alignment and the Endurance of American Hegemony." *Security Studies* 22, no. 2 (May): 330–64.

Seligman, Lara. 2016. "Boeing Showcases New Sub-Hunting Torpedo." *Defense News*, May 19.

Senate Foreign Relations Subcommittee on East Asian and Pacific Affairs. 2013. *China's Water Challenge: Implications for the U.S. Rebalance to Asia*, 1st, July 24.

Schwartz, Felicia. 2017. "U.S. to Send Antitank Weaponry to Ukraine, Entering New Phase in Conflict." *Wall Street Journal*. December 24.

Shambaugh, David L. 2002. *Modernizing China's Military: Progress, Problems, and Prospects*. Berkeley: University of California Press.

———. 2016. *China's Future*. Cambridge: Polity Press.

Shapiro, Joshua. 2013. "1,000 Paper Tigers: China's Conventional Missile Forces." *War on The Rocks*. October 9.

Sharma, Ruchir. 2012. *Breakout Nations: In Pursuit of the Next Economic Miracles*. New York: Norton.

———. 2014. "The Ever-Emerging Markets: Why Economic Forecasts Fail." *Foreign Affairs* 93, no. 1 (January–February): 52–57.

———. 2016a. *The Rise and Fall of Nations: Forces of Change in the Post-Crisis World*. New York: Norton.

———. 2016b. "How China Fell Off the Miracle Path." *New York Times*. June 3.

———. 2016c. "The Demographics of Stagnation: Why People Matter for Economic Growth." *Foreign Affairs* 95, no. 2 (March/April): 18–24.

Shepard, Wade. 2015. *Ghost Cities of China*. London: Zed Books.

Shifrinson, Joshua R. Itzkowitz. 2016. "Deal or No Deal? The End of the Cold War and the U.S. Offer to Limit NATO Expansion." *International Security* 40, no. 4 (spring): 7–44.

———. 2018. *Rising Titans, Falling Giants: How Great Powers Exploit Power Shifts*. Ithaca: Cornell University Press.

Shifrinson, Joshua R. Itzkowitz, and Miranda Priebe. 2011. "The Limits of an Iranian Missile Campaign against Saudi Arabian Oil." *International Security*. 36, no. 1 (summer): 167–201.

Shlapak, David A., and Michael W. Johnson. 2016a. *Reinforcing Deterrence on NATO's Eastern Flank*. Santa Monica, CA: RAND.

———. 2016b. "Outnumbered, Outranged, and Outgunned: How Russia Defeats NATO." *War on the Rocks*, April 20.

Shlapak, David A., David T. Orletksy, Toy I. Reid, Murray Scott Tanner, and Barry Wilson. 2009. *A Question of Balance: Political Context and Military Aspects of the China-Taiwan Dispute*. Santa Monica, CA: RAND Corporation.

Shor, Borris, and Nolan McCarty. 2015. "Measuring American Legislatures." Updated Data (v 4.0), released June. https://americanlegislatures.com.

Simon, Steven, and Jonathan Stevenson. 2015. "The End of Pax Americana: Why Washington's Middle East Pullback Makes Sense." *Foreign Affairs* 94, 6 (November/December): 2–10.

Sindreu, Jon, and Mike Bird. 2017. "A Decade after the Crisis, King Dollar Is the World's Tyrant." *Wall Street Journal*. November 26.

Singer, David J., Stuart Bremer, and John Stuckey. 1972. "Capability Distribution, Uncertainty, and Major Power War, 1820–1965." In *Peace, War, and Numbers*, edited by Bruce Russett, chapter 1. Beverly Hills, CA: Sage.

Smil, Vaclav. 2013. *Making the Modern World: Materials and Dematerialization*. New York: Wiley.

Smith, Adam. 1976. *An Inquiry into the Nature and Causes of the Wealth of Nations*. Vol. 1. Chicago: University of Chicago Press.

Smith, Jeff M. 2015. *Cold Peace: China-India Rivalry in the Twenty-First Century*. New York: Lexington Books.

Sng, Tuan-Hwee. 2014. "Size and Dynastic Decline: The Principal-Agent Problem in Late Imperial China, 1700–1850." *Explorations in Economic History* 54 (October): 107–27.

Snyder, Jack. 2003. "Imperial Temptations." *National Interest* 71 (spring): 29–40.

Snyder, Jack, and Keir A. Lieber. 2008. "Correspondence: Defensive Realism and the "New" History of World War I." *International Security* 33, no. 1 (summer): 174–94.

Sokoloff, Kenneth. 1988. "Inventive Activity in Early Industrial America: Evidence from Patent Records." *Journal of Economic History* 48, no. 4 (December): 813–50.

Song, Wei. 2010. "Guoji jinrong weiji yu Meiguo de danji diwei." *Shijie Jingji yu Zhengzhi* 5: 25–48.

———. 2017. "Daguo de zhengti guojia liyi: yizhong lilun fenxi." *Xiandai Guoji Guanxi* 3: 37–44.

Spence, Jonathan. 1991. *The Search for Modern China*. New York: Norton.

Stanway, David, and Kathy Chen. 2015. "More Than 60 Percent of China's Water Underground Water Rated Unfit for Human Contact." *Reuters*. June 4.

Stein, Arthur A. 1984. "The Hegemon's Dilemma: Great Britain, the United States, and the International Economic Order." *International Organization* 38, no. 2 (spring): 355–86.

Steinberg, James, and Michael E. O'Hanlon. 2014. *Strategic Reassurance and Resolve: U.S.-China Relations in the Twenty-First Century*. Princeton: Princeton University Press.

Stigler, George J. 1971. "The Theory of Economic Regulation." *The Bell Journal of Economics and Management Science* 2, no. 1 (Spring): 3–21.

Stockholm International Peace Research Institute (SIPRI). 2017a. "Military Expenditure Database."

———. 2017b. *Arms Transfers Database*.

Stocking, Andrew. 2015. "China's Growing Energy Demand: Implications for the United States." Congressional Budget Office Working Paper. June.

Storeygard, Adam. 2016. "Farther on Down the Road: Transport Costs, Trade, and Urban Growth in Sub-Saharan Africa." *Review of Economic Studies* 83, no. 3 (April): 1263–95.

Strauss, Valerie. 2016. "Most Literate Country in the World? Not the U.S., New Ranking Says." *Washington Post*. March 8.

———. 2017. "Mass Incarceration of African Americans Affects the Racial Achievement Gap." *Washington Post*. March 15.

Strittmatter, Anthony, and Uwe Sunde. 2013. "Health and Economic Development: Evidence from the Introduction of Public Health Care." *Journal of Population Economics* 26, no. 4 (October): 1549–84.

Subramanian, Arvind. 2011. *Eclipse: Living in the Shadow of China's Economic Dominance.* Washington, DC: Peterson Institute for International Economics.

Suisse, Credit. 2015. "Global Wealth Report Databook." October.

Sun, Yun. 2014. "U.S. Energy Independence: Disaster or Blessing for China?" *The Hill.* March 20.

Swartz, Spencer, and Shai Oster. 2010. "China Tops U.S. In Energy Use." *Wall Street Journal.* July 18.

Talmadge, Caitlin. 2008. "Closing Time: Assessing the Iranian Threat to the Strait of Hormuz." *International Security* 33, no. 1 (summer): 82–117.

Tao, Tao, and Kunlin Xin. 2014. "A Sustainable Plan for China's Drinking Water." *Nature.* July 30.

Tarrow, Sydney. 1995. "Bridging the Quantitative-Qualitative Divide in Political Science." *American Political Science Review* 89, no. 2 (June): 471–74.

Taylor, Adam. 2015. "A Russian Journalist Explains Why There Is No Corruption in Russia." *Washington Post.* January 28.

Taylor, Brian. 2011. *State Building in Putin's Russia: Policing and Coercion after Communism.* Cambridge: Cambridge University Press.

Tellis, Ashley, Janice Bially, Christopher Layne, and Melissa McPherson. 2000. *Measuring Power in the Postindustrial Age.* Santa Monica, CA: RAND.

Testimony before the U.S.-China Economic and Security Review Commission. 2014. *China's Social Unrest Problem.* May 15.

Tham, Engen. 2017. "'Ghost Collateral' Haunts Loans across China's Debt-Laden Banking System." *Reuters.* May 31.

Thayer, Carl. 2014. "Can Vietnam's Maritime Strategy Counter China?" *Diplomat.* September 29.

Thayler, Carlyle A. 2017. "Background Briefing: Vietnam—Evaluating Its Fleet of Six Kilo-Class Submarines." Australia: Thayer Consultancy.

Thomas, Jim. 2013. "Why the U.S. Army Needs Missiles: A New Mission to Save the Service." *Foreign Affairs* 92, no. 3 (May/June): 137–44.

Thomas, M. A. 2010. "What Do the Worldwide Governance Indicators Measure?" *European Journal of Development Research* 22, no. 1 (February): 31–54.

Tocqueville, Alexis de. 2000 [1835–1840]. *Democracy in America.* Chicago: University of Chicago Press.

Toje, Asle. 2010. *The European Union as a Small Power: After the Post-Cold War.* New York: Palgrave Macmillan.

Tomkins, Richard. 2016. "U.S. Orders Archerfish Counter-Mine System." *UPI.* April 14.

Torode, Greg. 2016. "Vietnam Moves New Rocket Launchers into Disputed South China Sea." *Reuters.* August 10.

Transparency International. 2016. *Corruption Perceptions Index.* Berlin.

———. 2017. *U.S. Corruption Barometer 2017.* Berlin.

Trump, Donald J. 2017a. "Remarks by President Trump to the 72nd Session of the United Nations General Assembly." *The White House.* The United States Government. September 19. https://www.whitehouse.gov/briefings-statements/remarks-president-trump-72nd-session-united-nations-general-assembly/.

———. 2017b. "Remarks by President Trump before a Briefing on the Opioid Crisis." *The White House.* The United States Government. August 8. https://www.whitehouse.gov/briefings-statements/remarks-president-trump-briefing-opioid-crisis/.

Truver, Scott C. 2011. "Taking Mines Seriously: Mine Warfare in China's near Seas." *Naval War College Review* 65, no. 2 (spring): 30–66.

Tsai, Kellee S. 2002. *Back-Alley Banking: Private Entrepreneurs in China.* Ithaca: Cornell University Press.

United Nations Environment Programme (UNEP) and United Nations University International Human Dimensions Programme on Global Environmental Change (UNU-IHDP). 2014. *Inclusive Wealth Report 2014.* New York: Cambridge University Press.

United Nations Population Division. 2015. *World Population Prospects 2015.* New York.

U.S. Bureau of the Census. 1991. *USA/USSR: Facts and Figures.* Washington, DC: U.S. Government Printing Office.

U.S. Central Intelligence Agency (CIA). 2015. *CIA World Fact Book.* Fairfax: VA.

———. 2017. *World Fact Book.* Fairfax: VA.

U.S.-China Business Council (USCBC). 2016. *USCBC China Economic Reform Scorecard October 2016.* Washington, DC.

U.S.-China Economic and Security Review Commission. 2017a. *Hearing on China's Military Modernization and Its Implications for the United States,* January 30.

———. 2017b. *2017 Report to Congress of the U.S.-China Security Review Commission.* November.

U.S. Commission on the Theft of American Intellectual Property. 2017. "Update to the IP Commission Report." Washington, DC: National Bureau of Asian Research.

U.S. Congressional-Executive Commission on China. 2017. *Political Prisoner Database.* Washington, DC: U.S. Government Printing Office.

U.S. Department of Defense. 2014. *2014 Demographics: Profile of the Military Community.* Washington, DC.

———. 2015. "Base Structure Report: Fiscal Year 2015 Baseline." Washington, DC.

———. 2016. "Annual Report to Congress: Military and Security Developments Involving the People's Republic of China 2016." Washington, DC.

U.S. Department of Energy, Energy Information Administration. 2016. *Annual Energy Outlook 2016.* Washington, DC.

U.S. Department of State. 2017. *Voting Practices in the United Nations 2016.* Washington, DC: U.S. Department of State.

U.S. Energy Information Agency. 2017. *Annual Energy Outlook 2017.* Washington, DC: U.S. Department of Energy.

U.S. Office of Naval Intelligence. 2015. *The PLA Navy: New Capabilities and Missions for the 21st Century.* Suitland, MD.

Vaishnav, Milan. 2017. *When Crime Pays: Money and Muscle in Indian Politics.* New Haven: Yale University Press.

van der Ploeg, Frederick. 2011. "Natural Resources: Curse or Blessing?" *Journal of Economic Literature* 49, no. 2: 366–420.

Verleger, Philip K., Jr. 2012. "The Amazing Tale of U.S." *International Economy* 26, no. 2 (spring): 8–62.

Vice, Margaret. 2017. "In Global Popularity Contest, U.S. and China—Not Russia—Vie For First." *FactTank*. Pew Research Center. August 23.

Villamor, Felipe. 2017. "Philippines Halts Work in South China Sea, in Bid to Appease Beijing." *New York Times*. November 8.

Vincent, Kenneth. 2016. "The Economist Costs of Persian Gulf Oil Supply Disruptions." In *Crude Strategy: Rethinking the U.S. Military Commitment to Defend Persian Gulf Oil*, edited by Charles L. Glaser and Rosemary A. Kelanic, chapter 3. Washington, DC: Georgetown University Press.

Vinik, Danny. 2015. "America's Secret Arsenal." *Politico*. December 9.

Voigt, Stefan. 2013. "How (Not) to Measure Institutions." *Journal of Institutional Economics* 9, no. 1 (March): 1–26.

Volodzko, David. 2016. "Why China Can't Quit Tobacco." *Diplomat*. January 12.

Vries, Peer. 2012. "Public Finance in China and Britain in the Long Eighteenth Century." London: London School of Economics and Political Science.

Wachman, Alan. 2007. *Why Taiwan? Geostrategic Rationales for Chinese Territorial Integrity*. Stanford: Stanford University Press.

Wade, Robert H. 1990. *Governing the Market*. Princeton: Princeton University Press.

Walker, Christopher. 2016. "The Hijacking of "Soft Power."" *Journal of Democracy* 27, no. 1 (January): 49–63.

Walker, Christopher, and Jessica Ludwig. 2017. "The Meaning of Sharp Power: How Authoritarian States Project Influence." *Foreign Affairs*. November 16.

Wall Street Journal. 2015. "Fake Peer Review Scandal Shines Spotlight on China." August 25.

———. 2016. "China's Rare-Earths Bust." July 18.

Wallace, Jeremy L. 2016. "Juking the Stats? Authoritarian Information Problems in China." *British Journal of Political Science* 46, no. 1: 11–29.

Walt, Stephen M. 1987. *The Origins of Alliances*. Ithaca: Cornell University Press.

———. 1989. "The Case for Finite Containment: Analyzing U.S. Grand Strategy." *International Security* 14, no. 1 (summer): 5–49.

———. 2005. *Taming American Power: The Global Response to U.S. Primacy*. New York: Norton.

———. 2013. "Applying the 8 Questions of the Powell Doctrine to Syria." *Foreign Policy*. September 3.

———. 2016. "The Case against Peace." *Foreign Policy*. June 17.

———. 2017a. "Stealing Elections Is All in the Game." *Foreign Policy*. January 10.

———. 2017b. "The Power of a Strong State Department." *New York Times*. May 12.

Waltz, Kenneth N. 1979. *Theory of International Politics*. Reading, MA: Addison-Wesley.

———. 1993. "The Emerging Structure of International Politics." *International Security* 18, no. 2 (autumn): 44–79.

Wang, Yuhua, and Carl Minzer. 2015. "The Rise of the Chinese Security State." *China Quarterly* 222 (June): 339–59.

Wei, Lingling, and Bob Davis. 2013. "China's "Shadow Banks" Fan Debt-Bubble Fears." *Wall Street Journal*, June 25.

Weissman, Stephen R. 2017. "Congress and War: How the House and the Senate Can Reclaim Their Role." *Foreign Affairs* 96, no. 1 (January/Feburary): 132–45.

Werrell, Kenneth P. 1988. *Archie, Flak, Aaa, and Sam: A Short Operational History of Ground-Based Air Defense*. Maxwell Air Force Base: Air University Press.

Whiting, Allen S. 1960. *China Crosses the Yalu: The Decision to Enter the Korean War.* Stanford: Stanford University Press.

Whittle, Richard. 2015. "New China Drone: Looks Like a Reaper But . . ." *Breaking Defense.* September 2.

Wike, Richard, Bruce Stokes, Jacob Poushter, and Janell Fetterolf. 2017. "U.S. Image Suffers as Publics around World Question Trump's Leadership." *Global Attitudes and Trends.* Pew Research Center. June 26.

Wildau, Gabriel. 2016. "The State-Owned Zombie Economy." *Financial Times.* February 29.

———. 2017. "China New Silk Road Investment Fell in 2016, Despite Policy Push." *Financial Times.* May 10.

Williamsen, Marvin. 1992. "The Military Dimension, 1937–1941." In *China's Bitter Victory: War with Japan, 1937–45,* edited by James C. Hsiung and Steven I. Levine, chapter 6. New York: Routledge.

Woetzel, Jonathan, Yougang Chen, Jeongmin Seong, Nicolas Leung, Kevin Sneader, and Jon Kowalski. 2016. *China's Choice: Capturing the $5 Trillion Productivity Opportunity.* New York: McKinsey Global Institute.

Wohlforth, William C. 1999. "The Stability of a Unipolar World." *International Security* 24, no. 1 (summer): 5–41.

———. 2001. "The Russian-Soviet Empire: A Test of Neorealism." *Review of International Studies* 27, no. 5 (December): 213–35.

Wolf, Charles, K.C. Yeh, Edmund D. Brunner, Aaron S. Gurwitz, and Marilee Lawrence. 1983. *The Costs of the Soviet Empire.* Santa Monica, CA: RAND Corporation.

Wolf, Martin. 2016. "Too Big, Too Leninist: A China Crisis Is a Matter of Time." December 13.

Wong, Chun Han. 2014. "The Miniscule Cost of Equipping a Chinese Soldier." *Wall Street Journal, China Real Time Report.* December 8

Wong, Edward. 2014. "Beijing Goes Quiet on Rise of Local Security Budgets." *New York Times.* March 6.

Wong, Chun Han, and Eva Dou. 2017. "Foreign Companies in China Get a New Partner: the Communist Party." *Wall Street Journal.* October 29.

World Bank. 2006. *Where Is the Wealth of Nations? Measuring Capital for the 21st Century.* Washington, DC: World Bank.

———. 2016. "World Development Indicators." Washington, DC: World Bank.

World Economic Forum. 2016. *The Global Competitiveness Report, 2015–2016.* Geneva: World Economic Forum.

Wright, Gavin. 1990. "The Origins of American Industrial Success, 1879–1940." *American Economic Review* 80, no. 4 (September): 651–68.

Wright, Gavin, and Jesse Czelusta. 2004. "The Myth of the Resource Curse." *Challenge* 47, no. 2 (March/April): 6–38.

Wright, Thomas. 2017. *All Measures Short of War: The Contest for the 21st Century and the Future of America's Power.* New Haven: Yale University Press.

Wrigley, E. A. 2010. *Energy and the English Industrial Revolution.* Cambridge: Cambridge University Press.

Wu, Harry X. 2014. "China's Growth and Productivity Performance Debate Revisited: Accounting for China's Sources of Growth with a New Dataset." The Conference Board Report No. EPWP1401. February.

———. 2016. "Sustainability of China's Growth Model: A Productivity Perspective." *China and World Economy* 24, no. 5 (September/October): 42–70.

Wu, Xiaojie. 2011. "60% of Scientific Research Funds Lost to Corruption and Embezzlement." *Guangming Daily*. September 7.

Wu, Xinbo. 2005–6. "The End of the Silver Lining: A Chinese View of the U.S.-Japanese Alliance." *Washington Quarterly* 29, no. 1 (winter): 117–30.

Wubbeke, Jost, Mirjam Meissner, Max J. Zenglein, Jaquelin Ives, and Bjorn Conrad. 2016. "Made in China 2025: The Making of a High-Tech Superpower and the Consequences for Industrial Countries." *Merics Papers on China*, no. 2 (December).

Xing, Yuqing. 2014. "Measuring Value Added in the People's Republic of China's Exports: A Direct Approach." Asian Development Bank Institute Working Paper No. 493. August.

Xinhua. 2015. "China's Education Spending on the Rise." November 20.

Xu, Jin. 2010. "Jinrong weiji nanyi dianfu yi chao duo qiang geju." *Shijie Jingji yu Zhengzhi* 12: 26–27.

Yang, Yuan. 2017. "China's Communist Party Raises Army of Nationalist Trolls." *Financial Times*. December 29.

Yang, Yuan, and Archie Zhang. 2017. "China Launches Crackdown on Academic Fraud." *Financial Times*. June 18.

Yergin, Daniel. 2013. "Congratulations, America. You're (Almost) Energy Independent." *Politico*. November.

Yglesias, Matthew. 2017. "We're Witnessing the Wholesale Looting of America." *Vox*. December 19.

Yoshihara, Toshi. 2015. "Sino-Japanese Rivalry at Sea: How Tokyo Can Go Anti-Access on China." *Orbis* 59, no. 1 (winter): 62–75.

Yoshihara, Toshi, and James R. Holmes. 2011. "Can China Defend a "Core Interest" in the South China Sea?" *Washington Quarterly* 34, no. 2 (spring): 45–59.

Yu, Hao. 2015. "Universal Health Insurance Coverage for 1.3 Billion People: What Accounts for China's Success?" *Health Policy* 119, no. 9 (September): 1145–52.

Yusuf, Moeed. 2009. "Predicting Proliferation: The History of the Future of Nuclear Weapons." *Brookings Institution Foreign Policy Paper Series*. No. 11. Washington, DC: Brookings.

Zakaria, Fareed. 1998. *From Wealth to Power: The Unusual Origins of America's World Role*. Princeton: Princeton University Press.

———. 2012. *The Post-American World: Release 2.0*. New York: Norton.

———. 2015. "Stop Swooning over Putin." *Washington Post*. October 15.

———. 2016. *In Defense of a Liberal Education*. New York: Norton.

Zarate, Juan. 2013. *Treasury's War: The Unleashing of a New Era of Financial Warfare*. New York: Public Affairs.

Zeihan, Peter. 2015. *The Accidental Superpower: The Next Generation of American Preeminence and the Coming Global Disorder*. New York: Hachette Book Group.

———. 2017. *The Absent Superpower: The Shale Revolution and a World without America*. New York: Amazon Digital Services.

Zhao, Xu, Junguo Liu, Qingying Liu, Martin R. Tillotson, Dabo Guan, and Klaus Hubacek. 2015. "Physical and Virtual Water Transfers for Regional Water Stress Alleviation in China." *Proceedings of the National Academy of Sciences* 112, no. 4 (January 27): 1031–35.

Zhou, Zhangyue, Weiming Tian, Jimin Wang, Hongbo Liu, and Lijuan Cao. 2012. "Food Consumption Trends in China, April 2012." Report Submitted to the Australian Government Department of Agriculture, Fisheries, and Forestry.

Zimmerman, William. 2014. *Ruling Russia: Authoritarianism from the Revolution to Putin*. Princeton: Princeton University Press.

Zubok, Valdislav M. 2010. "Soviet Foreign Policy from Detente to Gorbachev, 1975–1985." In *Westad, Odd Arne*, edited by Melvin P. Leffler, chapter 5. Cambridge: Cambridge University Press.

Zweig, David, and Huiyao Wang. 2013. "Can China Bring Back the Best? The Communist Party Organizes China's Search for Talent." *China Quarterly* 215 (September): 590–615.

Index

CPSIA information can be obtained
at www.ICGtesting.com
Printed in the USA
LVHW091720050521
686573LV00020B/557/J